Doctor Faustus

Continuum Renaissance Drama

Series editors: Andrew Hiscock, University of Wales Bangor, UK and Lisa Hopkins, Sheffield Hallam University, UK

Continuum Renaissance Drama offers practical and accessible introductions to the critical and performative contexts of key Elizabethan and Jacobean plays. Each guide introduces the text's critical and performance history but also provides students with an invaluable insight into the landscape of current scholarly research through a keynote essay on the state of the art and newly commissioned essays of fresh research from different critical perspectives.

Current titles:

A Midsummer Night's Dream, ed. Regina Buccola

'Tis Pity She's A Whore, ed. Lisa Hopkins

Forthcoming titles:

1 Henry IV, ed. Stephen Longstaffe

The Duchess of Malfi, ed. Christina Luckyj

King Lear, ed. Andrew Hiscock and Lisa Hopkins

Volpone, ed. Matthew Steggle

Women Beware Women, ed. Andrew Hiscock

DOCTOR FAUSTUS

A Critical Guide

Edited by Sara Munson Deats

continuum

Continuum
The Tower Building
11 York Road
London SE1 7NX

80 Maiden Lane, Suite 704
New York
NY 10038

www.continuumbooks.com

British Library Cataloguing-in-Publication Data
A catalogue record for this book is available from the British Library.

ISBN: 978-1-8470-6137-9 (Hardback)
        978-1-8470-6138-6 (paperback)

Library of Congress Cataloging-in-Publication Data
A catalog record for this book is available from the Library of Congress.

Typeset by BookEns Ltd, Royston, Hertfordshire
Printed and bound in Great Britain by CPI Antony Rowe, Chippenham, Wiltshire

Contents

Acknowledgements

First and foremost, I wish to express my gratitude to the eight studious artisans who have contributed chapters to this collection. These scholarly chapters have already given me abundant profit and delight and will, I am convinced, continue to provide pleasure and insight to students of *Doctor Faustus* for many years to come. I would also like to thank Rolland Elliot for permission to reprint his excellent photographs of the production of *Doctor Faustus* directed by Andrew James Hartley at the University of North Carolina, Charlotte.

Since the majority of the contributors to this volume are active members of the Marlowe Society of America, including a few presidents, both former and future, I would like to express my special appreciation to that Society for the encouragement and inspiration that it has provided to me and to all Marlowe scholars throughout the years. I am also much indebted to the general editors of this series, Lisa Hopkins and Andrew Hiscock, particularly Lisa Hopkins, who first recruited me for this endeavour and has guided me throughout this process. My deepest appreciation also goes to my editor, Colleen Coalter, whose beneficial advice and assistance have been crucial to the success of this project, and to my super-conscientious and organized research assistant, Robin Rogers, who scrupulously proof-read and formatted this manuscript.

And most of all, I wish to thank my Good Angel, my husband Gordon Deats, whose patience and support have sustained me throughout this and many other scholarly enterprises.

Series Introduction

The drama of Shakespeare and his contemporaries has remained at the very heart of English curricula internationally and the pedagogic needs surrounding this body of literature have grown increasingly complex as more sophisticated resources become available to scholars, tutors and students. This series aims to offer a clear picture of the critical and performative contexts of a range of chosen texts. In addition, each volume furnishes readers with invaluable insights into the landscape of current scholarly research as well as including new pieces of research by leading critics.

This series is designed to respond to the clearly identified needs of scholars, tutors and students for volumes which will bridge the gap between accounts of previous critical developments and performance history and an acquaintance with new research initiatives related to the chosen plays. Thus, our ambition is to offer innovative and challenging guides which will provide practical, accessible and thought-provoking analyses of Renaissance drama. Each volume is organized according to a progressive reading strategy involving introductory discussion, critical review and cutting-edge scholarly debate. It has been an enormous pleasure to work with so many dedicated scholars of Renaissance drama and we are sure that this series will encourage you to read 400-year old playtexts with fresh eyes.

Andrew Hiscock and Lisa Hopkins

Timeline

1564: Birth of Christopher Marlowe.

1579–80: Marlowe is a scholar at King's School, Canterbury.

17 March 1581: Marlowe matriculates at Cambridge.

7–11 May 1581: Marlowe is formally elected to receive the Archbishop Parker Scholarship at Cambridge.

1581–86: Marlowe is believed to be involved in secret service for the government.

1584: Marlowe is permitted to proceed to the BA.

1585–86: *Dido, Queene of Carthage* is written, perhaps with Thomas Nash.

31 March 1587: Marlowe is admitted to candidacy for the MA.

29 June 1587: Privy Council attests to Marlowe's 'good service' and petitions for him to be granted his MA degree.

1587–88: Marlowe probably writes *Tamburlaine, I and II*; *Tamburlaine, I and II* is performed by the Admiral's Men in London to great success.

1588–89: *Doctor Faustus* is probably written and perhaps performed (although some scholars favour a 1592–93 date).

18 September 1589: Marlowe is imprisoned with poet Thomas Watson for participation in a street brawl in which William Bradley is killed.

19 September 1589: The coroner's jury finds that Marlowe withdrew from combat and that Watson killed Bradley in self-defence.

1590: Publication of *Tamburlaine, I and II*; Marlowe may also have written *The Jew of Malta* (although both earlier and later dates have been proposed).

1591: Marlowe shares lodgings with Thomas Kyd.

26 January 1592: Marlowe is accused of counterfeiting money in the Netherlands.

9 May 1592: Marlowe is bound over to keep the peace; he probably writes *Edward II* and *The Massacre at Paris*.

15 September 1592: Marlowe fights William Corkine in Canterbury; after suits and countersuits, the case is dismissed.

1593: Marlowe probably writes *Hero and Leander*.

12 May 1593: Thomas Kyd is arrested on suspicion of libel and imprisoned; papers containing heretical opinions, which Kyd attributes to Marlowe, are found in Kyd's rooms.

20 May 1593: Marlowe is called before the Privy Council and is instructed to give his 'daily attendance'; he is not imprisoned.

30 May 1593: Marlowe is killed by Ingram Frizer at the house of Widow Bull in Deptford. According to witnesses, Marlowe attacked Frizer after a heated dispute over the 'reckoning', or bill.

1 June 1593: The coroner's jury finds that Frizer acted in self-defence. Marlowe is buried in the churchyard of St Nicholas's Church, Deptford.

1593: Publication of *The English Faustbook* by P. F. Gent (Gentleman). This chapbook is accepted by scholars as the source for Marlowe's *Doctor Faustus*.

1594: First recorded performance of *Doctor Faustus* by the Admiral's Men at the Rose Theatre.

1594: Publication of *Dido, Queene of Carthage* and *Edward II*.

1594: Publication of *Massacre at Paris*.

1595, 1596, 1597: *Doctor Faustus* is successfully performed by the Admiral's Men at the Rose Theatre.

1598: Publication of *Hero and Leander*.

1599: The Bishop of London and the Archbishop of Canterbury order a public burning of Marlowe's translation of Ovid's elegies.

1600: Publication of *The First Book of Lucan*, a classical translation.

1602: Philip Henslowe pays William Birde and Samuel Rowley £4 for additions to *Doctor Faustus*.

1604: The A-text of *Doctor Faustus* is published.

1616: The B-text of *Doctor Faustus* is published.

1633: *The Jew of Malta* is published with a dedication by Thomas Heywood.

1633: In *Histriomastix*, William Prynne makes reference to a production of *Doctor Faustus* held at the Belsavage Playhouse, probably in 1588 or 1589. This reference gives support for the early dating of the play.

1662: A farcical version of *Doctor Faustus* is performed at the Red Bull with Thomas Betterton as Faustus. Despite his admiration for Betterton, Samuel Pepys found the play 'so wretchedly and poorly done that we were sick of it'.

1688, 1723: Harlequin versions of *Doctor Faustus* that combined Marlowe's play with sizable portions of *Harlequin and Scaramouche* are performed at the Queen's Theatre, Drury Lane, and Lincoln's Inn Fields. However, these versions bear little resemblance to Marlowe's original version, and Marlowe's play virtually disappears from the stage for over a century.

1744: The revival of interest in Marlowe begins with the inclusion of *Edward II* in Robert Dodsley's *Old Plays*.

1780: Isaac Reed, editor of the second edition of *Old Plays*, adds *The Jew of Malta* to the collection.

1782: *The Baines Note*, attributed to Marlowe, is published by Joseph Ritson.

1885: An amalgamation of Marlowe's *Doctor Faustus* and Goethe's *Faust* is mounted at London's Lyceum Theatre.

1896: *Doctor Faustus* is staged by William Poel for the Elizabethan Stage Society with a prologue by Algernon Swinburne.

1903: *Doctor Faustus* is presented on a simple platform stage in Heidelberger Hebbelverein, Germany. This is the first of many German productions during the next 25 years.

1908: A spectacular production of *Doctor Faustus* is mounted by Herbert Beerbohm Tree at His Majesty's Theatre, London.

1910: Tucker Brooke edits *Doctor Faustus*. Like most of the nineteenth- and early twentieth-century editors, Brooke favours the A-text.

1928: A revival of *Doctor Faustus* is staged by the Phoenix Society at London's New Oxford Theatre.

1929: Nugent Monck's experimental Norwich Maddermarket Theatre performs *Doctor Faustus* three times at the Canterbury Theatre.

1932: Frederick S. Boas edits *The Tragical History of Doctor Faustus*, which includes a composite of the A- and B-texts; where the two texts are parallel, the B-text is favoured.

1936–37: Orson Welles stars in his own production of *Doctor Faustus* at the Maxine Elliott Theatre in New York.

1944: John Moody directs *Doctor Faustus* at the Old Vic.

1946–47: *Doctor Faustus* is included in the repertory of the Royal Shakespeare Company, starring Robert Harris and Hugh Griffith as Faustus and Mephistopheles, with Paul Scofield playing the role of Mephistopheles the second year.

1950: Welles revives his production of *Doctor Faustus* in Paris with Eartha Kitt in the role of Helen. W. W. Greg publishes *Marlowe's 'Doctor Faustus' 1604, 1616: Parallel Texts*. Greg argues that the A-text is a bad quarto and that the B-text reflects Marlowe's original play without the Birde-Rowley additions. For the next 25 years, editors favour the B-text.

1961: Michael Benthall directs *Doctor Faustus* for the Old Vic in Edinburgh.

1963: Jerry Grotowski produces the play for his Theatre Laboratory in Opole, Poland.

1966: Nevill Coghill directs *Doctor Faustus* for the Oxford University Society, starring Richard Burton and Elizabeth Taylor. The following year this production is transferred to film.

1968: The Royal Shakespeare Company again produces the play starring Eric Porter and Terrence Hardiman, with the first nude Helen in the history of the play's performance.

1970: The Royal Shakespeare Company's Theatregoround Troupe stages the play at Dublin's Abby Theatre and later at Stratford-upon-Avon, featuring David Warner and Alan Howard as Faustus and Mephistopheles.

1974: The Marlowe Society of American is founded by Jean Jofen.

1974–75: A version of *Doctor Faustus* conflating the A- and B-texts is produced by the Royal Shakespeare Company and directed by John Barton with Ian McKellen in the title role.

1980: Christopher Fettes stages *Doctor Faustus* at the Lyric Studio, Hammersmith, with an all-male cast.

1981: Adrian Noble directs the play for the Royal Exchange Theatre in Manchester with Ben Kingsley in the leading role.

1985, 1989, 1991: Three new editions of *Doctor Faustus* based solely on the A-text are published by David Ormerod and Christopher Wortham, Roma Gill, and Michael Keefer. These editions establish the critical preference for the A- text which currently dominates Marlowe scholarship.

1989: Another all-male production of *Doctor Faustus* is directed by Barry Kyle for the Swan Theatre at Stratford.

1993: Agreeing with many scholars that the A- and B-texts are best considered as two separate plays, David Bevington and Eric Rasmussen edit '*Doctor Faustus*': *A- and B-texts (1604, 1616)*.

2002: *Doctor Faustus* is directed at the Young Vic by David Lan, starring Jude Law as Faustus.

2004: A Chichester Festival modern dress production of *Doctor Faustus* is staged at the Minerva Theatre.

2005: The Working Group Company produces the play at the Belvoir Street Theatre in Sydney, Australia. *Doctor Faustus* makes its first appearance at the Elizabethan Theatre of the Oregon Shakespeare Festival.

Introduction

Sara Munson Deats

The Guide

Critical consensus identifies Christopher Marlowe's *Doctor Faustus*, probably written and performed around 1588, as the first great tragedy in the English language, a powerful drama that ushered in 30 years of unparalleled dramatic creativity on the English stage. For over 400 years, Marlowe's most often read and most frequently performed play has been surrounded by conjecture; indeed, few works of literature have evoked such violent critical controversy as Marlowe's *Doctor Faustus*. Almost every aspect of the play has been questioned: the text has been contested; the authorship has been challenged; the date has been disputed; and the meaning has been debated. This volume seeks to guide the teacher and student of Marlowe – and, of course, all successful teachers are also students – through the labyrinth of critical controversy associated with Marlowe's most popular play, and to aid all students of Marlowe in gaining a fuller appreciation of the originality and profundity of this work.

The book contains this Introduction and eight chapters designed to approach the play from multiple perspectives. The Introduction outlines the scope and goals of the volume, examining Marlowe's changing status in the canon of English literature, whereby during the past few decades he has become accepted as one of the most influential of early modern dramatists, second only to Shakespeare. The Introduction also explores the various influences – the magus legend, the morality play tradition, and the German and English *Faustbooks* – that combined to produce this fascinating fusion of native and classical dramatic conventions. Finally, it briefly analyses the characteristics that make this play one of the triumphs of the English Renaissance and a powerful influence on the development of the English drama.

In the first chapter, 'The Critical Backstory', Bruce E. Brandt traces the rich and varied critical history of *Doctor Faustus*, encompassing the enthusiastic responses of early modern audiences, the disregard of the play in the seventeenth century, its rediscovery in the eighteenth century, its resurrection by critics and poets in the nineteenth century, and the passionate engagement that the play has aroused in twentieth-century critics. This chapter also surveys the lively debates provoked by the play. These focus on the two very different extant versions, the A- and B-texts; the dating of the play; the authorship of the comic sections of the drama; and, most important of all, the theological ideology dominating the tragedy. This chapter not only summarizes traditional arguments concerning the meaning of the drama, but also examines the new perspectives offered by psychoanalytical, feminist and new historicist commentators on the play.

Although undoubtedly the most frequently performed of Marlowe's plays, *Doctor Faustus*, like so many of the dramas by Shakespeare's contemporaries, has experienced both overwhelming success and virtual neglect. In the second chapter of this volume, David Bevington reviews the diversity in the performance history of the play, ranging from its immediate popularity after its premier performance, probably in 1588 (although this is much debated), to its degeneration into farcical adaptations in the eighteenth century, to its complete disappearance from the stage in the nineteenth century, to its resurrection by William Poel in 1896 and the plethora of revivals in the twentieth and twenty-first centuries. This chapter focuses not only on highly touted productions by companies like the Royal Shakespeare Company and the Old Vic but also on the myriad of exciting experimental adaptations performed by repertory companies and college groups in Britain, Canada and the United States, as well as radio and television versions of the play.

The third chapter of this collection, 'The State of the Art: Current Critical Research', written by Robert Logan, provides readers with a broad overview of recent critical research on *Doctor Faustus*, demonstrating how during the past few decades interest in Marlowe has virtually exploded. Before examining the present state of the art in the scholarship and criticism of *Doctor Faustus*, Logan distinguishes between these two terms, using 'scholarship' to describe work that deals primarily with matters of text and print culture and 'criticism' as commentary on issues of interpretation. This chapter then focuses on three central topics: first, the tendencies reflected in twenty-first century scholarship and criticism of the play; second, recurrent patterns characterizing this scholarship and criticism; and, third, areas of critical neglect and possibilities for new and rewarding inquiry. This chapter also includes a detailed listing of all editions, collections, and individual essays and chapters on the play published in the new millennium.

The following four chapters, under the rubric 'New Directions', employ innovative analyses of this widely studied text. These include the discovery of a new ethos for the tragedy, a postcolonial reading of the play, a first-hand account of the problems facing a director attempting to produce the drama for a contemporary audience, and an examination of the play's relationship to print culture.

What exactly is the magic that Faustus practises, and how does it relate to both his ambition and his fall? These questions have been asked many times before but have generally been approached by equating Marlowe's protagonist with notable Renaissance occultists such as Cornelius Agrippa and John Dee. In 'Doctor Faustus and Renaissance Hermeticism', Andrew Duxfield posits a very different ethos for the play, discovering striking parallels between Marlowe's Doctor Faustus and key passages from the writings of Hermes Trismegistus, the pseudo-historical mystic whose ideas strongly influenced Renaissance occult thought. Duxfield argues that these parallels offer a new perspective on Faustus's aspirations and also a potential synthesis between reading the play as a celebration of an ambitious yet admirable human being and interpreting it as a moral tale about the punishment of a foolish and faithless sinner.

Characterizing Doctor Faustus as an anamorphic drama, in 'Imperialism as Devilry: A Postcolonial Reading of Doctor Faustus', Toni Francis assumes an untraditional perspective from which to view the tragedy. From this unconventional stance, Francis discovers a drama in which Marlowe adapts his morality play format to contemporary issues, establishing a direct relationship between Faustus's surrender of his soul to Lucifer and England's pursuit of imperialist power through the mechanism of colonialism. According to Francis, the play's multiple allusions to exploitation and colonialism suggest a subtle critique of the discourse of imperialism emerging in the early modern period. In her reading, therefore, necromancy is equated with imperialism and Faustus with the colonizer who sells his soul for the power and control intrinsic to the imperialist enterprise.

In Chapter 6, '"What means this show?" Staging *Faustus* on Campus', Andrew James Hartley describes the decisions that he faced in directing this problematic play at the University of North Carolina at Charlotte in April 2007. First, of course, any director must select from the two very different extant texts. Hartley chose the A-text as more compatible with his own vision of the production, which stressed Faustus's agency and responsibility for his contract. In an effort to make the play relevant to a contemporary audience, Hartley adopted modern dress and minimized Faustus's aspirations for power and forbidden knowledge while highlighting his yearning for celebrity, in this case, celebrity as both a magician and a rock star. Finally, Hartley cast a female actor in the role of Mephistopheles, emphasizing the inner conflict of this most undemonic of devils, who is obliged to tempt and damn a man for whom she feels pity.

According to Georgia E. Brown in Chapter 7, 'The Other Black Arts: *Doctor Faustus* and the Inky Worlds of Printing and Writing', Marlowe's play is obsessed with the relationship between writing, print and performance, and the ways that textuality and corporeality might overlap. Brown argues that for all the excitement generated by its angels, devils, magic and hell fire, *Doctor Faustus* is particularly concerned with the opportunities and dangers of writing. First performed during the period when drama became a print form, the play coincides with the tentative beginnings of a writerly drama, and Brown adapts the techniques of cultural materialism to interrogate the way in which Marlowe's play probes the nature of script and of print, and examines the relationship of writing to performance and to bodies.

Not only does *Doctor Faustus* continue to be Marlowe's most often performed and critically debated play, but it also remains a perennial favourite in anthologies and textbooks and thus appears more frequently than any other work by Marlowe on university and college syllabi. The final chapter in this volume, 'A Survey of Resources', is thus designed to assist the teacher in presenting *Doctor Faustus* in the university and college classroom and proposes educational approaches that might effectively be adopted in teaching this play. In this chapter, Sarah K. Scott offers a comprehensive selection of resources – which include editions of the play, critical studies, pedagogical essays and media-based material – to suggest critical approaches, teaching strategies.

As noted above, Marlowe's reputation as a dramatist has suffered multiple vicissitudes, ranging from the stunning success of his plays in the 1580s and 1590s to their loss of favour in the seventeenth and eighteenth centuries, to their reinstatement in the canon in the nineteenth and twentieth centuries. Due in part to the fervent advocacy of the Marlowe Society of America, founded in 1974, after centuries of neglect, the late twentieth century rediscovered this enigmatic figure, an *enfant terrible* in his own time. Throughout the past three decades, two or three scholarly books on Marlowe have appeared in print every year, in addition to a constant flow of critical essays, all passionately debating the political affiliations, religious attitudes and sexual preferences affirmed in both Marlowe's life and his work. Moreover, the life of this dashing yet mysterious figure has also inspired numerous biographical studies, historical novels and original dramas. Clearly, in the new millennium, Christopher Marlowe has become an increasingly hot property and *Doctor Faustus* has remained his most frequently anthologized and most often performed play.

The Sources

The roots of *Doctor Faustus* lie deep in the fertile loam of medieval legend. Many of the stories told about Faust appear in the accounts of earlier charismatic conjurers such as Simon Magus, St Cyprian and Theophilus, all of whom have been cited as possible forerunners of Faust.[1] The stories surrounding these magicians were typical magus legends, tales centring around a much-acclaimed conjurer whose magical feats were recounted with great zest and wonder. Simon Magus, the hubristic magician first mentioned in the Acts of the Apostles, sought to purchase from St Peter the power of the Holy Spirit and instead 'gained undying notoriety by lending his name to one of the great vices of the Church – simony'.[2] St Cyprian, whose provenance derives not from Scripture but from Church tradition, was consecrated by his parents to the devil at the age of 7, performed many miraculous deeds and was eventually converted, martyred and canonized. However, the most popular magus legend was the story of Theophilus, dating from 650 AD, which introduced into the tradition the diabolical blood pact. Theophilus, initially a godly man, angered at his unfair treatment by the Church, denied Christ and made a pact with the devil, signed in his own blood. Later, however, after a career of dazzling supernatural exploits, he repented and was redeemed through the intercession of the Virgin Mary.

If the magus legend provided one radical source for the Faust fable, the medieval morality play furnished another root of this literary mandrake. Morality plays flourished primarily in the fifteenth century using allegory to teach a moral lesson. These plays are peopled with abstractions like Mercy and Justice or Virtue and Vice, and the protagonist usually bears the name Mankind or Everyman to signify that he represents the entire human race. The typical plot of these plays focuses on the allegorical conflict for the spiritual allegiance of this Mankind figure. Mankind's chief tempter, commonly called the Vice, attempts to lure the Everyman hero from the straight and narrow road of virtue onto the primrose path of dalliance and sin, while the Virtue figures, often called Good Council or Mercy, urge the hero to follow the dictates of God or the Church. The entire drama thus occurs within the human psyche, which becomes a battleground on which good and evil contend for ascendancy. The morality play Vice descends from the Satan of the mystery play and like his infernal progenitor is a conniving, comic hypocrite who delights in chicanery for its own sake and speaks directly to the audience, inviting their complicity in his schemes to corrupt the Mankind figure. As a comedian par excellence, the Vice often usurps centre stage from the Virtue figure, and even from the Mankind protagonist, to become the real star of the show. Although humorous, the Vice, representing the devil, is also horrific, and the levity of his antics in no way diminishes the terror that he inspires, since a majority of the people in the medieval and early modern periods believed in the devil as a real presence – ubiquitous, malevolent, wily, lurking behind every wheat field, awaiting the chance to lure the unwary to their doom.[3]

Doctor Faustus both adopts and alters the schema of the morality play to its tragic format. Like the morality play, Marlowe's drama enacts the *psychomachia* between good and evil for the allegiance of the protagonist; however, as in classical tragedy, Marlowe's tormented hero is not an Everyman figure but an exceptional individual. Moreover, Marlowe imports a number of emblematic characters from the morality play: the Good and Evil Angels probably derive from the fifteenth-century morality *The Castle of Perseverance*; the Old Man assumes the customary role of Good Council or Mercy, contesting with the Vice Mephistopheles for the soul of the protagonist. However, in his Mephistopheles, Marlowe creates a tempter unlike any Vice that had ever trod the medieval or early modern stage, a potentially tragic devil capable of both compassion and suffering. In addition, despite the emblematic quality of the morality play figures and the comic characters, Marlowe brackets his tragedy with two of the most eloquent and internalized soliloquies in early modern drama, soliloquies more appropriate to classical tragedy than to the morality play. Finally, whereas the majority of the morality plays conclude with the redemption of the often-erring hero, Marlowe's drama, as relentless as classical tragedy, ends in a harrowing denouement.

Critics suggest that the religious controversies of the period between Catholic/Anglican/Lutheran free will and Calvinist pre-destination modify the play's morality *psychomachia*. David Bevington and Eric Rasmussen posit that Marlowe's tragedy departs markedly from early Catholic moralities like *Everyman* and more closely resembles the Calvinist morality plays of the 1560s and 1570s, which dramatize issues of election and reprobation.[4] Lily Bess Campbell offers another possible homiletic source for the play: Nathaniel Woodes's *The Conflict of Conscience*, a Calvinist work based on the spiritual biography of Francesco Spira.[5] Lastly, Susan Snyder interprets the play as an inversion of the saint's legend, staging Faustus's conversion to evil, his embrace of the sacraments of devil worship, his bogus miracles, his multiple repentances to Lucifer, his mystical vision of Helen and his final damnation. Moreover, Faustus's consistent inversion of Scripture supports Snyder's reading of the play as an ironic hagiography.[6]

Having briefly canvassed the literary sources of the Faust legend, I shall undertake a search for the historical Faust. Like the majority of humanity's myths, the Faust legend appears to have had some basis in fact. Records show that a Georgius of Helmstadt matriculated at the University of Wittenberg in 1483 and later became known as Johann Faustus. Bevington and Rasmussen suggest that 'Faustus', meaning 'auspicious', may have been a Latin cognomen granted the magician in recognition of his magical exploits.[7] Between 1507 and 1540, many references to a wonder-worker bearing the name Johann or Johannes Faustus appeared in contemporaneous letters and diaries. These documents limn the portrait of a widely-travelled, well-educated, rather shady miracle worker, who was also a braggart, a vagabond and something of a mountebank. After his death, this Faustus became a lodestone about which gathered a mass of superstition, the deposit of centuries, including tales associated not only with Simon Magus, St Cyprian and Theophilus, but also with Empedocles, Virgil and Roger Bacon.[8] This slightly disreputable figure has had an indelible impact on the literary imagination of the western world, through the alchemy of myth transformed into an archetypical symbol of humanity's aspirations, follies and impossible dreams.

Throughout the latter decades of the sixteenth century, oral and occasional written accounts of Faustus's magical feats circulated around Europe. It was not long before an enterprising publisher saw the commercial possibilities of the legend and in the year 1587 a German press produced the first coherent biography of *The Historie of the Damnable Life and Deserved Death of Doctor John Faustus*, compiled by a man named Johann Spies. *The German Faustbook*, as this work was popularly called, narrates the story of the insatiable speculator who taking to himself the wings of an eagle desires to fly over the whole world and to know the secrets of heaven and earth. In his obsession for forbidden knowledge and worldly pleasure, Faustus studies necromancy, conjures the devil and makes a blood pact with Mephistopheles, promising his soul to Lucifer in return for 24 years of hedonistic delight and intellectual satisfaction. The centre section of the book details the puerile practical jokes on which Faustus squanders his dearly purchased power and the final chapters conclude on a solemn, cautionary note, graphically recounting the 'deserved death' of the 'damnable' necromancer. *The German Faustbook* blends soaring aspiration and grovelling lust, rollicking humour and tragic despair, all combined in the hybrid figure of its hero. In 1592, or perhaps even earlier, *The German Faustbook* was adapted into English by a man known only to posterity as P. F. Gent (Gentleman), and critical consensus accepts this version as the source for Marlowe's great tragedy. P. F., in his free-wheeling, sometimes grossly inaccurate, but always sprightly rendering into English of Spies's biography, expanded, condensed, diverged and interpolated at will, and some of these modifications help to identify *The English Faustbook* rather than the German version as Marlowe's source. *The English Faustbook* retains the oxymoronic quality of the German original, both its mixed form – part tragedy, part jestbook – and its hybrid hero – part titan, part buffoon – and Marlowe adopts both the cross-bred genre and the hybrid hero to his tragedy.[9]

The Play

In *The Tudor Play of Mind*, Joel Altman situates the problematic dramas of the early modern period within the theatrical tradition of arguing on both sides of the question. According to Altman, the interrogative plays so popular at this period are constructed from a series of statements and counterstatements, both equally valid, thereby imitating the form of a sophistical debate in which thesis provokes antithesis, yet without resolving synthesis. Thus, these plays ask questions rather than provide answers and deliberately evoke mixed reactions from their audiences.[10] Although all of Marlowe's plays have traditionally incited multiple responses, none has provoked the heated controversy generated by *Doctor Faustus*. Establishing the polarities of these responses are Una Ellis-Fermor and George Santayana, at one extreme, who identify *Doctor Faustus* as the 'most nearly Satanic tragedy that can be found' and Faustus as a 'martyr to everything that the Renaissance prized – power, curious knowledge, enterprise, wealth, and beauty', and Leo Kirschbaum, at the other, who insists that 'there is no more Christian document in all Elizabethan drama'.[11] Although the majority of commentators assume less hyperbolic stances, Faustus still arouses widely disparate reactions in audiences and critics alike, ranging from breathless admiration for the magician's aspiring mind and eloquent verse to utter contempt for his inane tricks. These widely divergent responses suggest that in *Doctor Faustus* Marlowe has penned an interrogative drama that brilliantly argues on both sides of the question.

If we focus only on the action of the play, the Christian apologists have the stronger case. Critics advancing this position cite the many changes that Marlowe makes in his source, *The English Faustbook*, that tend to deflate Faustus and his heroic aspirations.

First, the shift in emphasis from a longing for forbidden knowledge (the trespass of Prometheus) to a desire for power (the sin of Lucifer) radically alters the nature of the magician's transgressions. Both *Faustbooks* offer two primary motivations for Faustus's fatal contract: an itch for sensual pleasure and a voracious curiosity. In his dramatic adaptation, Marlowe surpasses his source in deeply probing his hero's motivation during the first two acts of the play, allowing Faustus continuously to rhapsodize on his dreams. The majority of these passages centre not on sensual pleasure (although he does refer to this on more than one occasion) nor on forbidden knowledge (although he does make casual reference to the 'resolution of ambiguities' and the 'secrets of foreign kings'). Rather, Marlowe's magician revels in visions of power, glory and wealth, like Tamburlaine, another of Marlowe's titanic over-reachers, elevating the sweet fruition of an earthly crown above knowledge infinite and the puissance of a god above both. Therefore, so the argument goes, despite Faustus's frequent intellectual debates with Mephistopheles, the language of the play minimizes the lure of forbidden knowledge and such curiosity as Marlowe's Faustus does exhibit is strongly vitiated by the yearning for power, fame and wealth. Moreover, by magnifying his hero's aspirations (the necromancers of the *Faustbooks* never presume to be 'great emperor of the world' or strive 'to gain a Deity') and sharply curtailing his realization (Marlowe's Faustus gains few, if any, of his grandiose dreams), Marlowe stresses the hiatus between

Faustus's over-reach and grasp and thus arguably renders his hero more truly tragic.[12]

Marlowe's exclusion of extraneous elements from his source further clarifies Faustus's downward trajectory as he falls under the spell of magic. According to G. K. Hunter's schema, the play traces the magician's descent through activities, associates and adversaries.[13] The play initially presents Faustus as a type of polymath, an adept in the four doctoral-granting disciplines of the early modern period: philosophy, medicine, law and divinity. Having rejected these four disciplines and embarked on his perilous journey into necromancy, Faustus first requests information about astronomy as his reward, thus partially vindicating himself as a knowledge-seeker. However, he soon discovers that Mephistopheles, unable to discuss first causes, can provide only the rudimentary knowledge already available to Faustus, and even to Wagner. Frustrated in his attempt to discover astronomical truth, Faustus moves from heaven to earth, devoting himself to cosmography, or what we would today call geography, enjoying something equivalent to the Grand Tour as he visits the capitals of Europe. In Rome, Faustus progresses downward from cosmology into politics, since his activities in the papal court, although primarily involving slapstick antics, relate tangentially to politics, at least in the B-text.[14] In the emperor's court, he further descends from Pope-maker to court entertainer, conjuring simulacra of Alexander and his paramour for the pleasure of Emperor Charles; the man who earlier exulted, 'The emperor shall not live but by my leave', now serves the emperor. Faustus's status is further reduced in the court of Vanholt, where he performs the function of an errand boy, a type of 'greengrocer', sending Mephistopheles around the world to fetch grapes out of season for the pregnant duchess. Ultimately, he degenerates into comic shenanigans with horse coursers and carters. At the same time that his field of activity deteriorates, Faustus suffers a social demotion, as he moves from the court of the Pope to that of the emperor to that of the duke, and the status of his adversaries diminishes from Pope, to jesting knight, to horse coursers and carters. Although Faustus's professional and social decline is more carefully delineated in the B-text than in the A, the elements of descent pervade both versions and this consistent demotion stresses the degenerative effects of the contract.[15] Finally, both texts of the play include a farcical sub-plot that parodies and deflates the necromancer's achievements, thus further diminishing his heroic stature by associating him with clowns like Robin and Rafe in the A-text and Robin and Dick in the B.[16]

According to the Christian exegetes, Marlowe not only adapts

The English Faustbook to reflect the early modern obsession with power, but he further alters his source to accentuate Faustus's responsibility for the pact, presenting his hero as agent of his own damnation as he doggedly seeks to finalize the contract with the devil. In his opening soliloquy, a masterly exemplum of reason pandering will, the discontented divine rejects all learning as trivial and embraces damnation as unavoidable, thus providing a rationale for his infernal contract. Later, in order to make his contract appear less threatening, he convinces himself that hell is only a fable and confounds it in Elysium. When confronted with undeniable evidence to the contrary – Mephistopheles come from hell to seize his 'glorious soul' – Faustus employs fallacious reasoning to convince himself that the demon cannot really be in hell. Finally, Faustus ignores Mephistopheles's passionate warning 'to leave these frivolous demands | Which strike a terror to my fainting soul' (I.III.83–84).[17] Here, in one of the most stunning changes in his source, Marlowe reverses the roles of tempter and tempted. The tempter of both *Faustbooks*, like the morality Vice and like any savvy salesman, minimizes the liabilities and maximizes the advantages of his product until he has his victim's name on the dotted line, while the vacillating conjurer of the *Faustbooks* seeks the best bargain possible. Conversely, in Marlowe's tragedy, Mephistopheles even urges his 'customer' to abstain from purchasing his product at such an exorbitant price, and Marlowe's Faustus himself plays the devil's advocate.[18]

In addition, Christian advocates point out that the introduction of emblematic characters from the morality play further reinforces the centrality of human choice, stressing Faustus as an agent of his own fate rather than the victim of a malevolent deity. These morality play figures include the Good and Evil Angels as well as the Old Man. Christian expositors would insist that the two debating angels, as well as the Old Man, would be theologically and dramatically gratuitous were Faustus predestined to damnation as many heroic interpreters insist.

In summation, Christian interpreters assert that, despite the allegedly heterodox opinions of its author, *Doctor Faustus* is paradoxically the most orthodox of Marlowe's dramas. They further insist that the containment and ironic undercutting of Faustus's radical subversion of Christian authority constitute a reaffirmation of that authority.

Challenging this impressive array of evidence, exponents of a heroic reading assert that both verbal statement and visual imagery create an irony that undermines the ostensible orthodoxy of the tragedy. Heroic advocates find support in two quotations from the play that arguably problematize the drama's affirmation of free will and personal responsibility. The first of these occurs in the Prologue's description of Faustus's Icarian flight and his disastrous fall: 'Til, swoll'n with cunning of a self conceit. | His waxen wings did mount above his reach, | And melting heavens *conspired* his overthrow' (Prologue 20–22; emphasis added). The second quotation is Mephistopheles's boast to Faustus in Act V, in which the fiend accepts responsibility for inspiring Faustus's fatal fallacious syllogism in scene i:

> 'Twas I that, when you wert i'the way to heaven,
> Damned up thy passage. When thou took'st the book
> To view the Scriptures, then I turned the leaves
> And led thine eye.
>
> (B.V.ii.98–101)

The first of these quotations certainly seems to imply the presence of a malignant deity conspiring against Faustus and perhaps predestining him to damnation; the second, although contradicting Mephistopheles's fervent warning to Faustus to 'Leave these frivolous demands', definitely interrogates Faustus's free will. Heroic commentators further cite the threatening figures of the infernal trinity – Lucifer, Beelzebub and Mephistopheles – hovering over Faustus's initial conjuring (I.iii) and over his final desperate soliloquy (V.ii) to suggest a world presided over by malevolent forces. They also stress the appearance of Lucifer instead of Christ in answer to Faustus's desperate plea, 'Ah, Christ, my Saviour, | Seek to save distressèd Faustus' soul!' (A.II.iii.82–83; cf. B.II.iii.84, which reads, 'Help to save distressèd Faustus' soul!'), as an emblem of the absence of God or Christ and the presence of evil as the controlling force of the play. Lastly, heroic expositors adduce the didactic speeches of the two angels at the play's denouement, which confirm Faustus's inexorable damnation, pointing out that these diatribes call into question the omnipresent possibility of repentance asserted by the Christian exponents and thus their affirmation of a benevolent providence presiding over the play. Moreover, Kristen Poole asserts that rather than unequivocally affirming human agency, the two duelling angels represent the two different theologies – Catholic/Anglican free will and Calvinist predestination – informing the play. Critics of this persuasion insist, therefore, that the contrary signals embedded within the play create an ideological disjunction that implicitly subverts the orthodoxy explicitly endorsed in the drama.[19] However, since the sinister imagery of the infernal trinity presiding over the initial and final scenes, Mephistopheles's boast concerning the fallacious syllogism, and the final tirades of the two angels are all absent from the A-text, advocates of a Christian reading might rebut that this ostensible ambiguity results primarily from textual corruption rather than ideological contrariety.[20]

Ultimately, the heroic interpreters must rely primarily on something much less tangible than visual tableau or explicit statement, offering instead the sense of identification and sympathy with which readers and audiences alike have traditionally responded to Faustus, the fallible human being desperately seeking to transcend human limitation. Two recent books present new readings to support this audience identification with Faustus. Patrick Cheney gives a novel twist to the heroic reading of the play, interpreting the tragedy not only as a deconstruction of Calvinist theology but also as an affirmation of artistic freedom in the face of restrictive religious orthodoxy. By merging Faustus the magician with Marlowe the playwright, Cheney interprets the play as the 'author's affirmation of his own artistic power to be free from the orthodox Christian forces dangerously afoot in the universe'.[21] Conversely, adapting a feminist approach to the play, Alison Findlay suggests that female audience members would have particularly identified with Faustus who, like them, is bullied by a patriarchal authority figure and denied desired knowledge.[22] Although I find both of these interpretations intriguing, I locate the source of audience empathy elsewhere, in both Faustus's complexity and in his eloquence. For in *Doctor Faustus*, Marlowe has created not only a morality play but a lacerating tragedy, as revealed in the two soliloquies with which Faustus opens and concludes the play. In his opening soliloquy, Faustus rationalizes his reasons for rejecting traditional learning and fatally choosing magic over divinity; in his final soliloquy, he struggles between desire for repentance and despair. In both speeches, Faustus portrays an *interiority* that anticipates Hamlet's famous internal conflicts, and this psychological inwardness evokes from the audience both pity and terror. Moreover, I suspect that the empathy, pity and terror that audiences frequently feel when confronting the tragedy derive to a large extent from Faustus's glorious language. For Faustus, like so many Marlovian protagonists, pits the magnificent word against the ignoble or, in this case, the inane deed. Those listening with a sensitized ear to Faustus's sonorous rhetoric while turning a blind eye to his foolish escapades will adopt a heroic reading. Conversely, those turning a deaf ear to some of the most soaring poetry in the early modern theatre and seeing only the trivial action on the stage will judge Faustus fatally flawed. Spectators able both to hear and to see simultaneously, and thus to perceive both the swan and the crow of Marlowe's perspective painting,[23] will probably achieve the fullest experience of Marlowe's tragedy.[24]

With its interiorized protagonist and its double perspective, *Doctor Faustus* occupies a pivotal position in the development of the English drama. Scholars have long credited Marlowe with introducing into the drama a flexible and dynamic verse through which emotion could be communicated and character created. I further assert that in the person of his tormented hero Marlowe creates the first fully internalized character on the early modern stage. Finally, I speculate that in *Doctor Faustus* Marlowe may be the first English playwright to script a dialogical drama that inscribes the multiplicity and indecidability of human experience, thereby anticipating, and perhaps even precipitating, the greater achievements of Elizabethan and Jacobean tragedy. On many levels, I suggest, reading or viewing *Doctor Faustus* allows us to participate in the creation of the English drama.

Notes

1   For a full account of the forerunners of Faust, see the excellent study by Philip Mason Palmer and Robert Patterson More, *The Sources of the Faust Tradition* (1936) (New York: Octagon Books, 1966), pp. 9–77, to which this brief summary is deeply indebted.

2   Palmer and More, *Sources*, p. 10.

3   For two definitive discussions of the distinctive characteristics of the morality play, see David Bevington, *From 'Mankind' to Marlowe* (Cambridge, MA: Harvard University Press, 1962) and Bernard Spivack, *Shakespeare and the Allegory of Evil* (New York: Columbia University Press, 1958).

4   David Bevington and Eric Rasmussen, Introduction to *'Doctor Faustus': A- and B-texts (1604, 1616)* (1993) (Manchester: Manchester University Press, 1995), p. 10.

5   Lily Bess Campbell, '*Doctor Faustus*: A Case of Conscience', *PMLA* 67 (1952), pp. 219–39.

6   Susan Snyder, 'Marlowe's *Doctor Faustus* as an Inverted Saint's Life', *Studies in Philology* 63 (1966), pp. 565–77.

7   Bevington and Rasmussen, Introduction to *Doctor Faustus*, p. 4.

8   Palmer and More, *Sources*, pp. 81–126, evaluate the historical evidence for a magician named Johannes or Johann Faustus in considerable detail. My brief summary draws freely from this valuable study. See also useful discussions by William Rose in his introduction to *The Historie of the Damnable Life and Deserved Death of Doctor John Faustus* (Notre Dame: University of Notre Dame Press, 1963), pp. 3–22, and by Bevington and Rasmussen, Introduction to *Doctor Faustus*, p. 4.

9   See the discussion by E. M. Butler of the German and English *Faustbooks* in *The Fortunes of Faust* (Cambridge: Cambridge University Press, 1952), pp. 3–41. See

also William Rose, Introduction to *Historie*, pp. 23–45. For the definitive examination of the sources and background of Marlowe's tragedy, see Bevington and Rasmussen, Introduction to *Doctor Faustus*, pp. 3–15. For a detailed comparison of *The English Faustbook* to Marlowe's *Doctor Faustus*, see Sara Munson Deats, '*Doctor Faustus*: From Chapbook to Tragedy', *Studies in Literature* 3 (1976), pp. 3–16.

10 Joel Altman, *The Tudor Play of Mind: Rhetorical Inquiry and the Development of Elizabethan Drama* (Berkeley, CA: University of California Press, 1978).

11 For the heroic interpretation of the play, see Ellis-Fermor, *The Frontiers of Drama* (New York: Oxford University Press, 1946), p. 143, and Santayana, *Three Philosophical Poets: Lucretius, Dante, and Goethe* (Cambridge, MA.: Harvard University Press, 1910), p. 147. For the Christian reading, see Kirshbaum, 'Marlowe's *Faustus*: A Reconsideration', *Review of English Studies* 19 (1943), p. 229.

12 For a more detailed analysis of Marlowe's changes in his source, see Douglas Cole, *Suffering and Evil in the Plays of Christopher Marlowe* (1962) (New York: Gordian Press, 1972), pp. 191–231, and Deats, '*Doctor Faustus*: From Chapbook to Tragedy', pp. 3–16.

13 G. K. Hunter, 'Five Act Structure in *Doctor Faustus*,' *Tulane Drama Review* 8.4 (1964), pp. 84–99.

14 In the papal court, the A-text Faustus limits himself to high jinks and practical jokes without political implications and thus Hunter's schema works much better in the B-text than in the A-text.

15 Although Hunter offers the most detailed analysis of Faustus's descent down the ladder of early modern professions, the term 'greengrocer' derives from Helen Gardner's 'Milton's Satan and the Theme of Damnation in Elizabethan Tragedy', *English Studies* (1948), p. 48.

16 The most comprehensive treatment of the deflative comic sub-plot in both texts can be found in Robert Ornstein, 'The Comic Synthesis in *Doctor Faustus*', *ELH* 22 (1955), pp. 165–72.

17 All quotations from the play are taken from the A-text in the edition by Bevington and Rasmussen; citations will be included within the text.

18 See Deats, '*Doctor Faustus*: From Chapbook to Tragedy', pp. 7–9.

19 For an insightful defence of the anti-Christian reading, particularly the contrariety produced by the sinister supernatural figures, see Max Bluestone, '*Libido Speculandi*: Doctrine and Dramaturgy in Contemporary Representations of *Doctor Faustus*', in *Reinterpretations of Elizabethan Drama*, ed. Norman Rabkin (New York: Columbia University Press, 1969), pp. 33–88. Poole further supports the interrogative nature of the play in '*Dr. Faustus* and Renaissance Theology,' in *Early Modern English Drama: A Critical Companion*, ed. Garrett A. Sullivan, Jr, Patrick Cheney and Andrew Hadfield (Oxford: Oxford University Press, 2006), pp. 96–107.

20 Leah Marcus in 'Textual Indeterminacy and Ideological Difference: The Case of *Doctor Faustus*', *Renaissance Drama* 20 (1989), pp. 1–29, argues that the differences in the two texts are so significant that we cannot legitimately discuss the single play *Doctor Faustus* but should treat the two versions as two separate dramas.

21 Patrick Cheney, *Marlowe's Counterfeit Profession: Ovid, Spenser, Counter-Nationhood* (Toronto: University of Toronto Press, 1997), pp. 190–220.

22 Alison Findlay, *A Feminist Perspective on Renaissance Drama* (Oxford: Backwell, 1999), pp. 11–25.

23 The allusion is to the 'couzening picture, which one way | Shows like a crow, another like a swan,' from George Chapman, *All's Fools*, I.IV.47, quoted in Ernest B. Gilman, *The Curious Perspective: Literary and Pictorial Wit in the Seventeenth Century* (New Haven, CT: Yale University Press, 1987), p. 36.

24 For a fuller discussion of the interrogative tone of Marlowe's *Doctor Faustus*,

see my essay, 'Marlowe's Interrogative Drama: *Dido, Tamburlaine, Doctor Faustus*, and *Edward II*', in *Marlowe's Empery: Expanding His Critical Contexts*, ed. Sara Munson Deats and Robert A. Logan (Newark, DE: University of Delaware Press, 2002), pp. 117–20.

CHAPTER ONE

The Critical Backstory

Bruce E. Brandt

This chapter traces the rich and varied critical history of *Doctor Faustus* from its beginning to the end of the twentieth century. It examines the strongly contested issues of text, date, authorship and structure; surveys the evolution of critical perspectives since Marlowe's rediscovery in the mid-eighteenth century; and concludes with a brief look at the theological issues that predominate in discussion of the play. Necessarily selective rather than comprehensive, the majority of the scholars it refers to are mentioned only once, despite the range of their contributions to Marlowe studies.

The Two Texts

The two early editions of *Doctor Faustus* pose a complex textual problem. The first, commonly referred to as the A-text, was published in 1604, and the second, known as the B-text, was published in 1616. The B-text is substantially longer than the A-text, and significant differences exist between the parallel portions of the two texts. Complicating the textual issue is the fact that in 1602 Philip Henslowe paid William Birde and Samuel Rowley to write additions to *Doctor Faustus*. The nature of the copy underlying each of the two editions has been much debated, and over the years both the A- and B-texts have been seen as the best choice for an editor to use as the copytext. An early nineteenth-century preference for the longer B-text (Dilke 1814; Oxberry 1818; and Robinson 1826) was followed by a long list of editors who chose the A-text because they perceived that the extra length of the B-text reflected Birde and Rowley's additions (Dyce 1850; Wagner 1877; Ward 1878; Bullen

1885; Ellis 1887; and Tucker Brooke 1910).[1] Cunningham's edition (1870) reprinted the B-text, but he too thought that the A-text was closer to Marlowe's original play.[2]

The editorial consensus in favour of the A-text switched to the B-text in the mid-twentieth century, and then changed back. The transition began in 1932, with Frederick Boas, who maintained that both texts have independent authority, that B contains Birde and Rowley's additions but preserves the main features of the play's original form and that where the texts are parallel, the 1616 readings are preferable.[3] In 1946, J. M. Nosworthy suggested that the two versions are Marlowe's first and second drafts, that Marlowe died leaving the play unfinished, and that neither text has an absolute claim to priority.[4] In that same year, Leo Kirschbaum asserted that the A-text is a bad quarto, that it 'reports the 1616 text, which is a good quarto; and that since it existed in 1594, the 1616 version is very close to Marlowe's original'.[5] W. W. Greg's monumental parallel-text edition of the two versions in 1950 also contended that the A-text is a bad quarto. Further, he maintained that the B-text reflects Marlowe's original play and does not contain the Birde-Rowley additions, which he suggested had been lost without being printed.[6] In 1973, Fredson Bowers agreed that the A-text is a memorial reconstruction but felt that it reports the form of the play as it was originally acted. He insisted that the B-text is based on Marlowe's foul papers, although it includes the 1602 additions, and concluded that any valid edition of the play had to be based on the B-text.[7] Other mid-century editions also featured the B-text, including those by Irving Ribner (1963), Roma Gill, in her first New Mermaids edition (1965), and John D. Jump (1976).[8]

In the last quarter of the twentieth century, the tide of critical opinion turned away from the B-text. Particularly influential in the transition were textual analyses by Constance Brown Kuriyama (1975) and Michael J. Warren (1981).[9] Kuriyama demonstrated that both texts are bad and refuted Greg's argument that the B-text does not contain the 1602 additions. Warren re-examined the assumptions underlying editorial distinction between the two texts, the differences in interpretation that they yield and the problem of distinguishing Marlowe's part of each text. He found that the textual problem cannot be resolved and that, in essence, we have two plays, both requiring study. The change in preference was cemented by four new editions of *Doctor Faustus* based on the A-text: Ormerod and Wortham (1985); Gill (1989 and 1990); and Keefer (1991).[10] Agreeing with Warren that the A- and B-texts are best considered as two separate plays, Bevington and Rasmussen include both in their edition. They posit that the A-text is not a memorial reconstruction but was set from an authorial manuscript. It is therefore 'closer in most ways to the original work of Marlowe and his collaborator' than the B-text, but '[b]ecause the B-text incorporates a thorough if intermittent reworking of concept and language, it deserves to be treated as a text by itself'.[11]

A number of other critics have weighed in on this debate, with many advancing additional textual arguments in favour of the A-text, or finding it superior to the B-text for other reasons. Bernard Beckerman explores the differences in organization between parallel scenes from the A- and B-texts and suggests on dramaturgical grounds that the B-text more likely contains additions to the A-text rather than the A-text being a contracted version of the B-text.[12] Seeing performances based on both A and B convinced George Geckle that 'the A-text version provides the superior aesthetic and emotional experience for a theatergoer'.[13] Examining the use of colloquialisms and contractions within the texts, D. J. Lake argues that the A-text is closer to Marlowe's autograph than the B-text and that the latter was revised after 1600, probably by Birde and Rowley.[14] Kenneth Muir sees the A-text as abridged, but not a memorial reconstruction.[15]

Some critics have continued to prefer the B-text. Roy Eriksen's *The Forme of Faustus Fortunes* defends the textual and authorial integrity of the B-text and concludes that it represents Marlowe's final conception of the play.[16] He also maintains that the B-text's Bruno material, often thought to be an addition, was written in 1592–93.[17] Doris Adler finds that the B-text's numerous allusions to John Foxe's *Acts and Monuments* contribute to the play's meaning and thematic unity and support the greater authority of the B-text since they would no longer have been relevant when the play was revised in 1602.[18] Robert A. H. Smith asserts that the allusion to three Doctor Faustuses in the *Folio Merry Wives of Windsor* indicates that the lines that Shakespeare refers to must have been written before 1602, and that therefore the Birde-Rowley additions restore lines that were most likely cut from the A-text.[19] Smith reaches a similar conclusion concerning similarities between passages in Lodge's *The Wounds of Civil War* and the B-text scene in which the scholars discover Faustus's dismembered body, suggesting that the parallels date this scene to the early 1590s or earlier.[20] Using computer analysis of relative vocabulary overlap and new word frequency, Louis Ule infers that the B-text is closer to Marlowe's other works than is the A-text.[21] One novel interpretation that sees both versions as distant from Marlowe's original vision is Francis Covella's assertion that *Doctor Faustus* was initially a short play consisting only of two parts, the covenant and the final reckoning, connected by Wagner's choral speech. She interprets the A-text as some other writer's expansion of the play, with the B-text reflecting the Birde-Rowley additions.[22] Gill's speculation that Marlowe died having completed only the beginning and ending of his play produces a similar textual situation, although without Marlowe's having felt that the play was complete.[23]

Bevington and Rasmussen warn that accepting that the two versions each merit independent study means that 'Editors and critics alike need to be wary of claims based on a conflated text'.[24] Historically, of course, most studies have been based on conflated texts, since editors believed that such texts brought one as close as possible to Marlowe's original. However, the new paradigm insists on the difference in vision embodied in the two texts. Thus, Warren observes that the variations in the scene with the Old Man reflect two different visions of Christianity,[25] and Ormerod and Wortham confirm this difference in their edition.[26] They also discover differences in the depictions of magic, interpreting the pact as binding in the B-text, but not in the A-text.[27] Keefer maintains that the A-text 'is shorter, harsher, more focused and more disturbing than that version of the play which readers and play-goers have for much of this century been taught to regard as Marlowe's'.[28] He also argues both that the A-text's depiction of magic shows Faustus becoming trapped by words, a theme that becomes muddled in the B-text,[29] and that supposedly objective bibliographical decisions can be ideological, suggesting that Greg's preference for the B-text reflects his preference for its theology.[30] Anne Mette Hjort similarly asserts that what the New Bibliography (which includes Greg and Bowers) accepts as self-evident terms are actually cultural constructs. Greg in particular is perceived as assuming that the goals of finding the author's original formulation and the aesthetically best play must coincide.[31] Like Keefer, Leah Marcus observes generational differences in scholarly preferences for the A- or B-texts.[32] She also contends that the A-text's Wertenberg refers to the duchy of Württemberg, a more Calvinistic locale than the B-text's Wittenberg, and that this corresponds with the A-text's more Protestant vision and the B-text's more Anglican orientation,[33] demonstrating that apparently small differences in parallel sections of the two texts may have large implications.

Thus, led to choose one text or the other, most critics began to base their arguments on the A-text. For example, both Stephen Greenblatt and C. L. Barber comment that their own work accords with the conclusions of Warren and Kuriyama, and both argue that the 1604 play is superior.[34] Nonetheless, some critics prefer the textual variations in B or find their interpretations supported by either text. For example, Rosador contends that the Elizabethan understanding of how temptation works is apparent in either the A- or B-text but that it is more fully developed in the B version.[35] Similarly, Fred B. Tromly discovers Tantalian motifs in both the A- and B-texts but finds they are most fully elaborated in the last act of the B-text.[36]

Date

Was *Doctor Faustus* written in 1588–89, in the heady aftermath of Marlowe's rousing success with *Tamburlaine, Parts I* and *II*, or was it written in 1592–93, shortly before Marlowe's untimely death in 1593? Critical opinion has veered back and forth, although, over the years, a majority has favoured the earlier date. John Bakeless's summary of scholarly opinion from 1831 to 1936 lists only two advocates of a later date, Tucker Brooke in 1922 and Boas in 1932.[37] Greg endorses the later date in his *Parallel Texts* edition, and Bowers supports Greg's opinion, noting that 'This view may well be the true one, for the mature style of Marlowe's part certainly agrees with a late instead of an early date'.[38] Irving Ribner follows 'most authorities' in preferring the later date.[39] The split continues among the recent editors advocating the A-text. Keefer thinks that the late date is more probable; Ormerod and Wortham opt for an early date; Gill believes that a date cannot be assigned; and Bevington and Rasmussen state that 'Stylistically and thematically, the case for a date in 1588–89 is as strong as for 1592 and probably no stronger'.[40]

The argument for the earlier date rests on a number of possible allusions to *Doctor Faustus* in works that predate 1592. Critics have noted striking parallels with *Doctor Faustus* in two early comedies, the anonymous *Taming of a Shrew* (performed some time between 1588 and 1593) and Robert Greene's *Friar Bacon and Friar Bungay* (probably first performed in 1589), in which Friar Bacon, like Faustus, plans to enclose his native land with a wall of brass. Others have identified debts to Marlowe's style and language in *A Knack to Know a Knave* (performed on 10 June 1592) and in *A Looking-Glass for London and England*, written by Thomas Lodge and Robert Greene (performed in August 1591). However, conclusions based on dramatic allusions are complicated by textual problems, dating problems and questions of who borrowed from whom.[41] Eric Sams proposes an early date for *The Taming of a Shrew*, but Raymond Houk explains the parallels by positing a common source, and, more recently, Robert A. H. Smith has suggested that the allusions in *A Shrew* point to an acting version preceding both the A- and B-texts.[42] Bakeless describes Greene's probable debt to Marlowe's walls of brass but notes that Greene's verbal debts are all to *Tamburlaine, I and II*.[43] Curt Zimansky identifies an allusion to *A Knack to Know a Knave* in *Doctor Faustus* and dates the play in 1589.[44] Roma Gill maintains that parallels in the Clown's part in *A Looking-Glass for London* and *Doctor Faustus* originate from the actor who played both parts.[45] This possibility reflects Thomas Pettitt's theory of 'dramaturgical formulas' that are repeated from play to play.[46]

Non-dramatic evidence includes the anonymous 'A ballad of the life and deathe of Doctur Faustus the great Cunngerer', entered in the Stationers' Register on 28 February 1589. Only the title is known, but its contents may be reflected in later seventeenth-century broadsides.[47] A reference in *The Black Book* (1604) to the appearance of an actual devil on stage at the Belsavage Playhouse during a performance of the *History of Faustus* has been taken to imply that *Doctor Faustus* was enacted in 1590, although Rasmussen has recently concluded that it alludes to *The Second Report of 'Doctor Faustus'* and not to an actual performance.[48] Finally, it seems probable that certain historical allusions in the play, such as references to the Duke of Parma, would have lost their point after 1590.[49] Each of these dramatic and non-dramatic parallels is subject to debate, and none is conclusive, but their combined evidence constitutes a strong case for the early composition and performance of this immensely influential play.

The case for *Doctor Faustus* being written late rather than early in Marlowe's career is based primarily on the fact that the earliest extant edition of Marlowe's primary source, *The Historie of the Damnable Life and Deserved Death of Doctor John Faustus*, was published in 1592. Obviously Marlowe could not have written his play before reading this translation, and for critics such as Greg, the publication date is definitive.[50] Other scholars have suggested that Marlowe may have had access to the work prior to 1592. The title page describes the book as being 'newly imprinted, and in convenient places imperfect matter amended', which may imply that there was an earlier edition.[51] Harold Jantz has proposed that there may have been a lost Latin version, and Paul Kocher surmises that an edition of the *English Faustbook* may have appeared in 1589 or 1590.[52] Bakeless endorses the possibility that Marlowe had read P. F.'s translation in manuscript, pointing out that Marlowe had clearly read Paul Ive's *Practise of Fortification*, one of his sources for *Tamburlaine, Part II*, prior to its publication.[53]

Co-authorship, Structure and Comedy

Whether *Doctor Faustus* was written early or late in his all-too-short career, the overwhelming majority of critics and editors concur that Marlowe did not write the play in its entirety. Editors do not agree entirely on which portions are by Marlowe and which are not, but in general they attribute the poetically powerful beginning and ending to Marlowe, while awarding the farcical clownage scenes and a good portion of Faustus's comic adventures to a collaborator.[54] Such collaboration was not uncommon in the early modern theatre. Typically the collaborators simply divided the task, with each then going off and writing his portion, and some inconsistencies between the tragic and comic portions of this play suggest that the two playwrights did not work closely together.[55] Who Marlowe's collaborator may have been is not known, but scholars have suggested a number of candidates. Samuel Rowley is frequently mentioned since he was later asked to write additions to the play.[56] Thomas Nashe is championed by Kocher,[57] and Bevington and Rasmussen speculate that the collaborator may been Henry Porter.[58]

Early commentators focused primarily on the specific passages considered to be Marlowe's, but as interest shifted to the play as a whole, critics began seeing it as structurally unified and thematically consistent. Greg avers that it was Marlowe 'who planned the whole' and 'that his collaborator or collaborators [. . .] carried out his plan substantially according to instructions'.[59] G. K. Hunter persuasively contends that the B-text of the play reveals a five-act structure, and the editions by Keefer and Bevington and by Rasmussen demonstrate that the same five-act structure is present in the A-text.[60] Moreover, numerous studies have found ways in which the comedy of the middle scenes contributes to and reinforces the thematic unity of *Doctor Faustus*. Thinking primarily of the B-text, Nicholas Brooke submits that Faustus 'is burlesqued by Wagner and the Clowns, and the impact of their activities on the main theme must be observed'.[61] Warren D. Smith maintains that the comedy of the A-text is essential to the play.[62] Harry Levin, Robert Ornstein, Roland M. Frye, John H. Crabtree, Jr., Charles Beall, Cleanth Brooks and Nigel Alexander insist that the comedy is an integral part of the play.[63] David Hirst goes so far as to suggest that 'No play provides a finer example than *Doctor Faustus* of the careful integration and employment of comic techniques in tragedy'.[64]

The Birth of Marlowe Studies

The popularity of *Doctor Faustus* from its first recorded performance in 1594 up to the closing of the theatres in 1642 is evident from the 'takings' recorded in Henslowe's diary, from the fact that extensive additions were considered commercially viable in 1602 and from the numerous reprintings of both the A- and B-texts.[65] However, Restoration adaptations of the play bore little resemblance to the original, and Marlowe's play disappeared from the stage.[66] Marlowe himself was nearly forgotten until the mid-eighteenth century and remained largely unknown to readers and scholars until the beginning of the nineteenth century. The revival of interest in him began in 1744 with the inclusion of *Edward II* in Robert Dodsley's *Old Plays*. Isaac Reed, the editor of the second edition, added *The Jew of Malta* in 1780. Unfortunately, the biographical information then available was dominated by the antagonistic account in Thomas Beard's *The Theatre of God's Judgments*, the idea promulgated by Anthony à Wood that Marlowe had died in a brawl over a serving woman, and the information in the Baines note, which was published by Joseph Ritson in 1782.[67] The result, as Thomas Dabbs has shown, was that by the end of the eighteenth century, 'Marlowe had become more prominent in the estimation of scholars, critics, and collectors, but his reputation as a depraved atheist may have put off critical estimation of his works'.[68]

In the early nineteenth century, *Doctor Faustus* was still considered to be inferior to *Edward II* and *The Jew of Malta*, but interest in Marlowe and *Doctor Faustus* was growing, and by the middle and latter parts of the century many critics judged it the best of Marlowe's plays.[69] Dabbs observes two dimensions to this increasing popularity. First, educators establishing a literary canon for a mass curriculum were concerned to show that the study of literature had socially redeeming value. *Doctor Faustus* benefited from this concern since it could not only be read as an exemplum of traditional Christian morality, but could be taught without confronting the issues of homosexuality and anti-Semitism raised by *Edward II* and *The Jew of Malta*. Moreover, Marlowe's acceptability was enhanced by Victorian academics who began to see him as a Romantic in the mould of Shelley and Byron.[70] A contrasting vision of Marlowe arose in the late nineteenth century when writers such as A. C. Swinburne, J. A. Symonds and Havelock Ellis created 'wild and extravagant images of the playwright in order to maintain an ongoing resistance against Victorian political and social values'.[71] This Marlowe was a rebel and free thinker or sceptic, driven, in Symonds's phrase, by 'l'amour de l'impossible'.[72]

Sceptic or Moralist?

The Victorian split between seeing Marlowe as a free thinking sceptic or an orthodox moralist has continued to inform Marlowe studies throughout the twentieth century.[73] The Romantic perspective, as it has come to be called, was highly influential during the first half of the century. Its most prominent early exponent was Una Ellis-Fermor, who presented Marlowe as a daring and audacious artist who projected his own sceptical ideas and frustrations onto his characters and interpreted the plays primarily as a means of insight into Marlowe's own rebellious mind. According to Ellis-Fermor, Marlowe was driven by conflicting thoughts and passions that he never resolved.[74] At mid-century Paul Kocher was also as much concerned with Marlowe's mind as with his drama, judging him 'one of the most highly subjective playwrights of his age'.[75] He discerns in *Doctor Faustus* both a knowledgeable description of orthodox Christianity and an anti-Christian bias made evident in Marlowe's ironical mockery.[76] Harry Levin's groundbreaking *The Overreacher* falls into the Romantic camp, although as Ribner says, it 'extends that tradition and develops it in new directions'.[77] Levin sees Marlowe as expressing Renaissance aspirations for sensation, power and knowledge (*libido sentiendi, libido dominandi* and *libidi sciendi*),[78] setting *Doctor Faustus* 'within a Christian framework, even while hinting that the framework is arbitrary and occasionally glancing beyond it'.[79] Ribner too affirms a Romantic reading of *Doctor Faustus*, viewing it as a protest against the religious system that it so accurately depicts.[80] Late twentieth-century exponents of the Romantic perception that 'Marlowe is deeply implicated in his heroes' include Greenblatt and Ian McAdam.[81]

Critical reaction against the notion that Marlowe's treatment of religion in *Doctor Faustus* is subversive gained strength near mid-century. In 1939, James Smith proposed that *Doctor Faustus* was an orthodox Christian allegory and suggested that thinking otherwise reflected twentieth-century prejudices.[82] A few years later Leo Kirschbaum urged that Marlowe's reputation for atheism and his presumed support for the Renaissance superman had skewed the interpretation of the play: 'Whatever Marlowe was himself, there is no more obvious Christian document in all Elizabethan drama than Doctor Faustus.'[83] Emphasizing the necessity of explaining Renaissance drama phenomenologically in terms of its social, intellectual and religious background, Clifford Davidson agrees that twentieth-century prejudices have affected the interpretation of *Doctor Faustus*, maintaining that to regard Faustus 'as the prototype of the striving individual who yearns for progress in this world against all the superstitions of the past' is to ignore all that we know about the way that Renaissance men and women thought about humanity's place 'in the scheme of things'.[84] Martin Versfeld, G. I. Duthie, James T. F. Tanner and Michael Hattaway concur that the play must be read in its sixteenth-century Christian context.[85] Margaret Ann O'Brien submits that Marlowe's position is thoroughly Christian even if it was not always seen as such by his contemporaries. Marlowe was, she asserts, 'much like the *avant garde* men in the era of Vatican II'.[86]

Some critics contend that *Doctor Faustus* was not only conservative in its values, but was, in fact, an attack on Renaissance humanism. M. M. Mahood argues that humanism was a disaster, that Marlowe was acutely aware of its defects and that his tragedies record its disintegration.[87] Robert Ornstein judges Marlowe more medieval than modern and more anti-humanistic than humanistic.[88] L. T. Fitz perceives Faustus as 'a commentary on the new vistas of hypocrisy and rationalization opened to mankind by Neoplatonism'.[89] Finally, Wolfgang Riehle suggests that while Marlowe's poetic powers have led to his being identified with the new ideas of the Renaissance, the ideas presented in *Doctor Faustus* are actually medieval and conservative.[90]

Marlowe and Early Drama

In the 1960s an emphasis on the relationship of Marlowe's drama to earlier English drama emerged, but the conclusions reached were often very different. Douglas Cole's *Suffering and Evil in the Plays of Christopher Marlowe* strongly insists on the Christian orthodoxy of Marlowe's canon.[91] Cole finds that the plays explain human suffering as divine retribution for sinfulness and argues that Marlowe's religious perspective strongly reflects both the theology he studied at Cambridge and the traditions of earlier English drama, including the cycle plays and the morality tradition. David Bevington's seminal study *From 'Mankind' to Marlowe* appeared in the same year as Cole's book and also analysed Marlowe's debt to the earlier drama. Bevington establishes a canon of early popular drama, examines the structural implications of the conditions and methods of performance, and traces dramaturgical development from the Middle Ages to Marlowe's time. Unlike Cole, he does not see Marlowe as constrained by the theology of the moralities, and, indeed, Bevington endeavours 'to correct the common misapprehension that popular dramatic structure was a simple, constant entity, to which one might refer statically as "the Morality pattern" '.[92] Bevington discovers an ambiguity in Marlowe's plays that arises from a tension between their apparent dramatic aims and the morality structures that Marlowe uses. James Reynolds locates the source of such tension within Protestant thought, noting that from around 1550 the morality plays began to emphasize divine retribution for sin while Catechisms, the Prayerbook, the Articles and sermons continued to stress the possibility of salvation. He interprets *Doctor Faustus* as paralleling this later kind of morality and presenting the damnation of a sinner who does not repent.[93] Stephen Rayburn traces *Doctor Faustus*'s indebtedness to the Judgement Day plays in the Corpus Christi cycles, including the juxtaposition of the good and bad angels, the alternations of comic and serious scenes, the use of the seven deadly sins and the appearance of devils on stage.[94] Lorraine Kochanske Stock contends that the depiction of gluttony in *Doctor Faustus* is rooted in the medieval association of gluttony with Adam's Fall, that the gluttony motif pervades and unites both the comic and tragic portions of the play and that the language of Faustus's final soliloquy is filled with images of gluttony.[95] Margaret E. Owens focuses on *Doctor Faustus*'s visual depictions of dismemberment (more prevalent in the B-text), relating them to theatrical traditions deprecated or suppressed by reformers: juggling, folk play and saint play.[96] The use of gluttony and dismemberment in the play is also explored by Barber and Edward Snow, and Susan Snyder sees Faustus's life as an inverted version of the conventional saint's life.[97] Robert Weimann argues that the artistic potential of Renaissance humanism was enriched through its merger with the popular dramatic tradition and that *Tamburlaine* and *Doctor Faustus* reveal 'a new confidence in man's capacity for self-determining action'.[98] John D. Cox's study of the demons in *Doctor Faustus* and Shakespeare's 1 and 2 *Henry VI* notes that a sixteenth-century play could not have been too openly heterodox and suggests that Marlowe's 'dramaturgical appearance of conformity may in fact have been a stalking horse for defiance' and that the play's demonology appears 'defensively orthodox' while being, in fact, 'ambiguous and subversive'.[99]

The End of the Century

The heterodoxy attributed to Marlowe by Cox differs from the critical perceptions offered earlier in the century in that Cox regards Marlowe as an objective rather than as a subjective artist and suggests that any ambiguity in his plays is intentional.[100] This recognition of objective artistry and deliberate irony plays a large role in Marlowe studies during the last quarter of the century. Judith Weil asserts that Marlowe deliberately 'mocks his heroes in a remarkably subtle fashion'.[101] Joel B. Altman contends that 'Marlowe's plays are literally dramatized *suppositions*', a reflection of Renaissance rhetorical training in arguing both sides of a proposition.[102] Thomas McAlindon demonstrates that Marlowe manipulates key words to create a deeply ironic perspective of Faustus.[103] Lawrence Danson maintains that Marlowe's use of rhetorical questions reveals his artistic objectivity and control and that in *Doctor Faustus* his questions are subversively satirical.[104] Carol Leventen Duane urges that the moral ambiguity of Marlowe's plays is the product of the playwright's deliberate 'manipulation of multiple perspectives and divided responses'.[105]

The latter quarter of the century also witnessed the rise of new historicism, inaugurated in Marlowe studies by *Renaissance Self-fashioning*, Greenblatt's seminal exploration of the interplay between cultural values and a writer's sense of selfhood.[106] Jonathan Dollimore and Simon Shepherd are also concerned with the cultural context of Renaissance drama, both focusing on the way in which it questions and subverts the era's dominant religious and political ideologies.[107] Thomas Cartelli, drawing on historical and critical analyses of Elizabethan thought and behaviour, maintains that far from being resistant to unorthodox ideas within the drama, most Elizabethan playgoers would have found pleasure in transgressive or heterodox materials.[108] Examining Marlowe's use of 'alien' characters such as Oriental despots, Jews and homosexuals in the context of England's nascent imperialism, Emily C. Bartels concludes that Marlowe helped to 'transform the theater into one of the most popular and powerful arenas for social and political comment and dissent'.[109]

Psychoanalytic criticism also emerged as an important aspect in late twentieth-century criticism. Constance Brown Kuriyama's notable *Hammer or Anvil* proposes that Marlowe's plays are a symbolic working out of his intense homosexual conflicts.[110] Philip Wion explains Faustus's aspirations and anxieties in terms of Oedipal wishes and fears.[111] Peter Donaldson adopts the perspective of Heinz Kohut and argues that Marlowe's tragic vision arises from the interplay of conflict and coherence.[112] Matthew Proser utilizes aggression theory to explain Marlowe's creative process and the thematic implications of his plays.[113] Other interesting studies include Emil Roy's dream analysis of Faustus's final speech, Kenneth

Golden's Jungian interpretation of *Doctor Faustus* and William Stull's assertion that Adlerian insights clarify Marlowe's tragic vision.[114] Adapting Greenblatt's new historicist notion of self-fashioning and exploring it from a psychoanalytic perspective, Ian McAdam's *Irony of Identity* concludes that Marlowe's 'plays are orthodox in their exposure of human limitation, but heterodox in their treatment of traditional religious doctrine'[115] and that the failures of Marlowe's protagonists are rooted in 'Marlowe's own religious and sexual conflicts'.[116] During the last quarter of the century, feminist theory had become important to Renaissance studies in general. However, the first book-length study to explore Marlowe's dramatization of sexuality and gender relations, as opposed to homosexuality and sexual transgressiveness, was by Sara Munson Deats in 1997.[117]

Helen

The source of the thousand ships in Faustus's rhapsodic speech to Helen is Lucian's *Eighteenth Dialogue of the Dead*,[118] but while Marlowe's language emphasizes Helen's incomparable beauty, in Lucian her rotting skull is indistinguishable from any other. Harry Levin suggests that Marlowe could not have been insensitive to the *Ubi sunt* mood of the original and that the contrast is a reminder that Faustus's vision of Helen is merely skin-deep.[119] More recently, Pompa Banerjee argues that the ironic contrast with Lucian shows that Faustus has chosen death rather than life.[120] The same allusion appears in *Tamburlaine* (Part II: II.iii.88) and Hobart Jarrett submits that Faustus's speech to Helen more effectively creates a sense of beauty than Tamburlaine's praise of Zenocrate because of its verbal ambiguities.[121]

The courtship of Helen has inspired a variety of critical responses. Neil Forsyth concludes that Marlowe uses the traditional ambivalence of the Helen figure as a way to extend the paradox of destructive beauty to language itself and to challenge the very idea of *limit* and *term*.[122] Beach Langston interprets Helen as the temptation of the world and the flesh within the *Ars Moriendi* tradition.[123] Patrick Cheney contends that Helen embodies and deliberately undercuts the type of neoplatonism found in Spenser's poetry, thus indicting Spenser's idealism.[124] Kuriyama points out that the blurred gender distinctions in the similes at the end of Faustus's speech to Helen may reflect Marlowe's subconscious grappling with his own homosexuality: *she* is 'flaming Jupiter'; *he* is 'hapless Semele'.[125] Kay Stockholder also treats the supernatural and diabolic elements of

Doctor Faustus as revelatory of the psychological state of the protagonist, presenting him as having sublimated his sexuality to his desire for knowledge and reputation and arguing that this 'one kiss [...] is all that he realizes of the limitless sensual pleasure he anticipated'.[126] For Bartels, Faustus's desire for Helen reflects not repressed sexuality but his grappling with the idea of immortality.[127] Drawing on Joseph Campbell to explore the Helen myth and the mythological allusions in Faustus's courtship speech, Sallye Sheppeard concludes that *Faustus* 'says less about the consequences of actual sin in such a culture than it does about the condemnation visited upon those who challenge the orthodoxy of such a culture'.[128] Christopher Wortham asks how a Renaissance humanist would have responded to Helen since Troy was aligned with English nationalism, while Helen, despite her beauty, was identified with destruction and 'sensuality unchecked by moral restraint'.[129] For Barber the Helen episode is both rhapsodically erotic and blasphemous. His discussion of Helen is a portion of a larger discussion of Marlowe's exploration of the tensions within Protestant theology and worship, especially as they relate to the communion service.[130]

Deats excludes Helen from consideration in her seminal feminist analysis of Marlowe's works precisely because Helen is a demon and not a woman.[131] However, others have seen gender division within the play. Barbara Baines argues that all of Marlowe's plays show feminine qualities being suppressed so that a masculine ideal can be achieved and that the process is powerfully internalized in *Doctor Faustus*: 'As Faustus confronts himself, he is simultaneously masculine aggressor and feminine victim'.[132] Lucy De Bruyn's examination of how woman and the devil are depicted in sixteenth-century literature moves between two poles: Mary of Nemmegen, a female Faust figure who is saved by the Virgin Mary and who embodies the contemporary ideal of womanhood, and Marlowe's Helen, who is 'the woman in league with the Devil, working for man's damnation'.[133]

The Faustus-Helen relationship climaxes in their kiss. Martin Puhvel suggests that when Faustus asks Helen to make him 'immortal with a kiss' he is thinking of Helen as a classical goddess who could grant immortality to her human lover.[134] Bruce E. Brandt proposes that the kiss is far more ironic, drawing upon the traditions of the liturgical kiss of peace, the chaste kiss of Castiglione's Pietro Bembo and the use of the kiss to symbolize mystical rapture, including the neoplatonic understanding of the *mors osculi*.[135] Philip Traci concludes that Faustus's search to know good and evil is an artist's search and that Faustus hopes to find artistic immortality in Helen's kiss.[136]

Despair

Since Helen is not a mortal woman but a demon impersonating Helen, Greg famously asserts that the kiss constitutes the sin of demoniality, which he defined as the unforgivable sin against the Holy Ghost, and thus the sin for which Faustus is damned.[137] However, Nicholas Kiessling points out that demoniality was never considered an unforgivable sin and Gerard Cox identifies six meanings of 'sin against the Holy Ghost' (presumption, despair, impenitence, hardness of heart, resisting a previously known truth and envying other men who have made better use of God's grace), and finds that Faustus has committed all six.[138] Lily B. Campbell argues that Faustus sins in his estrangement from God but that his conclusive sin is despair, which is unforgivable in the sense that one in its grip feels unworthy of repentance and therefore does not repent. She compares his case to that of Francis Spira, an Italian lawyer who converted to Lutheranism, recanted under the threat of prosecution for heresy and then died in a state of despair, a story dramatized in England in Nathaniel Woodes's *A Case of Conscience*.[139] R. H. Bowers supports Campbell's thesis of the role of despair in *Doctor Faustus* by comparing it to Tirso's *El Condenado por Desconfiado*, a play in which a hermit sins through pride and presumption and falls into despair and damnation.[140] John C. McClosky and Arieh Sachs discuss the Reformation understanding of despair and its role in the play.[141] Greg's suggestion that Faustus had literally become a spirit is refuted by T. W. Craik, who argues that Greg is wrong to attach more weight to demoniality than to pride and despair.[142] Kiessling, J. C. Maxwell and James Smith also discuss pride's role in Faustus's fall.[143]

Si Pecasse Negamus

The numerous inaccuracies in Faustus's survey and rejection of all other fields of learning in favour of magic have engendered divergent readings. For example, Joseph McCullen is certain that the Elizabethan audience would have recognized the sophistry of Faustus's rejections and would not have seen him as learned; R. W. Ingram suggests that the initial soliloquy leaves the audience convinced of Faustus's learning, but in a way that reveals his moral error in rejecting God; and Phoebe Spinrad argues that the opening soliloquy reveals Faustus as merely a dilettante, a superficial dabbler who perceives himself to be an expert in all fields.[144] Critics focus on the syllogism based on Romans 6:23 and 1 John 1:8 that Faustus employs to convince himself to bid Divinity adieu, insisting that its refutation would have been well known to Marlowe's audience: Kocher notes the use of the same syllogism by Thomas Becon and Cole points out that the passage from John was used in the second of the official Elizabethan sermons and homilies.[145] In fact, as Gill observes, the words of Faustus's 'translation' of Jerome's Bible actually derive from the 1599 Book of Common Prayer.[146] Indeed, the refutation is so obvious that John Wilks asserts that 'Faustus does not actually believe what he is saying'.[147] Claude J. Summers and Ted-Larry Pebworth suggest that episode ironically mirrors St Augustine's conversion to Christianity and is an attack on the doctrine of predestination.[148]

Predestination and Free Will

The question of whether Faustus is predestined to damnation or if he is free to repent looms large in Marlowe studies. Those who see Faustus as free to repent rely on the assertions of the Good Angel and the Old Man that grace is available if Faustus repents.[149] Those favouring predestination emphasize the Calvinist orientation of Reformation theology. The latter readings participate in the same orthodox/heterodox debate as do the former. Thus, Paul Sellin suggests that Faustus embodies the plight of the reprobate, while Alan Sinfield concludes that although Faustus is predestined to hell the play ironically condemns the God who sends him there.[150] Many critics, however, have come to feel that the true point is Marlowe's exploitation of these theological tensions. Martha Tuck Rozett notes that Marlowe brings 'his audience to an extraordinary degree of emotional involvement with a soul whose damnation is certain.'[151] Pauline Honderich stresses the interplay that Marlowe creates between Calvinist and Anglican understandings of spiritual destiny.[152] Robert G. Hunter believes that Marlowe forced Christian playgoers of all stripes (Semi-Pelagian, Augustinian and Calvinist) to examine imaginatively what it is they believe.[153] Roy Eriksen insists that Faustus's answer to the theological dilemma posed by the Calvinist-Augustinian debate over free will lies in the moral philosophy and rhetorical strategies of Giordano Bruno.[154] King-Kok Cheung maintains that the dialectic between despair and the possibility of salvation creates real suspense about the outcome of the play, and Phoebe Spinrad argues that the stricter Calvinists would have shunned the play and that Marlowe was writing for an audience that was inclined to see Faustus's despair not as a natural function of his predestined state but as a headstrong refusal to acknowledge his sin, turn to God and amend his life.[155] If repentance is possible, then so is salvation. Among others, Max Bluestone contends that Faustus's end is ambiguous and David C. Webb submits that 'the play flaunts a number of possible reasons why Faustus might be damned, yet never allows the audience the satisfaction of certainty'.[156] However, the vast majority of both predestination and free will critics agree that Faustus is damned and that, justly or unjustly, he has paid the price for his sin.

On to the Future

Tracing the form of *Faustus*'s critical fortunes has meant touching upon many of the most ardently debated issues in the play's critical heritage. Some of them, such as the questions of date and edition, might initially appear to be merely technical, but as this chapter has shown, they are contentious because they relate to the play's core meaning: what did Marlowe himself write; how youthful or mature is the play's vision; is one text or the other more authentically Marlovian? These have proven to be daunting questions and they will likely remain so. The same is true of the debates over the play's theology: does Faustus have free will or not; is he predestined to damnation; is the audience meant to applaud Faustus's aspirations or condemn them; does the play endorse Faustus's damnation, or does it subtly criticize the Christian vision? Marlowe's grappling with the nature of the human condition looms large in the play's critical backstory, and one suspects that the vitality of these questions will endure for readers and audiences of the twenty-first century.

Notes

1   David Bevington and Eric Rasmussen, eds, '*Doctor Faustus*': A- and B-texts *(1604, 1616)*, (Manchester: Manchester University Press, 1993), p. 63.
2   Bevington and Rasmussen,' *Faustus*'.
3   Frederick S. Boas, *The Tragical History of Doctor Faustus* (New York: Lincoln MacVeagh; Dial Press, 1932), pp. 33–34.
4   J. M. Nosworthy, 'Some Textual Anomalies in the 1604 *Doctor Faustus*', *Modern Language Review* 41 (1946), pp. 1–8.
5   Leo Kirschbaum, 'The Good and Bad Quartos of *Doctor Faustus*', *The Library*, 4th ser., 26 (1946), p. 294.
6   W. W. Greg, ed., *Marlowe's 'Doctor Faustus' 1604, 1616: Parallel Texts* (Oxford: The Clarendon Press, 1950).

7   Fredson Bowers, 'Marlowe's *Doctor Faustus*: The 1602 Additions,' *Studies in Bibliography* 26 (1973), pp. 1–18; *The Complete Works of Christopher Marlowe*, vol. 2 (Cambridge: Cambridge University Press, 1973).

8   Irving Ribner, ed., *The Complete Plays of Christopher Marlowe* (New York: Odyssey, 1963); Roma Gill, ed., *Dr Faustus*, New Mermaids (London: Ernest Benn, 1965); John D. Jump, ed., *The Tragical History of the Life and Death of Doctor Faustus*, The Revels Plays (1962) (Manchester: Manchester University Press, 1968).

9   Constance Brown Kuriyama, 'Dr. Greg and *Doctor Faustus*: The Supposed Originality of the 1616 Text', *English Literary Renaissance* 5 (1975), pp. 171–97; Michael Warren, '*Doctor Faustus*: The Old Man and the Text,' *English Literary Renaissance* 11 (1981), pp. 111–47.

10 David Ormerod and Christopher Wortham, eds, *Christopher Marlowe: 'Dr Faustus': The A-Text* (Nedlands: University of Western Australia Press, 1985); Roma Gill, ed., *Dr Faustus*, 2nd edn, New Mermaids (London: A & C Black, 1989); Roma Gill, ed., *The Complete Works of Christopher Marlowe*, vol. 2, *Dr Faustus* (Oxford: The Clarendon Press, 1990); Michael Keefer, ed., *Christopher Marlowe's 'Doctor Faustus': A 1604-version Edition* (Peterborough, Ontario: Broadview Press, 1991).

11 Bevington and Rasmussen, '*Faustus*', pp. 64, 77. Rasmussen lays out the textual arguments more fully in 'Rehabilitating the A-text of Marlowe's *Doctor Faustus*,' *Studies in Bibliography* 46 (1993), pp. 221–38; and *A Textual Companion to 'Doctor Faustus'*, The Revels Plays Companion Library (Manchester: Manchester University Press, 1993).

12 Bernard Beckerman, 'Scene Patterns in *Doctor Faustus* and *Richard III*', in *Shakespeare and His Contemporaries: Essays in Comparison*, ed. E. A. J. Honigmann, The Revels Plays Companion Library (Manchester: Manchester University Press, 1986), pp. 31–41.

13 George L. Geckle, 'The 1604 and 1616 Versions of *Dr. Faustus*: Text and Performance', in *Subjects on the World's Stage: Essays on British Literature of the Middle Ages and the Renaissance*, ed. David G. Allen and Robert A. White (Newark, DE: University of Delaware Press, 1995), p. 147.

14 D. J. Lake, 'Three Seventeenth-Century Revisions: *Thomas of Woodstock*, *The Jew of Malta*, and *Faustus B*', *Notes and Queries* 30 (1983), pp. 133–43.

15 Kenneth Muir, 'Three Marlowe Texts', *Notes and Queries* 43 (1996), pp. 142–44.

16 Roy T. Eriksen, *The Forme of Faustus Fortunes: A Study of 'The Tragedie of Doctor Faustus' (1616)* (Oslo: Solum Forlag A.S.; Atlantic Highlands, NJ: Humanities Press International, 1987).

17 Roy T. Eriksen, 'Giordano Bruno and Marlowe's *Doctor Faustus* (B)', *Notes and Queries* 32 (1985), pp. 463–65.

18 Doris Adler, 'The Acts of Doctor Faustus as Monuments of the Moment', *Selected Papers from the West Virginia Shakespeare and Renaissance Association* 10 (1985), pp. 1–24.

19 Robert A. H. Smith, '*Doctor Faustus* and *The Merry Wives of Windsor*', *Review of English Studies* 43 (1992), pp. 395–97.

20 Robert A. H. Smith, ' "Faustus End" and *The Wounds of Civil War*', *Notes and Queries* 32 (1985), pp. 16–17.

21 Louis Ule, 'Recent Progress in Computer Methods of Authorship Determination', *Association for Literary and Linguistic Computing Bulletin* 10.3 (1983), pp. 73–89.

22 Frances Dolores Covella, 'The Choral Nexus in *Doctor Faustus*', *Studies in English Literature, 1500–1900* 26 (1986), pp. 201–15.

23 Gill, *The Complete Works of Christopher Marlowe*, p. xviii.

24 Bevington and Rasmussen, '*Faustus*', p. 77.

25 Warren, '*Doctor Faustus*: The Old Man and the Text', p. 139.

26 Ormerod and Wortham *Christopher Marlowe: 'Dr Faustus': The A-Text*, p. xxv.

27 Ormerod and Wortham, *Christopher Marlowe: 'Dr Faustus': The A-Text*, pp. xli–xlii.
28 Keefer, *Christopher Marlowe's 'Doctor Faustus': A 1604-version Edition*, p. vii.
29 Michael H. Keefer, 'Verbal Magic and the Problem of the A- and B-Texts of *Doctor Faustus*', *Journal of English and Germanic Philology* 82 (1983), pp. 324–46.
30 Michael H. Keefer, 'History and the Canon: The Case of *Doctor Faustus*', *University of Toronto Quarterly* 56 (1987), p. 510.
31 Anne Mette Hjort, 'The Interests of Critical Editorial Practice', *Poetics* 15 (1986), pp. 259–77.
32 Leah S. Marcus, *Unediting the Renaissance: Shakespeare, Marlowe, Milton* (London: Routledge, 1996), p. 44.
33 Marcus, *Unediting the Renaissance: Shakespeare, Marlowe, Milton*, pp. 41–54.
34 Stephen Greenblatt, *Renaissance Self-Fashioning: From More to Shakespeare* (Chicago: University of Chicago Press, 1980), p. 290; C. L. Barber, *Creating Elizabethan Tragedy: The Theater of Marlowe and Kyd*, ed. Richard P. Wheeler (Chicago: University of Chicago Press, 1988), p. 94.
35 K. Tetzeli von Rosador, 'Supernatural Soliciting: Temptation and Imagination in *Doctor Faustus* and *Macbeth*', in *Shakespeare and His Contemporaries: Essays in Comparison*, ed. E. A. J. Honigmann, Revels Plays Companion Library (Manchester: Manchester University Press, 1986), pp. 42–59.
36 Fred B. Tromly, *Playing with Desire: Christopher Marlowe and the Art of Tantalization* (Toronto: University of Toronto Press, 1998), p. 134.
37 John Bakeless, *The Tragicall History of Chistopher Marlowe*, vol. 1 (Cambridge, MA: Harvard University Press, 1942; reprinted Westport, CT: Greenwood, 1970), pp. 277–78; C. F. Tucker Brooke, 'The Marlowe Canon', *PMLA* 37 (1922), p. 384; Boas, *The Tragical History of Doctor Faustus*, p. 8.
38 Greg, *Marlowe's 'Doctor Faustus' 1604, 1616: Parallel Texts* , p. 10; Bowers, *The Complete Works of Christopher Marlow*, p. 124.
39 Ribner, *The Complete Plays of Christopher Marlowe*, pp. xxiii–iv.
40 Keefer, *Faustus*, p. lv; Ormerod and Wortham, *Faustus*, p. xv; Gill, *Works*, p. xii; Bevington and Rasmussen, *Faustus*, p. 3.
41 See the overviews in Ormerod and Wortham, *Faustus*, pp. xiii–xv; Keefer, *Faustus*, pp. lv–ix; Bevington and Rasmussen, *Faustus*, pp. 1–3; Jump, *Tragical History*, pp. xxii–iv; and Greg, *Parallel Texts*, pp. 1–10.
42 Eric Sams, 'The Timing of the *Shrews*', *Notes and Queries* 32 (1985), pp. 33–45; Raymond A. Houk, '*Doctor Faustus* and *A Shrew*', *PMLA* 62 (1947), pp. 950–57; Robert A. H. Smith, 'A Note on *Doctor Faustus* and *The Taming of a Shrew*', *Notes and Queries* 26 (1979), p. 116.
43 Bakeless, *Tragicall History*, pp. 307–8.
44 Curt Zimansky, 'Marlowe's Faustus: The Date Again', *Philological Quarterly* 41 (1962), pp. 181–87. See also Greg, *Parallel Texts*, p. 53; Kuriyama, 'Dr. Greg', pp. 181–97; William Empson, *Faustus and the Censor: 'The English Faust-book' and Marlowe's 'Doctor Faustus'* (Oxford: Basil Blackwell, 1987), pp. 185–95.
45 Gill, *Works*, pp. xix–xi.
46 Thomas Pettitt, 'Formulaic Dramaturgy in *Doctor Faustus*', in *'A Poet and a filthy Play-maker': New Essays on Christopher Marlowe*, ed. Kenneth Friededreih, Roma Gill and Constance B. Kuriyama (New York: AMS Press, 1988), pp. 167–91.
47 Mac D. P. Jackson, 'Three Old Ballads and the Date of *Doctor Faustus*', *AUMLA* 35 (1971), pp. 187–200.
48 Eric Rasmussen, 'The Black Book and the Date of *Doctor Faustus*', *Notes and Queries* 37 (1990), pp. 168–70.
49 Bakeless, *Tragicall History*, p. 276.
50 Greg, *Parallel Texts*, p. 10.
51 But see Boas, *Tragical History*, p. 6.
52 Harold Jantz, 'An Elizabethan Statement on the Origin of the German Faust Book', *Journal of English and Germanic Philology* 51 (1952), pp. 137–53; Paul

H. Kocher, 'The English *Faust Book* and the Date of Marlowe's *Faustus*', *Modern Language Notes* 55 (1940), pp. 95–101; and Paul H. Kocher, 'The Early Date for Marlowe's *Faustus*', *Modern Language Notes* 58 (1943), pp. 539–42.

53   Bakeless, *Tragicall History*, p. 277.

54   Dissenters from the majority opinion include Leo Kirschbaum, 'The Good and Bad Quartos of *Doctor Faustus*', *The Library*, 4th ser., 26 (1946), p. 274, and J. T. McNeely, 'The Integrated Design of *Dr. Faustus*: An Essay in Iconoclasm', *Cahiers Élisabéthains* 41 (1992), pp. 1–2.

55   Bevington and Rasmussen, *Faustus*, pp. 70–1.

56   For example, Boas, *Tragical History*, pp. 27–31; Greg, *Parallel Texts*, pp. 133–39; Leslie M. Oliver, 'Rowley, Foxe, and the *Faustus* Additions', *Modern Language Notes* 60 (1945), pp. 391–94.

57   Paul H. Kocher, 'Nashe's Authorship of the Prose Scenes in *Faustus*', *Modern Language Quarterly* 3 (1942), pp. 17–40. See also Gill, *Works*, pp. xviii–xi.

58   Bevington and Rasmussen, *Faustus*, p. 72.

59   W. W. Greg, 'The Damnation of Faustus', *Modern Language Review* 41 (1946), p. 99.

60   G. K. Hunter, 'Five-Act Structure in *Doctor Faustus*', *Tulane Drama Review* 8.4 (1964), pp. 77–91; Keefer, *Faustus*, pp. lxxi–ii; Bevington and Rasmussen, *Faustus*, p. 38.

61   Nicholas Brooke, 'The Moral Tragedy of *Doctor Faustus*', *Cambridge Journal* 5 (1952), p. 673.

62   Warren D. Smith, 'The Nature of Evil in *Doctor Faustus*', *Modern Language Review* 60 (1965), pp. 171–75.

63   Harry Levin, *The Overreacher: A Study of Christopher Marlowe* (Cambridge, MA: Harvard University Press, 1952; reprinted Boston, MA: Beacon Press, 1964); Robert Ornstein, 'The Comic Synthesis in *Doctor Faustus*', *ELH* 22 (1955), pp. 165–72; R. M. Frye, 'Marlowe's *Dr. Faustus*: The Repudiation of Humanity', *South Atlantic Quarterly* 55 (1956), pp. 322–28; John H. Crabtree, Jr, 'The Comedy in Marlowe's *Dr. Faustus*', *Furman Studies* 9 (1961), pp. 1–9; Charles Beall, 'Definition of Theme by Unconsecutive Event: Structure as Induction in Marlowe's *Doctor Faustus*', *Renaissance Papers* (1962), pp. 53–61; Cleanth Brookes, 'The Unity of Marlowe's *Dr. Faustus*', in *To Nevill Coghill from Friends*, ed. John Lawler and W. H. Auden (London: Faber & Faber, 1966), pp. 109–24; Nigel Alexander, 'The Performance of Christopher Marlowe's *Dr. Faustus*', *PBA* 62 (1971), pp. 331–49.

64   David L. Hirst, *Tragicomedy*, The Critical Idiom 43 (London: Methuen, 1984), p. 38.

65   Bevington and Rasmussen, *Faustus*, pp. 48–50.

66   Bevington and Rasmussen, *Faustus*, pp. 51–52.

67   Thomas Dabbs provides a detailed discussion of the changes in the perception of Marlowe: *Reforming Marlowe: The Nineteenth-Century Canonization of a Renaissance Dramatist* (Lewisburg, WV: Bucknell University Press, 1991). For Dodsley, Reed and Ritson see pp. 25–27.

68   Dabbs, *Reforming Marlowe*, p. 18.

69   Dabbs, *Reforming Marlowe*, p. 89.

70   Dabbs, *Reforming Marlowe*, p. 91.

71   Dabbs, *Reforming Marlowe*, p. 21.

72   J. A. Symonds, *Shakespeare's Predecessors in the English Drama*, 1884. The passage on Marlowe is reprinted in Miller MacLure, *Marlowe: The Critical Heritage 1588–1896* (London: Routledge & Kegan Paul, 1979), p. 135. See also Dabbs, *Reforming Marlowe*, p. 122.

73   For the continuing impact of Victorian thought on twentieth-century Marlowe studies, see Dabbs *Reforming*; MacLure, *Marlowe*; Kenneth Friedenrich's introduction to *Christopher Marlowe: An Annotated Bibliography of Criticism Since 1950* (Metuchen, NJ: Scarecrow, 1979); and Irving Ribner, 'Marlowe and the Critics', *Tulane Drama Review* 8.4 (1964), pp. 211–24.

74 Una Ellis-Fermor, *Christopher Marlowe* (London: Methuen, 1927), p. 67.

75 Paul Kocher, *Christopher Marlowe: A Study of his Thought, Learning, and Character* (1946) (New York: Russell & Russell, 1962), p. 4.

76 Kocher, *Christopher Marlowe*, pp. 118–19.

77 Ribner, 'Marlowe and the Critics', p. 216.

78 Levin, *Overreacher*, pp. 26–27.

79 Levin, *Overreacher*, p. 134.

80 Irving Ribner, 'Marlowe's "Tragic Glasse"', in *Essays on Shakespeare and Elizabethan Drama in Honor of Hardin Craig*, ed. Richard Hosley (Columbia, MO: University of Missouri Press, 1962), p. 109.

81 Greenblatt, *Self-Fashioning*, p. 221; Ian McAdam, *The Irony of Identity: Self and Imaginiation in the Drama of Christopher Marlowe* (Newark, DE: University of Delaware Press, 1999), p. 244.

82 James Smith, 'Marlowe's *Dr. Faustus*', *Scrutiny* 8 (1939), pp. 36–55.

83 Leo Kirschbaum, 'Marlowe's *Faustus*: A Reconsideration', *Review of English Studies* 19 (1943), p. 228.

84 Clifford Davidson, 'Renaissance Dramatic Forms, Cosmic Perspective, and Alienation', *Cahiers Elisabéthains* 27 (1985), p. 10.

85 Martin Versfeld, 'Some Remarks on Marlowe's *Faustus*', *English Studies in Africa* 1 (1958), pp. 134–43; G. I. Duthie, 'Some Observations on Marlowe's *Doctor Faustus*', *Archiv für das Studium der Neueren Sprachen und Literaturen* 203 (1966), pp. 81–96; James T. F. Tanner, '*Doctor Faustus* as Orthodox Christian Sermon', *Dickinson Review* 2 (1969), pp. 23–31; Michael Hattaway, 'The Theology of Marlowe's *Doctor Faustus*', *Renaissance Drama* 3 (1970), pp. 51–78.

86 Margaret Ann O'Brien, 'Christian Belief in *Doctor Faustus*', *ELH* 37 (1970), p. 11.

87 M. M. Mahood, *Poetry and Humanism* (1950) (Port Washington, NY: Kennikat, 1967), pp. 85–86.

88 Robert Ornstein, 'Marlowe and God: The Tragic Theology of Dr. Faustus', *PMLA* 83 (1968), pp. 1378–85.

89 L. T. Fitz, 'Humanism Questioned: A Study of Four Renaissance Characters', *English Studies in Canada* 5 (1979), p. 395.

90 Wolfgang Riehle, 'Marlowe's *Doctor Faustus* and Renaissance Italy: Some Observations and Suggestions', in *Medieval Studies Conference, Aachen 1983: Language and Literature*, Bamberger Beitrage zur Englischen Sprachwissenschaft 15 (Frankfurt: Peter Lang, 1984), pp. 185–95.

91 Douglas Cole, *Suffering and Evil in the Plays of Christopher Marlowe* (Princeton, NJ: Princeton University Press, 1962).

92 David Bevington, *From 'Mankind' to Marlowe: Growth of Structure in the Popular Drama of Tudor England* (Cambridge, MA: Harvard University Press, 1962), p. 4.

93 James A. Reynolds, *Repentance and Retribution in Early English Drama*, Jacobean Drama Studies 96 (Salzburg: Universität Salzburg, Institut für Anglistik und Amerikanistik, 1982).

94 Stephen E. Rayburn, 'Marlowe's *Doctor Faustus* and Medieval Judgment Day Drama', *Publications of the Mississippi Philological Association* (1985), pp. 33–39.

95 Lorraine Kochanske Stock, 'Medieval *Gula* in Marlowe's *Doctor Faustus*', *Bulletin of Research in the Humanities* 85 (1982), pp. 372–85.

96 Margaret E. Owens, 'Desperate Juggling Knacks: The Rehearsal of the Grotesque in *Doctor Faustus*', *Medieval and Renaissance Drama in England* 8 (1996), pp. 63–93.

97 Barber, *Creating Elizabethan Tragedy*; Edward A. Snow, 'Marlowe's Doctor Faustus and the Ends of Desire', in *Two Renaissance Mythmakers: Christopher Marlowe and Ben Jonson*, ed. Alvin Kernan, Selected Papers from the English Institute, 1975–76, n.s. 1 (Baltimore, MD: Johns Hopkins University Press, 1977), pp. 41–69; Susan Snyder, 'Marlowe's Doctor Faustus as an Inverted Saint's Life', *Studies in Philology* 63 (1966), pp. 565–77.

98 Robert Weimann, *Shakespeare and the Popular Tradition in the Theater: Studies in the Social Dimension of Dramatic Form and Function*, ed. Robert Schwartz (Baltimore, MD: Johns Hopkins University Press, 1978), p. 179.

99 John D. Cox, 'Devils and Power in Marlowe and Shakespeare', *The Yearbook of English Studies* 23 (1993), pp. 47, 49.

100 Cox, 'Devils and Power in Marlowe and Shakespeare', p. 47.

101 Judith Weil, *Christopher Marlowe: Merlin's Prophet* (Cambridge: Cambridge University Press, 1977), p. 2.

102 Joel B. Altman, *The Tudor Play of Mind: Rhetorical Inquiry and the Development of Elizabethan Drama* (Berkeley, CA: University of California Press, 1978), p. 322.

103 Thomas McAlindon, 'The Ironic Vision: Diction and Theme in Marlowe's *Doctor Faustus*', *Review of English Studies* 32 (1981), p. 129. See also his *English Renaissance Tragedy* (Vancouver: University of British Columbia Press, 1986).

104 Lawrence Danson, 'Christopher Marlowe: The Questioner', *English Literary Renaissance* 12 (1982), pp. 3–29.

105 Carol Leventen Duane, 'Marlowe's Mixed Messages: A Model for Shakespeare?', *Medieval & Renaissance Drama in England* 3 (1986), p. 51.

106 Greenblatt, *Self-Fashioning*.

107 Jonathan Dollimore, *Radical Tragedy: Religion, Ideology and Power in the Drama of Shakespeare and His Contemporaries* (Chicago: University of Chicago Press, 1984); Simon Shepherd, *Marlowe and the Politics of Elizabethan Theatre* (New York: St Martin's, 1986).

108 Thomas Cartelli, *Marlowe, Shakespeare, and the Economy of Theatrical Experience* (Philadelphia, PA: University of Pennsylvania Press, 1991).

109 Emily C. Bartels, *Spectacles of Strangeness: Imperialism, Alienation, and Marlowe* (Philadelphia, PA: University of Pennsylvania Press, 1993), p. xiii.

110 Constance Brown Kuriyama, *Hammer or Anvil: Psychological Patterns in Christopher Marlowe's Plays* (New Brunswick, NJ: Rutgers University Press, 1980).

111 Philip K. Wion, 'Marlowe's *Doctor Faustus* the Oedipus Complex, and the Denial of Death', *Colby Library Quarterly* 16 (1980), pp. 190–204.

112 Peter S. Donaldson, 'Conflict and Coherence: Narcissism and Tragic Structure in Marlowe', in *Narcissism and the Text: Studies in Literature and the Psychology of Self*, ed. Lynne Layton and Barbara Ann Schapiro, Psychoanalytic Crosscurrents (New York: New York University Press, 1986), pp. 36–63.

113 Matthew N. Proser, *The Gift of Fire: Aggression and the Plays of Christopher Marlowe* (New York: Peter Lang, 1995).

114 Emil Roy, 'Faustus' Dream of Punishment', *American Imago* 34 (1977), pp. 158–69; Kenneth L. Golden, 'Myth, Psychology, and Marlowe's *Doctor Faustus*', *College Literature* 12 (1985), pp. 202–10; William L. Stull, 'Marlowe's Adlerian Tragedies', *Soundings* 73 (1990), pp. 443–64.

115 McAdam, *Irony of Identity*, p. 244.

116 McAdam, *Irony of Identity*, p. 243.

117 Sara Munson Deats, *Sex, Gender, and Desire in the Plays of Christopher Marlowe* (Newark, DE: University of Delaware Press, 1997).

118 Frederick Tupper, Jr, 'Legacies of Lucian', *Modern Language Notes* 21.3 (1906), pp. 76–77.

119 Levin, *Overreacher*, p. 127.

120 Pompa Banerjee, 'I Mephastophilis: Self, Other, and Demonic Parody in Marlowe's *Doctor Faustus*', *Christianity and Literature* 42 (1993), pp. 221–41.

121 Hobart S. Jarrett, 'Verbal Ambiguities in Marlowe's *Dr. Faustus*', *College English* 5 (1944), pp. 339–40. The edition cited is J. S. Cunningham, ed., *Tamburlaine the Great, by Christopher Marlowe*, Revels Plays (Manchester: Manchester University Press, 1981).

122 Neil Forsyth, 'Heavenly Helen', *Etudes de Lettres* 4 (1987), pp. 11–21.

123 Beach Langston, 'Marlowe's *Faustus* and the *Ars Moriendi* Tradition', in *A*

Tribute to George Coffin Taylor, ed. Arnold Williams (Chapel Hill, NC: University of North Carolina Press, 1952), pp. 148–67.

124 Patrick Cheney, 'Love and Magic in *Doctor Faustus*: Marlowe's Indictment of Spenserian Idealism', *Mosaic* 17.4 (1984), p. 107.

125 Kuriyama, *Hammer or Anvil*, p. 119.

126 Kay Stockholder, ' "Within the massy entrailes of the earth": Faustus's Relation to Women', in *'A Poet and a filthy Play-Maker': New Essays on Christopher Marlowe*, ed. Kenneth Friedenreich, Roma Gill and Constance B. Kuriyama (New York: AMS Press, 1988), p. 216.

127 Bartels, *Spectacles of Strangeness*, p. 135.

128 Sallye Sheppeard, 'Faustus and the Fall of Troy,' *CCTE Studies* 54 (1994), p. 74.

129 Christopher Wortham, ' "Read, Read the Scriptures": *Doctor Faustus* and the Retreat from Humanism', *The Aligarh Critical Miscellany* 6.2 (1993), p. 166.

130 Barber, *Creating Elizabethan Tragedy*.

131 Deats, *Sex, Gender, and Desire*, p. 202.

132 Barbara J. Baines, 'Sexual Polarity in the Plays of Christopher Marlowe', *Ball State University Forum* 23.3 (1982), p. 4.

133 Lucy De Bruyn, *Woman and the Devil in Sixteenth-Century Literature* (Tisbury, Compton, 1979), p. xi.

134 Martin Puhvel, 'Marlowe's *Doctor Faustus*, V.i', *Explicator* 46.4 (1988), pp. 3–5.

135 Bruce E. Brandt, 'Marlowe's Helen and the Soul-in-the-Kiss Conceit', *Philological Quarterly* 64 (1985), pp. 118–21.

136 Philip J. Traci, 'Marlowe's Faustus as Artist: A Suggestion about a Theme in the Play', *Renaissance Papers* (1966), pp. 3–9.

137 Greg, 'Damnation', pp. 97–107.

138 Nicholas Kiessling, 'Doctor Faustus and the Sin of Demoniality', *Studies in English Literature* 15 (1975), pp. 205–11; Gerard H. Cox, III, 'Marlowe's *Doctor Faustus* and "Sin against the Holy Ghost" ', *Huntington Library Quarterly* 36 (1973), pp. 119–37.

139 Lily B. Campbell, 'Doctor Faustus: A Case of Conscience', *PMLA* 67 (1952), pp. 219–39.

140 R. H. Bowers, 'Marlowe's *Dr. Faustus*, Tirso's *El Condenado por Desconfiado*, and the Secret Cause', *Costerus: Essays in English and American Language and Literature* 4 (1972), pp. 9–27.

141 John C. McCloskey, 'The Theme of Despair in Marlowe's *Faustus*', *College English* 4 (1942), pp. 110–13; Arieh Sachs, 'The Religious Despair of Doctor Faustus', *Journal of English and Germanic Philology* 63 (1964), pp. 625–47.

142 Greg, 'Damnation'; T. W. Craik, 'Faustus' Damnation Reconsidered', *Renaissance Drama*, n.s. 2 (1969), pp. 189–96.

143 Kiessling, 'Demonality', pp. 205–11; J. C. Maxwell, 'The Sin of Faustus', *The Wind and the Rain* 4 (summer 1947), pp. 49–52; Smith, 'Marlowe's *Dr. Faustus*', pp. 36–55.

144 Joseph T. McCullen, 'Dr. Faustus and Renaissance Learning', *Modern Language Review* 51 (1956), pp. 6–16; R. W. Ingram, ' "Pride in Learning goeth before a fall": Dr. Faustus' Opening Soliloquy', *Mosaic* 13.1 (1979), pp. 73–80; Phoebe S. Spinrad, 'The Dilettante's Lie in *Doctor Faustus*', *Tulane Studies in Language and Literature* 24 (1982), pp. 243–54.

145 Kocher, *Christopher Marlowe*, pp. 106–7; Cole, *Suffering and Evil*, p. 199.

146 Gill, *Works*, p. xxv.

147 John S. Wilks, *The Idea of Conscience in Renaissance Tragedy* (London: Routledge, 1990), p. 148.

148 Claude J. Summers and Ted-Larry Pebworth, 'The Conversion of St. Augustine and the B-Text of *Doctor Faustus*', *Renaissance and Renascences in Western Literature* 1.2 (1979), pp. 1–8.

149 Kocher strongly asserts that a strict Calvinistic reading is untenable (p. 108).

150 Paul R. Sellin, 'The Hidden God: Reformation Awe in Renaissance English Literature', in *The Darker Vision of the Renaissance*, ed. Robert S. Kinsman,

UCLA Center of Medieval and Renaissance Studies VI (Berkeley, CA: University of California Press, 1974), pp. 177–84; Alan Sinfield, *Literature in Protestant England, 1560–1660* (London: Croom Helm; Totowa, NJ: Barnes & Noble, 1983). T. McAlindon argues that either understanding misreads the play: '*Doctor Faustus*: The Predestination Theory', *English Studies* 3 (1993), pp. 215–20.

151 Martha Tuck Rozett, *The Doctrine of Election and the Emergence of Elizabethan Tragedy* (Princeton, NJ: Princeton University Press, 1984), p. 239.

152 Pauline Honderich, 'John Calvin and Doctor Faustus', *Modern Language Review* 68 (1973), pp. 495–519.

153 Robert G. Hunter, *Shakespeare and the Mystery of God's Judgments* (Athens, GA: University of Georgia Press, 1976), p. 66.

154 Eriksen, *Forme of Faustus Fortunes*, pp. 26–58.

155 King-Kok Cheung, 'The Dialectic of Despair in *Doctor Faustus*', in '*A Poet and a filthy Play-Maker*': *New Essays on Christopher Marlowe*, ed. Kenneth Friedenreich, Roma Gill and Constance B. Kuriyama (New York: AMS Press, 1988), pp. 193–201; Phoebe S. Spinrad, *The Summons of Death on the Medieval and Renaissance English Stage* (Columbus, OH: Ohio State University Press, 1987), p. 161.

156 Max Bluestone, '*Libido Speculandi*: Doctrine and Dramaturgy in Contemporary Interpretations of Marlowe's *Doctor Faustus*', in *Reinterpretations of Elizbethan Drama: Selected Papers from the English Institute*, ed. Norman Rabkin (New York: Columbia University Press, 1969), pp. 73–83; David C. Webb, 'Damnation in *Doctor Faustus*: Theological Strip Tease and the Histrionic Hero', *Critical Survey* 11.1 (1999), p. 31.

CHAPTER TWO

The Performance History

David Bevington

William Prynne, in 1633, attests to

> the visible apparition of the devil on the stage at the Belsavage
> playhouse, in Queen Elizabeth's days, to the great amazement
> both of the actors and spectators, whiles they were there
> playing the History of Faustus, the truth of which I have heard
> from many now alive, who well remember it, there being some
> distracted with that fearful sight.[1]

Conceivably, this is the earliest indication of performance of *Doctor
Faustus*, since the Belsavage playhouse was in use only until 1588 or
1589, normally by the Queen's Men but also by Lord Strange's Men
and Pembroke's Men, both of which are associated on title pages
with Marlowe. Admittedly, Prynne writes some decades later, but he
does insist on the veracity of stage tradition. Thomas Middleton
similarly refers to devils on stage 'in Dr. Faustus when the old
Theatre cracked and frighted the audience'. If Middleton is referring
to the building known as The Theatre in Shoreditch, he could be
alluding to performances there by the Admiral's Men during the
years 1590 to 1594. *The Second Report of Dr. John Faustus*, 1594,
similarly refers to a 'cracking' in the theatre; perhaps that is where
Middleton got the idea.[2] Prynne's account, if it may be trusted,
perhaps adds some weight to the argument in favour of an original
date for the play around 1588–89, though the case for 1592 is still a
viable possibility. In either event, we have evidence that the play was
in repertory prior to the first documentary recorded performance, in
Philip Henslowe's diary, on 30 September 1594, by the Lord

Admiral's Men at the Rose Theatre. This took place shortly after the formation in June of that year of the Lord Chamberlain's Company acting at the Theatre in Shoreditch. From this point on, the two companies were separate and were the chief contenders in the public market for London's theatrical clientele. Henslowe's entry notes his having received 'iij^{ll} xij^{s}' for 'docter ffostose' – a tidy sum. Edward Alleyn, married to Henslowe's stepdaughter, took the part of Doctor Faustus. Marlowe's play was to be the Admiral's Men's chief money-maker for a considerable time.

Prynne and Middleton attest not only to the early and instant success of this play in the theatre, but to its ability to titillate audiences by scaring them out of their wits. 'The visible apparition of the devil on the stage' was 'a fearful sight', says Prynne. Middleton tells us that the old theatre 'cracked and frighted the audience'. Presumably the cracking refers to the '*Thunder and lightning*' that accompanies the arrival of Lucifer, Mephistopheles, and other devils to claim Faustus's soul in the final scene of the A-text (V.ii.117), an impressive sound effect reiterated in the B-text's '*Thunder, and enter the* Devils' (V.ii.187). An attempt to argue for an early urtext of *Faustus* on the assumption that the cracking may refer to an actual earthquake is unconvincing,[3] but if an earthquake did occur it surely would have added to the frisson experienced by audiences.

Belief in devils was widespread, and Marlowe's play seemed to provide the opportunity to see the real thing. According to a popular story, during a performance at Exeter (date uncertain), the actors in *Faustus* 'were all dashed, every one hearkening other in the ear, for they were all persuaded there was one devil too many amongst them'.[4] John Aubrey fancied this story so much that he retold it in *The Natural History and Antiquities of the County of Surrey* (1718–19), including Edward Alleyn among the cast of those who were so frightened, but then marring the reliability of the account by attributing it to one of Shakespeare's plays.[5] The story is so manifestly a tale-type about theatre and about devils that it cannot be taken as gospel historically, but no matter for that; it is part of the legend that grew up around *Doctor Faustus* as diabolical. One more such anecdote tells of a spectator who threw a tobacco pipe at Mephistopheles, prompting the actor in that role to respond that he hoped 'e'er long' to see the 'son of a whore' fellow 'as bad as I am', i.e., packed off to hell.[6]

Such a formidable reputation was presumably the underlying motivation for Henslowe's decision to commission William Birde (or Borne) and Samuel Rowley in 1602 to provide some 'adicyones in doctor fostes'. The B-text appears to incorporate these additions, and they are pretty uniformly in the direction of augmenting the play's notorious scare factor, delighting in 'black magical' stunts.

The evidence of the play's early success in the theatre is abundantly clear. Henslowe records seven performances in all in 1594, seven each in 1595 and 1596, and one in 1597, with happy remunerative results, albeit trailing off a bit toward the end.[7] In concert with Pembroke's Men, the Admiral's Men staged a revival in 1597 at the Rose. Presumably on several occasions between 1596 and 1603 the play was acted (as announced on the 1604 A-text title page) 'by the Right Honourable the Earl of Nottingham his Servants', that is, by the Admiral's Company as renamed when their patron, Charles Howard, appointed Lord High Admiral in 1585, was then created first Earl of Nottingham in 1596 for his role as naval commander against the Spanish Armada in 1588 and in subsequent naval actions. The commissioning by Henslowe of the 1602 additions bespeaks both the play's great popularity and a fervent desire on the part of the audience to see even more. A total of nine quartos (first, of the A-text, and then, in 1616 and afterwards, of the B-text) appeared between 1604 and 1631. Performances in Graz (Austria) and Dresden by travelling players are recorded in 1608 and 1626. Prince Charles's Men were still performing *Doctor Faustus* at the Fortune Theatre a year or so before the closing of the theatres in 1642. Not many other plays of the English Renaissance can touch that record.

In its original staging, the A-text seems to have required only a raised platform in front of a tiring-house facade with two doors. As the play commences, Doctor Faustus is revealed to the audience by the Prologue ('And this the man that in his study sits'), perhaps by means of the pulling back of a curtain. Faustus presumably comes forward so that the entire stage becomes imaginatively his study. When the action cuts back and forth between high seriousness and below-stairs comedy, or requires the presence of the Good and Evil Angels, nothing is needed scenically other than the departure of one actor or set of actors and the entrance of those who come on next. Faustus needs a book with which to conjure. Probably the B-text illustration printed on the title page of the 1619 quarto (B2) gives a visual impression of the scene; the opening action of the A-text is essentially unaltered in the B-text. Faustus holds a book in one hand and a staff in the other. He stands inside a cabalistic conjuring circle. A globe is discernible on the wall, near a window, along with more books on a shelf and a crucifix. An ugly black devil, presumably Mephistopheles before he is bidden by Faustus to go away and return in the more tolerable shape of an old Franciscan friar (I.iii.24–27), emerges as though through the floor of Faustus's study. As in presentational theatre generally, scenic effects are minimal. In their place, costuming and hand props tell the story of where the action is located. Mephistopheles and other devils enter, '*giving crowns and rich apparel to Faustus, and dance and then depart*' (A-text, II.i.83). A devil dressed as a woman is brought in '*with fireworks*', presumably squibs (151). Mephistopheles brings Faustus '*a chafer of coals*' (II.i.69). Books are important in the comic scenes as well (II.ii.0, III.ii.0).

As the action moves forward with Faustus's travels to Rome and other parts of the world, the staging continues to exploit the presentational simplicity and flexibility of the theatre space. Information on Faustus's travels is provided in narrative form by the choruses to Acts III and IV, the first of these identified as Wagner, and by Faustus's recounting to Mephistopheles the wonders he has seen along the Rhine River down to Venice, Naples, and Rome (III.i.1–19). The scene in the Pope's chamber requires only the actors, most in clerical garb, a 'robe for to go invisible' for Faustus as included in the Admiral's inventory (Henslowe's *Diary*, p. 325), dishes of food and drink to be snatched away from the Pope by Faustus, perhaps a table temporarily brought on by stagehands, and more fireworks. Faustus's demonstration of his magical skills for the delectation of the German emperor depends for its effects on his ability to conjure up the wraiths of Alexander and his paramour (requiring nothing other than that actors enter in those roles) and Faustus's causing a pair of horns to sprout on the forehead of the obstreperously sceptical knight. The actual adorning with horns is accomplished behind the scenes, so that the actor need only stick out his horned head to offer visual demonstration of Faustus's formidable magical powers. The chorus has told us that the action is now located in the 'palace' of 'Carolus the Fifth'; no further stage contrivance is needed to set the scene. (Historically, the court of Charles V of Spain could be in Madrid or Germany or elsewhere; the imaginative world of the play takes no note of this matter.)

The Horse-Courser episode follows in Act IV without a break or change of scene, though the audience understands that it is now to imagine Faustus on his return journey to Wittenberg. When the Horse-Courser, convinced that he has been bamboozled by Faustus, pulls at a leg of the sleeping Faustus, it comes off in his hands – an easy enough stage device ('*Pull him by the leg, and pull it away*', IV.i.174). To impress the Duke and Duchess of Vanholt (i.e. Anholt, a duchy in central Germany) with his magical might, Faustus need only bid Mephistopheles to go and fetch grapes; he tells his astonished audience (on stage and in the theatre auditorium) that the grapes are from India, Saba, or some eastern country enjoying summer while Europe is in winter, but theatrically all that happens is that the actor playing Mephistopheles exits behind the scene and picks up some grapes as his prop. The brief and wordless two appearances of Helen happen when the presumably boy actor playing that part '*passeth over the stage*' (V.i.25); in her second appearance, she twice makes Faustus 'immortal' with a kiss (93–95). A clock strikes 11 o'clock (presumably offstage) and then half past the hour and then 12 to warn Faustus that his last hour is upon him (V.ii.64–115). With '*Thunder and lightning*', the devils comes to take Faustus away. That is all the staging that is required for the original A-text.

The B-text's considerable augmentations of the staging need to be regarded as early stage history, not a record of what Marlowe, his collaborator, and his original acting company had in mind. The B-text generally calls for more characters (including devils) on stage and more special effects. The presence of more devils appears to stack the deck unremittingly against Faustus and to augment a chillingly sardonic atmosphere. Appearances 'above' call for use of the gallery surmounting the main stage, as when Benvolio enters '*above at a window, in his nightcap, buttoning*' (IV.i.23). Machinery for effects of lowering and raising are required when '*the throne descends*' (V.ii.110) to show Faustus the 'bliss without end' that he has forfeited, and then, after that throne has presumably re-ascended at line 120, '*Hell is discovered*' in the full horror of 'that vast perpetual torture-house' and 'This ever-burning chair'. No less spectacularly, in an added scene not in the A-text, one scholar says, 'See, here are Faustus' limbs, | All torn asunder by the hand of death' (V.iii.6–7), suggesting by the deictic 'See' that some gruesome depiction of dismemberment is visually displayed on stage.

To judge from the testimonials of Edward Phillips and William Winstanley, performances in the Restoration period were, if anything, even more noisy than what is called for in the B-text. 'None made such a great noise as his comedy of *Doctor Faustus* with his devils and suchlike tragical sport', wrote Winstanley in 1687, 'which pleased much the humors of the vulgar'. Phillips, who saw the play in 1663, was substantially of the same opinion.[8] Samuel Pepys found the play 'so wretchedly and poorly done that we were sick of it' (20 May 1662, at the Red Bull), despite the opportunity to see Faustus played by Thomas Betterton, whom Pepys usually admired. Adaptation, so common an affliction in the Restoration, only made matters worse. Charles Mountfort, who had played Mephistopheles to Betterton's Faustus in 1675 for the Duke of York's Company, mounted a farcical version in 1688 at the Queen's Theatre in Dorset Garden that adulterated what was left of Marlowe's play by splicing in sizable portions of *Harlequin and Scaramouche*. This adulterate beast inspired in turn two rival pantomimes of 1723 and afterwards, one by John Thurmond entitled *Harlequin Dr Faustus,* at Drury Lane, and the other an anonymous piece called *The Necromancer, or Harlequin Doctor Faustus*, at Lincoln's Inn Fields. Alexander Pope, aghast at the continued popularity of these confections, drew in his *Dunciad* a satirical portrait of Colley Cibber mesmerized by a performance:

> [He] looked and saw a sable sorcerer rise,
> Swift to whose hand a wingèd volume flies.
> All sudden, gorgons hiss and dragons glare,
> And ten-horned fiends and giants rush to war.
> Hell rises, heav'n descends and dance on earth;
> God, imps, and monsters, music, rage, and mirth,
> A fire, a jig, a battle, and a ball,
> Till one wide conflagration swallows all.
>
> (3.229–36)

The rising of hell and descent of heaven sounds rather precisely like the last act of the B-text.

Under the weight of this trivialization, Marlowe's play disappeared from the London stage entirely until 1885, when, at London's Lyceum Theatre, it emerged in a form that showed the influence of Goethe's long philosophical poem, *Faust*, and Charles Gounod's operatic version based on Goethe. In part, the influence was in staging: the producer, W. G. Wills, reduced the number of scenes markedly to accommodate massive sets in the style of grand opera. With Henry Irving, famed for his Shakespearean roles, cast in the role of Mephistopheles, this *Doctor Faustus* focused on the central characters and the emotional highpoints of the story, again as in nineteenth-century opera (and also in many a Shakespeare production of the age). Marlowe's concentration on his two central male roles, Faustus and Mephistopheles, lent itself readily to nineteenth-century staging methods. What the Marlovian play had neglected to supply in the way of leading female roles, Goethe and Gounod were again able to provide. The era of celebrated divas like Ellen Terry, Sarah Bernhardt, and Charlotte Cushman demanded major roles for women.

A production of *Doctor Faustus* at His Majesty's Theatre in 1908, under the direction of Herbert Beerbohm Tree, similarly went in for opulence and a text freely adapted to make room for big scenes and spectacular scenic effects. The actor-managers of the late nineteenth century, when they finally got around to Marlowe's play, approached it as they did Shakespeare's: big, costly, centred on the star actor-manager.

The understandable parallelism between productions of *Doctor Faustus* and of Shakespeare's plays continued into the important theatrical revolution of the early twentieth century, when the brilliant visionary eccentric, William Poel, founded the Elizabethan Stage Society in order to stage Elizabethan plays in as authentically original a form as he could muster. Along with his scholarly revivals of *Hamlet* in 1881 (based on the unauthorized 1603 quarto), *Measure for Measure* in 1893 (at the Royalty Theatre, converted into a near replica of the old Fortune Playhouse of 1600), *The Comedy of Errors* in 1895 (at Gray's Inn, where the play had been performed in December of 1594) and *Troilus and Cressida* in 1912 (at the King's Hall, Covent Garden), among others, Poel staged Marlowe's *Doctor Faustus* on 4 July 1896, at the reconstructed Fortune Playhouse that had housed his *Measure for Measure* some three years earlier. A simple platform stage in the style of the Elizabethan public playhouses featured at its centre a raised structure built to resemble the pageant scaffolds of medieval cycle plays. The script, combining elements of the A- and B-texts in a way that minimized the buffoonery of the comic characters, was nonetheless closer to some kind of Marlovian original than what audiences had seen in Wills's 1885 revival and were to see in Tree's extravaganza of 1908. Poel's was definitely an experimental small-theatre movement, dwarfed by the costly splendour of the professional theatres, but his was the wave of the future. George Bernard Shaw and Harley Granville-Barker were among Poel's admirers and supporters generally, though Shaw did say, *à propos* of the 1896 production, that he regarded Marlowe as 'childish in thought, vulgar and wooden in humour and stupid in his attempts at invention'. (This diatribe was part of Shaw's objection to 'the whole obscene crew of these blank-verse rhetoricians', not excluding Shakespeare, with his 'bombast and drivel'.)[9] Algernon Swinburne wrote a prologue for the 1896 production. Poel's *Doctor Faustus* was in fact something of a success, at least in small-theatre terms: it was mounted again in October 1904 by the Elizabethan Stage Society at the Court Theatre and then at Terry's Theatre in December, following which it was taken on a six-week tour of England and

Scotland.[10] Later, in 1924, he agreed to direct a production at Canterbury designed to support the erecting of a memorial to Marlowe.

The appeal of the relatively unadorned open stage, providing as it did the opportunity for non-traditional presentational staging and rapid sequencing between scenes, proved immensely attractive to the experimentalists who were also staging Strindberg and Chekhov. On the continent, in Germany especially, *Doctor Faustus* appeared on a simple platform stage in December 1903, as directed by Ernst Leopold Stahl for the Heidelberger Hebbelverein, and then in Göttengen, Essen, and Frankfurt in 1910, Hamburg the following year, and for a meeting of the German Shakespeare Society in 1928. In England, the Phoenix Society did a revival of *Doctor Faustus* at London's New Oxford Theatre, capitalizing on the freedom of the unadorned stage and bringing back some of the farcical routines of the clowns that earlier directors had found vulgar and distasteful. Nugent Monck's experimental Norwich Maddermarket Theatre performed *Doctor Faustus* three times in the Chapter House at Canterbury Cathedral, during a festival of music and drama there in 1929. More revivals took place in 1934 at the Malvern under the directorship of H. M. Prentice, in 1937 at the Tavistock Little Theatre and in 1940 at the Rudolf Steiner Hall. In the United States, productions were staged in New York in 1910 (directed by Ben Greet), Detroit in 1918, Cleveland in 1922, and again in 1927–28 (running throughout that season), and New Orleans and Atlanta in 1937 (directed by Walter Armitage).[11]

Universities provided a venue for academic productions during these same years: at Cambridge University in 1907 (with the poet Rupert Brooke and George Mallory, who was later to die on Everest and may have been one of the first to conquer it, among the cast, leading to the founding of the Marlowe Society the following year), at Princeton in 1907 (supervised by the Chaucer scholar Robert K. Root), at Williams College on numerous occasions in 1908 and 1912, at the Carnegie Institute in 1921, Cambridge again in 1924 and 1934, Yale University in 1932, Stanford University in 1934, Dartmouth and Brown in subsequent years, and still more. Robert Frost directed his prize students in a compressed version of *Doctor Faustus* (along with four other plays, including two by Yeats) in 1909–10, while he was teaching at the Pinkerton Academy in Derry, New Hampshire. (The experience evidently prompted Frost to write some time later, in his poem 'New Hampshire', 'Kit Marlowe taught me how to say my prayers: | "Why this is Hell nor am I out of it" '.)[12]

Orson Welles starred in his own production at the Maxine Elliott

Theatre in New York city in 1936–37. Something of an event, it ran for six months and gave credibility to the labours of the Federal Theatre Project (part of the New Deal's Works Projects Administration, or WPA) in sponsoring adventuresome enterprises of this sort. When Welles revived his *Doctor Faustus* in 1950 in Paris, he cast the famous black singer, Eartha Kitt, in the silent but glamorous role of Helen. She told a *Life Magazine* reporter what the role had meant for her: 'I made him [Faustus] immortal with a kiss'.[13] Indeed she did. The production did much for Welles's reputation as a serious theatre artist in his self-proclaimed role as champion of the United States' challenge to British hegemony in the world of repertory classical theatre. The music was by Duke Ellington. Simon Callow, in his biography of Welles (New York: Viking, 1996), has pointed to the ironic relevance of the Prologue's opening speech to Welles's own career: 'Till, swoll'n with cunning of a self-conceit, | His waxen wings did mount above his reach, | And melting heavens conspired his overthrow' (A-text, lines 20–22).

By the 1940s and 1950s, the play had become part of the standard classical repertory. The Old Vic produced it in 1944 at the Playhouse Theatre in Liverpool under the direction of John Moody, with D. A. Clarke-Smith as Faustus and Noel Willman as Mephistopheles. In 1948, John Burrell directed a production for the Old Vic at the New Theatre, London, with Cedric Hardwicke and Robert Eddison in the same lead roles. At Stratford-upon-Avon in 1946–47, *Doctor Faustus* won the status of being included in the season's repertory along with Shakespeare's masterpieces. Robert Harris and Hugh Griffith took the major roles in 1946, with Walter Hudd as director; Paul Scofield memorably took over the role of Mephistopheles in the second year. John Crockett directed a production on tour for the Compass Players in 1950.

In much the same way that Shakespeare's plays were enlisted in the controversies of the mid- and later-twentieth century, *Doctor Faustus* took on a polemical edge. Even in traditional Elizabethan costuming, as in Michael Benthall's Old Vic production at the Assembly Hall in Edinburgh in 1961, Marlowe's play was discovered to have explosive potential for juxtaposing ceremonial seriousness with banality and raunchy humour. The contrasts had, of course, been there all along in the Marlovian script, but in the context of post-World War II and Korean War disillusionment, the play gained a new sense of cultural relevance.

Jerzy Grotowski's 1963 production for his Theatre Laboratory in Opole, Poland (some 60 miles from Auschwitz) burst onto the scene at about the time the controversy over the Vietnam war was heating up in earnest. The play was performed in Polish, with programme notes provided by Grotowski in French. Without excising Marlowe's language or substituting new dialogue, but with considerable rearrangement of scenes, Grotowski fashioned the play's script into a 'montage' designed to represent the whole event as a flashback passing through Faustus's tormented mind as he confronted his final destiny. Two long tables and one smaller table ran the length of a rectangular, low-ceilinged theatre in a space that could accommodate only about 60 spectators. Action was in the round. The audience members, greeted by Faustus as they entered and invited by him to sit on the side at the long tables, were intimately, even claustrophobically, involved. Costuming was spare, drab, monastic, without make-up, in accord with Grotowski's concept of an essentialized, stripped-down 'poor theatre.'

Inverted religious images took the form of an extended metaphor comparing the life of Faustus (ambivalently as Antichrist or as Promethean tragic hero) to that of Christ. Mephistopheles's first appearance to Faustus, for example, was a sardonic re-enactment of the scene of the Annunciation, in which the angel Gabriel (Luke 1:26) brings to Mary the news that she is to bear God's son. An angelic choir accompanied Mephistopheles's chanted address to Faustus-as-Mary. A mortification and a baptism of sorts (acted between the tables) prepared Faustus for his role as a thoughtful rebel capable of perceiving that God's laws were nothing more than 'traps contradicting morality and truth' and that therefore Faustus was duty-bound to martyr himself by defying divine authority. Only this could redeem his soul – that is, his self-awareness as a sentient, living creature.

This Faustus examined the diabolical 'wife' that Mephistopheles brought to him as though her bodily parts were the planets and the spheres. His temptation in the wilderness took the form of a series of interrogations by Mephistopheles as both Good and Evil Angels transformed into a Jesuit and a police informer. Mephistopheles also played the Seven Deadly Sins, whom Faustus absolved with liturgical gestures. At Rome, Faustus converted the Pope into a holy man. At the court of Charles V, Faustus transformed Benvolio (of the B-text) into a little child. At a representation of the Last Supper, Helen became Faustus's lover, giving birth instantly to an infant and then herself wailingly demanding the breast. In the familiar image of the Pietà, a motherly Mephistopheles comforted Faustus in his agony of approaching dissolution. Faustus's last monologue was an 'outrageous provocation of God', yielding him the moral victory but at the expense of martyrdom in hell 'where all is taken from him, even his dignity'.[14] Charles Marowitz's production for the Glasgow Citizens' Theatre in 1965 consciously echoed Grotowski's revisionary production in its use of a long refectory table.[15]

Another notable *Doctor Faustus* of the 1960s took place at Oxford, when the Merton Professor of English, Nevill Coghill, who had directed the play for the Oxford University Dramatic Society (OUDS) in 1957, persuaded his former tutee Richard Burton to return in 1966 to his old haunts in the role of Faustus. Burton, by now famous as an actor, brought along his glamorous Hollywood wife, Elizabeth Taylor, to undertake the silent role of Helen of Troy. Undergraduates supplied the supporting cast. Tickets were hard to come by, though whether because they afforded the chance to see Burton as Faustus or Taylor simply as Taylor was hard to say. Burton's sad reputation for being an alcoholic who would ultimately undo his brilliant achievement as an actor seemed all too well fitted to the role of the doomed magician. His manly, sardonic, intelligent voice (preserved on an LP recording, as is his splendid Coriolanus) gave to the role of Faustus a fine sense of scepticism, sensual self-indulgence, and bitter disappointment at himself for grandly wasted opportunities. This Faustus was a decidedly unheroic figure, obsessed with practical joking. He was his own worst enemy, acting out his frustrated sexual fantasies. Observers were not slow to point out 'the disquieting parallels between the performer and the role'.[16] One can hardly imagine a more apt fable for that disillusioning era in the wake of the assassinations of the Kennedys and of Martin Luther King, the escalating and often violent controversy over the Vietnam war, and so much more.

A film version, co-directed by Burton and his tutor Coghill, appeared in the year following the stage production.[17] An advertisement for this film on the internet states that Elizabeth Taylor, taking all the women's parts in the play, including Helen, Faustus's devil-wife, and Alexander's paramour, 'appears throughout the film in various states of undress as Doctor Faustus stands firm'. One reviewer, Renata Adler for the *New York Times*, pronounced the film to be 'of an awfulness that bends the mind'. Transparently, this was a 'vanity production', with a wooden supporting cast mostly of students. But Taylor is there, in her 1960s glitter eye-shadow and everything else, and Burton, even on an off day, is still Burton.

Clifford Williams's production for the Royal Shakespeare Company at Stratford-upon-Avon in 1968 captured a mood of apocalypse that seemed relevant both to the era in which the production was mounted and to the late medieval world of spiritual crisis depicted by Hieronymus Bosch, Pieter Bruegel the Elder, and Lucas Cranach in their representations of the torments of hell. Those artists' images were in fact the inspiration for the set designed by (Abd' Elkader) Farrah. The Seven Deadly Sins were 'weird skeletal figures' portentously anticipating the grisly dissolution that lay in wait for the protagonist. An ominous mood of impending catastrophe hung over him, as though by way of putting the audience in mind of its own prophetic anxieties. Faustus's dreadful end was both a personal tragedy and a fable of twentieth-century Europe. As Nigel Alexander aptly put it, in describing the final scene of the production,

> Faustus finished his final speech grovelling in abject terror on the ground. The clock finished striking. Nothing happened. After a long moment Faustus raised his head and looked round the totally empty stage. He started to laugh. As he reached the hysteria of relief, the back wall of the stage gave way and fell forward in sections revealing an ominous red glow and a set of spikes like the dragon's teeth of the Siegfried Line. The denizens of hell emerged with a kind of slow continuous shuffle until Faustus was surrounded by a circle of these skeletal figures – including the seven deadly sins. He was then seized and carried shrieking through the teeth of hell mouth which closed leaving the wall of Faustus's study again intact.[18]

Eric Porter was suitably sonorous and fierce-eyed as Faustus. Terrence Hardiman was a bitter Mephistopheles, attractively good-looking and yet tormented with unhappiness, 'as quiet and powerful as a coiled spring', in the words of Irving Wardle.[19] Stage trickery was impressive: grape seeds exploded when Mephistopheles spat them out; a turban belched smoke; a hand emerged suddenly from a plate of food. Helen, played by Maggie Wright, was briefly and tantalizingly visible in all her nakedness – widely reported to be the first nude ever to move on the British stage. This production went on a tour of six cities in the United States in early 1969. Williams had previously directed a studio production of the play in 1962 at the Conference Hall of the Royal Shakespeare Theatre in Stratford.

The Royal Shakespeare Company's Theatregoround troupe production directed by Gareth Morgan at Dublin's Abbey Theatre and then at Stratford-upon-Avon in 1970 was deliberately small scale, with a cut text of some two and a half hours and 12 actors doubling in some 49 roles. The set, designed by Stephanie Howard, wife of Alan Howard, consisted of a black-hung stage, on which, according to the *Cork Examiner*, 'a raised platform, tilted forward, held several boxes of varying sizes which were used to suggest whatever was needed in the way of props'. Costuming was generally in sombre black, with an occasional splash of colour in a cloak. David Warner as Faustus was destined from the start for a tragic fall; though defiant and arrogant, he was clearly outnumbered and outclassed by his diabolical adversaries in a cosmic battle of temptation and failure. Slightly flabby and burly, speaking in a foghorn voice with a northern accent, this Faustus was no match for the Mephistopheles of the sophisticated Alan Howard. Audiences perceived in this devil the ruins of a once-great and princely angelic figure, now forced to confront the appalling prospect of an eternity without grace. His contempt for the man he was obliged to serve for a time was matched only by his determination to reduce that sinner to the spiritual agony that Mephistopheles himself could not escape or forget. Val Mulkern wrote for the *Irish Press* that Howard's 'sinister flutelike voice suggested more depths of evil than all the Seven Deadly Sins put together. He moved like a dancer and his sense of timing was nothing short of diabolical'. Mephistopheles and Faustus, joined in an unhappy union of despair, indulged joylessly in practical joking that became more and more meaningless and tawdry: the throwing of a custard pie in slapstick comic fashion; a Mardi Gras display in which the Seven Deadly Sins were outfitted with massive carnival heads; sleazy sexual joking reminiscent of music hall stand-up comedy; and so on. No devils dragged Faustus off to his doom in the final scene; instead, his cloak simply dropped to the ground as a token of his soul's departure for an eternity of torment. Brechtian touches like these endowed the production with a vivid sense of alienation and defeat.[20]

John Barton cut and conflated the A- and B-texts of Marlowe's play and added some 600 lines of his own for his RSC production of 1974–75 at the Nottingham Playhouse, Newcastle, Edinburgh, Stratford, the Aldwych Theatre in London, and still other locations. His aim, by cutting back on the farce and adding new material from Marlowe's source, *The History of the Damnable Life and Deserved Death of Doctor John Faustus*, was to provide a consistent theology of damnation, focusing on Faustus's inner life. To that end Barton staged the entire action of the play in Faustus's study. Michael Annals's set also suggested the interior of a skull. The relative absence of sub-plot low comedy left this production with a Faustus who was in himself a travesty of the great magician that he had hoped to become. By showing the audience less of Faustus's exuberant travels in Italy and Germany, as John Barber has observed, the production concentrated on Faustus's internal schizophrenia.[21] Ian McKellen was this mental invalid, stunned by his own indecisiveness as he listened in turn to the Good and Evil Angels who were, in this production, glove puppets held and operated by McKellen himself as he spoke their lines. Were they voices from the cosmos, taking opposite sides in a cosmic struggle for possession of Faustus's soul, or were they projections of his interior and divided state of mind? In other ways as well, the figures that appeared to him were theatrical wraiths, perhaps figures of his hyperactive imagination, certainly projections of the theatre and its ability to conjure up magical shows. Helen was a blonde-wigged marionette in a mask and nightdress, carried in to Faustus's study by Mephistopheles (played by Emrys Jones). The life-sized Seven Deadly Sins (created by Jennifer Carey) were marionettes as well, described by Michael Billington as 'wispy, trailing, Bunraku-like creatures that underline the illusory nature of Faustus' pleasure'.[22] 'The incarnation of the silent Helen of Troy', McKellen writes, 'was a beautiful flowing chiffon [also a puppet] that I carried across the stage to Faustus's bed – a cunning revelation of the deceitful nature of the devilish delights which entrance the poor sexually frustrated academic'. Hell was thus at once a place of unimaginable physical torture and a state of mind, as Mephistopheles insists when he says to Faustus, 'Why, this is hell, nor am I out of it' (I.iii.78) and 'I am damned and am now in hell' (II.i.140). Barton's metatheatrical devices reinforced this double consciousness at every turn: evil was both an eternal force grappling for the soul of humanity and a slick theatrical display of showmanship. When Faustus approached his final moment, his twitching body became suddenly lifeless as it sank from his chair, leaving in its wake the empty, shroud-like robe of the once-great scholar. This *coup de théâtre* was at once a theatrical stunt and an emblem of spiritual loss. The overall effect, according to Irving Wardle, was of 'a nightmare of blindness and appetite'.[23]

Ben Kingsley was Faustus in Adrian Noble's production at the Royal Exchange Theatre, Manchester, in 1981. This version succeeded in making theatrical sense of the play's many thematic and gestural links between serious and buffoonish action. Mephistopheles, played by James Maxwell, was continuously involved in the scenes of clowning. He invisibly turned the pages of Robin's book in a scene that does not specify his presence in the original script (II.ii in both texts), thus matching what he had explicitly done for Faustus in the immediately preceding action (A.II.i.172, 176, 180, '*There turn to them,*' '*Turn to them*'; B.II.i.158ff.). He helped Robin pronounce hard words like 'Demogorgon' (B.III.iii.33) and whis-

pered blandishments in his ear, as before with Faustus. Wagner's
saucy banter with two scholars (I.ii in both texts) consciously
mirrored the specious logic of Faustus's disquisition on the Bible and
other authoritative texts in I.i. Noble kept most of the language of
the B-text, but reordered one sequence (as does the 1993 Revels
edition) so that Robin and Dick's fooling around with Doctor
Faustus's conjuring books and their smarmy talk about dancing
naked (B.II.ii) followed immediately after the scene in which Faustus
rejects Mephistopheles's offer of a 'hot whore' for his wife (II.i.149;
the effect in the A-text is similar; originally, in both texts, the comic
scene was printed after III.i and a misplaced chorus to Act IV). The
devils named Baliol1 (i.e., Belial) and Belcher whom Wagner invokes
in I.iv (A.46; 'Banio' and Belcher in the B) appeared in Noble's
production as 'evil-faced choirboys armed with rods' on black
bicycles, thus echoing the clerical procession of the opening scene
from which Faustus broke away from his fellow scholars to
contemplate instead his books of magic. The Good and Evil Angels
wore black gowns, adding reinforcement to the visual parallelism.

These jarring juxtapositions characterized the protagonist at
every turn. When Faustus asked to have a wife and was presented
with a seeming beauty, she was discovered to have, beneath her
attractive crinoline, a biting simian mouth. Lechery, the presumed
embodiment of sensual desire, entered in the procession of the
Deadly Sins, pushing Sloth in a pram, as though to signify the
unwholesome family connection between these sins of the flesh.
Faustus thrust a meringue into the Pope's face, and took impish
pleasure in his other pranks as well. The overall effect, according to
Russell Jackson, was 'not reductive irony, showing Faustus
squandering his powers on trivial shows, but an impression of the
honour, pleasure and pageantry' he enjoyed. The 'ultimate
emptiness' of Faustus's amusements was thus 'the greater for their
temporary satisfaction'. Faustus's three encounters with female
figures (the 'hot whore,' Lechery, and Helen) were 'properly
reminiscent of one another'. The production lent support to the
contention 'that Marlowe was a good judge of theatrical effect and
that the shows – if not the language – of the middle part of *Faustus*
have variety and richness'.[24]

When Christopher Fettes staged *Doctor Faustus* at the Lyric
Studio, Hammersmith (later the Fortune Theatre), opening on 25
February 1980, an all-male cast included John Aubrey as Faustus
and David Rappaport as the Pope. Helen was played by a boy,
'exquisitely decadent', according to Michael Scott, with 'a white
linen trouser costume with gold fastenings around the ankles and the

back slit to the waist'. Faustus 'was a slave to her but the audience was far from convinced of her beauty and was rightly uneasy at her appearance'.[25] As Faustus encountered Helen, the strains of Richard Wagner's *Liebestod* could be heard in the background. The set was a 'black box' reminiscent of Grotowski's 1963 Polish production. In his programme notes, Fettes cited Jean-Paul Sartre's enigmatic epigram, '*La jeunesse?*' as a source of inspiration. In his last hour, Faustus was stripped and dismembered to the accompaniment of a Bach musical score and the voice of President Richard Nixon speaking to the astronauts on the moon.

Another all-male production, with unmistakable homoerotic overtones, was directed by Barry Kyle for the Royal Shakespeare Company, opening in May 1989, at Stratford's Swan Theatre (of which Kyle was the first artistic director) and then in November at The Pit in London. Gerard Murphy was Faustus and David Bradley was Mephistopheles. As in Grotowski's 1963 version, extensive visual parallels to the life of Christ transformed the protagonist into an ambivalent martyr and AntiChrist. When he stabbed himself to obtain the blood needed to write his deed of gift of his soul to Lucifer (II.i in both texts), Faustus collected his own blood in a chalice. He greeted his devil-'wife', 'A plague on her for a hot whore!' (II.i.153), to the accompaniment of the 'Sanctus'. When the white-robed protagonist collapsed amidst his tormentors, the iconography blasphemously imitated the Pietà. Mephistopheles first appeared to him not as a monk but as another Christ-like figure in a loincloth, identifiable by his stigmata and crown of thorns. In the play's finale, Faustus was lowered down into hell in a cruciform cage. The effect of this was, as Michael Schmidt put it, to emphasize the sacrifice, the 'sensual reality of Faustus's fantasy, the sterility of his contract, and his early sense that he has short-changed himself with trivial powers'.[26]

The play opened with an all-male chorus of damned souls boiling up out of hell to recite the prologue. This same ensemble officiated as Faustus's fellow students, as the Seven Deadly Sins (portrayed through body language, not masks), as angels, as half-naked, writhing devils who groaned whenever the words 'God' or 'heaven' were spoken, and as the final chorus. As Michael Billington observed, they transformed themselves from robed scholars into red devils clawing and caressing Faustus's body 'as in an erotic dream'.[27] Masturbatory fantasies and hallucinatory anxieties of sexual impotence characterized the production throughout. Helen was visibly masculine, as in Fettes's 1980 production. Voyeuristic devils joined Faustus, along with the audience, in gaping at this transvestite male. Faustus and Mephistopheles were often physically close to each other, with hugs and embraces. Mephistopheles (David Bradley) was reptilian, cadaverous, glacial, stiff, as though, in Michael Schmidt's words, he was 'carrying Hell with him in his bones'. He watched Faustus 'like a ferret'. A deliberately slow pace gave emphasis to the scenes of high tragedy rather than to slapstick. The set, designed by Ashley Martin-Davis, was austere, monochromatic, open, with a raised platform stage, at times a throne-like chair, a trapdoor centre stage, and a crane menacingly overhead ready to lower Faustus into hell. The effect suggested both the bare grey walls of Faustus's study and the interior of his feverous mind. The production was, all in all, pointedly postmodern, interpreting Faustus's tragedy as a story for a contemporary world of radically redefined sexual ambiguities.

Simon Trussler saw this 1989 production as a fable of 'a modern man, the ultimate consumer believing that he could work miracles, but who was in fact switched on to a satanic TV set tuned into Channel Seven for the Deadly Sins and to the Helen of Troy Show'. It was thus 'a perfect metaphor for the Thatcherite era, one in which we sold our souls for the sake of consumption, and in which there was supposedly no desire that we could not, given sufficient wealth, realize'. The show made brilliant capital of Peter Brook's idea that theatre should create magic from the physical resources of the stage.[28]

The celebrity film star Jude Law was for many viewers the main attraction of a Young Vic production in 2002 under the direction of David Lan, who had previously directed Law in John Ford's *'Tis Pity She's a Whore* for the Young Vic in 1999. The Young Vic collaborated in this show with the National Nylon Theatre Company, a recently formed group of young actors that included Law and his wife, Sadie Frost. Law, voted by one periodical as the third sexiest man in the world and described from his performance in *The Talented Mr Ripley* as 'unbearably handsome', grew a beard for the part of Faustus. Law saw the play as about rebellion against the establishment and about embracing the darker side of humankind. 'We're relaying an extraordinary journey in a way that will remind people of their own lives, of the world we live in,' he said, adding, 'whether they be junkies or head of Enron'.

Contemporary relevance and updated psychological interpretation were thus the keys to this production. At the end, Faustus had to face not the conventional horrors of hell but the disillusionment of realizing that his book, handed to him once again by Mephistopheles (Richard McCabe), no longer meant to him what it once had; he was left with only his inner torment. When he attempted to console himself by seeking a kiss from Helen, he kissed his own reflection in a mirror. So much for the face that launched a thousand ships. This obsessive narcissist was destined to learn that the prize he sought was illusory. The two angels, one black and one white, were two sides of the same coin. The set design by Richard Hudson featured a long narrow strip of raised bare platform with a pit for detritus cast aside by the characters. The cut script (less than two hours without interval) was a composite of the A- and B-texts. Costuming began in a Tudor vein but ended with Mephistopheles in a red tuxedo outfit. Gwyneth Paltrow, who saw the show, was impressed.[29]

Martin Duncan, Edward Kemp, Stephen Pimlott, and Dale Rooks directed a Chichester Festival modern-dress production of the play at the Minerva Theatre, in the autumn of 2004. The show began in the 300-seat theatre, then promenaded through the atmospheric locations of Chichester, with devils as ushers, and ended with a hellish finale in the cathedral. Many townsfolk were involved. Faustus (Samuel West) smoked a joint and sniffed glue. His hugging and kissing relationship with Mephistopheles (Michael Feast) was decidedly homoerotic. At the Abbey bank, to illustrate the Deadly Sin of greed, devils slithered over the ATM machines. At a baker's shop, Lucifer and his minions made their point about gluttony by handing out jam-filled doughnuts to the spectators. The cathedral bell tolled 12 times to announce Faustus's fateful end, as Mephistopheles claimed his prize with a lingering kiss.[30]

Philip Wilson directed a production at the Liverpool Playhouse in February 2005, with Nicholas Tennant as Faustus and Jamie Bamber as Mephistopheles. With no intermission, this show chose the A-text as shorter and more coherent than the B-text. The set was a claustrophobic and fusty university library, occupied by filing clerks and bibliophiles and filled with massive folio volumes suggesting both the attractiveness and the dangers of learning. Faustus was dressed at first as a university lecturer of the 1960s, sitting at a table with a postgraduate student, Mr Wagner. Later, the Pope tried to eat at one of the library tables. Helen and Alexander walked across the desks. Bamber played Mephistopheles, according to Alfred Hickling, 'with the louche detachment of a Hoxton drug courier: all sleek suit, dirty trainers and looks which smoulder so hard they present a fire hazard amongst all these stacks of dusty paper'. Faustus burned himself on the arm so convincingly with a cigarette lighter to obtain a sample of blood that the audience winced. Doubling and skilful impersonation created the aura of illusoriness, as when Robert

Brown played Helen, Alexander's paramour, Pride, Lechery, and the Duchess of Vanholt, as well as Wagner. In the final scene, the desperate Faustus set fire to a massive volume, filling the stage and the auditorium with dense smoke and leaving in its wake only the burnt shell of the library, its timbers rear-stage forming a cross.[31]

The Working Group Company, in association with B Sharp Company at the Belvoir Street Theatre in Sydney in March and April of 2005 gave Australians a rare opportunity to see the play (very freely adapted) in production. Robert Couch, promising that the show would be 'uncompromising, irreverent and wildly theatrical', made changes to accommodate the script to five actors performing in an intimate, 80-seat house. Fewer than 50 lines of the A-text original were retained, mainly in Faustus's final soliloquy. The Good and Evil Angels, the Seven Deadly Sins, and the Old Man all disappeared. A female Mephistopheles (Amie McKenna) was the only devil. Couch retold the story as one not of damnation so much as a search for 'faith' in a meaningless world. A visit to Tycho Brahe's astronomical observatory led to a serious mathematical discussion of the solar system. Faustus (Eden Falk) and Mephistopheles were physically intimate with each other, suggesting unresolved sexual tensions that were accentuated by Mephistopheles's being played by an actress. At the end, Mephistopheles kneeled and kissed Faustus before leading him offstage. Faustus's faithful servant Robin (Paul Ashton), in an expanded role, was intuitive, practical and sensible enough to resist the blandishments of the devil – the very antithesis, in other words, of the doomed magician that he served. (The play seems also to have been produced at Sydney's Warehouse Theatre between 1986 and 1992 with John Bashford as director.)[32]

Doctor Faustus made its first appearance at the Elizabethan Theatre of the Oregon Shakespeare Festival in the summer and autumn of 2005. James Edmondson directed, with Jonathan Haugen as Faustus and Ray Porter as Mephistopheles. Some of the comic action, including the Horse-Courser and leg-pulling business, was deleted for want of actors and costume-shop resources. Nonetheless, fireworks, roaring devils, thunder and lightning, and Philip Henslowe's dragon-machine were plentifully in evidence. The centre-stage trap became the hellmouth of the final scene, billowing smoke and glowing red. Mephistopheles initially appeared as a huge dragon. Lucifer (Brent Harris) was a Rod Stewart rock star in mid-thigh white boots and a mammoth lime-green codpiece. The Good and Evil Angels were first seen in alcoves above the stage, as though in a diptych.[33]

At the University of Notre Dame on 18–19 April 2008, in the Decio Theatre in the DeBartolo Performing Arts Centre, Professors Anton Juan, Jesse Lander, and Mark Pilkington directed four performances of *Doctor Faustus* in conjunction with a scholarly conference on 'Faust at Notre Dame'. A notable feature of the production was the sending-up of anti-Catholic humour in the scene in the Pope's chambers and at every point when anti-Catholicism emerges in the text. The Pope's associates and followers were tall, awkward figures surmounted by grotesque papier-mâché heads and shoulders. The Pope himself was short and ridiculous; the actor's real head was cloaked, while a masked head located in his midriff grimaced and shrieked petulantly at the invasion of his sacred dignity. The audiences knew what this was all about and roared with laughter. A professional was called in to play Mephistopheles, but most of the actors were Notre Dame students. Also in the same theatre, on 18–20 April, Mark Beudert directed a reconstruction of the original 1859 version of Charles Gounod's opera *Faust*.

Other Productions in Brief

Doctor Faustus has proved itself to be remarkably durable in the theatre in the twentieth and twenty-first centuries, after more than 250 years of almost total neglect. The point can be documented by shorter reports on some lesser-known productions of the last half century. What follows is doubtless not a complete list, though it attempts to be extensive. For more information, consult a checklist of 'Renaissance Drama Productions' begun by G. K. Hunter in 1972–73, continued in 1977 and afterwards by Tony Howard in the pages of *Research Opportunities in Renaissance Drama* (*RORD*). Many of these performances took place in colleges and universities or in small experimental theatres.

The Farnham Repertory Company staged a production at the Castle Theatre, Guildford, in 1964.

Andre van Gyseghem directed a production at the Nottingham Playhouse in 1966, opening on 25 May.

Ann Stutfield directed a production at the Newcastle Playhouse in 1969, opening on 28 October.

A performance took place at Clare College, Cambridge, on 4 December 1975.

Another is recorded at St Peter's College, Oxford, in the summer of 1976.

Andrew McKinnon adapted and directed an Australian production for the Perth Repertory Theatre on 10–27 November 1976, with new material taken from the Faust legend.

Mary Washington College in Virginia mounted a production in February 1977, making use of heavy doubling and a short film and electronic soundtrack to evoke the atmosphere of hell.

A 90-minute version of the play was offered in 1977 by the York Theatre Royal Company at York's Arts Centre as directed by Alan Drury. It featured two Faustuses, one of them a hopeless alcoholic who 'sat in his ubiquitous hell with his back to the audience' for the entire performance, 'watching the events of his life unfold on stage' (as reviewed by Tony Howard in *RORD* 20 [1977], pp. 68–70).

The Young Vic staged the play in the autumn of 1977 using hand glove-puppets, controlled by three puppeteers, for Faustus and other human figures and with more elaborate demons for the Seven Deadly Sins. Alan Judd directed.

David Thacker directed a production for the Chestergateway Theatre Company at the Chester Arts Centre, 28 November–10 December 1977.

Sue Wilson directed a production for the Nuffield Theatre, Southampton, in February 1978. Patrick Sandford directed a subsequent production there with the Resident Company from 14 April– 7May 1984.

The Belgrade Theatre Company in Coventry put on a condensed version of the play called *Faustus's Last Supper* in February and March 1978, under the direction of Andrew Tuckey, with a minimalist set inspired by the productions discussed above by Jerzy Grotowski and Charles Marowitz.

Ron Huebert directed the play for the Dalhousie Dramatic Society, New Brunswick, in 1978, with Faustus as a man who, having lost his respect for the objects of experience in the very act of desiring them, tries 'to reduce them to properties or puppets under his control'. He thereby becomes a 'spiritual junkie' for whom the renunciation of desire would be to 'annihilate the person he has become'.[34]

At the Oxford Playhouse in November 1978, with Jeremy Howe as director, the devils doubled all the other roles by availing themselves of costumes from an onstage costume rack.

Also in November 1978, Duncan Miller and Frances Brookes directed a production at the Sherman Theatre, Cardiff.

Pembroke College, Cambridge, staged a production in November 1979, in which Mephistopheles doubled all the other parts except Faustus, who witnessed in this fashion an hour-long series of dream-temptations acted out by the devil. Richard Spaul directed.

Nicholas Young directed a production at the Connaught Theatre, Worthing, that ran from 31 October–17 November 1979.

In the chapel of Jesus College, Cambridge, in October 1980, two huge representations of the Good and Evil Angels stood originally as gigantic figures flanking the choir-screen. The Pope was ludicrously deaf and drunk. Alexander and Darius engaged in a boxing match. The chapel bell was pressed into service to toll the final hours of Faustus's fateful odyssey. Headless devils carried Faustus out into the cloister court, chanting the Requiem, leaving the audience in total darkness as the chanting receded. Tom Cribb directed.[35]

James Madison University's School of Theatre and Dance produced the play in early 1981.

A slideshow proclaiming such milestones as the moon landings and nuclear holocaust, together with a nightclub act of the Seven Deadly Sins, enlivened a production of the play at the Swan Theatre, Worcester, directed by Ian Granville Bell, in April 1982.

A transvestite and homosexual all-male cast that included giggling monks, a 'maiden-aunt' Mephistopheles, a beautiful but malevolent Lucifer, and a vampish paramour-consort of Alexander was the central feature of a Nottingham Playhouse production, directed by Michael Winter and Jeremy Howe, at York in April and then at Nottingham in May 1983. Compare Barry Kyle's 1989 production.

David Parry, a major force in the staging of medieval theatre at Cambridge and then at the University of Toronto, directed members of Cambridge's Marlowe Society in a production at the Arts Theatre in March 1984. Modern touches abounded. Faustus (Tim Pemberton) indulged in Groucho Marx-like wagging of bushy eyebrows and thumbs-up gestures. The actors frenetically chased one another around the auditorium. Lucifer reminded audiences of the British rock and pop star Gary Glitter. Pride sprayed the front-seat spectators with spittle. With the below-stairs comedy on full display, this production brought the play together as a whole.[36] In a production at the Royal Lyceum Theatre, Edinburgh, in July and

August 1984 and again in 1985, the Sins were particularly disgusting, having been based on the paintings of Hieronymus Bosch. Faustus, at the end, was electrocuted in an iron chair with a blaze of light calculated to shock the audience. Ian Wooldridge directed.

Andy Johnson adapted and directed the play for Nervous Theatre at the Bridge House, London, from 15 October–3 November 1984.

A production at the Edinburgh Festival in August 1986 featured a four-member Cambridge-based touring company. Faustus acted out the routines of the Seven Deadly Sins under Mephistopheles's hypnotic suggestion. A 30-minute street theatre version by the Wooden O Company acted at the Edinburgh Festival in August 1985.

The St Magnus Players from Orkney also presented a *Doctor Faustus* at the same Edinburgh Festival, featuring cage-like balances from which the Good and Evil Angels sparred with each other, demons with Minotaur-like and eagle-like heads, and a large fishing net used by the devils to ensnare Faustus at the end.

The Park Bench Theatre Company performed the play at the Cambridge Festival Fringe in the summer of 1986.

At Magdalen College, Oxford, in June 1987, the Oxford University Dramatic Society put on a lavish production in one of the main quadrangles. Faustus (Piers Gibbon) appeared high up on the top of the clock tower, brandishing flaming torches in both hands as he began his incantations. The Good and Evil Angels were disembodied voices. Faustus and Mephistopheles (Mark Roberts) mounted the walls so that they could witness the Pope (Mark Senior, doubling as Wagner) put on a show of rock-and-roll dancing. Helen was a figure of clay. Magdalen's clock chimed the fatal hour for the protagonist. Sad to say, a downpour of rain dampened the fireworks that were intended to signal the triumph of hell.[37]

The Actors Touring Company staged *Doctor Faustus* at the Lyric Studio, Hammersmith, in November and December 1987 (where Christopher Fettes had produced the play in 1980; see above) and then returned to the Lyric Studio the following May. Mark Brickman directed. This version added a visit to the underworld by the protagonist, under the guidance of Charon. Much of the play's middle action was omitted. Faustus's study had a stereo stand. George Anton played Mephistopheles as a bored intellectual, impatient with his charge. The scene of the Seven Deadly Sins featured Wagner as a waiter carrying a tray with glasses of beer.

Faustus drank and smoked as he watched Mephistopheles impersonate each of the Sins in turn. Helen was a yard-high hand puppet ghost.[38]

'Clowning does not come naturally to the earnest, overreaching members of the Shaliko Company', wrote Mel Gussow in the *New York Times* of a production under Leonardo Shapiro's directorship at La Mama Annex (74A East Fourth Street, NYC) in April 1988. The only member of the cast who was remotely able to invoke the power of Marlowe's script, in Gussow's view, was Christopher McCann as Faustus. The Good Angel, Mia Kanazawa, appeared naked, and then later, 'unconvincingly', as Helen. Faustus dressed as an astronaut for his visit to the Pope.[39]

The Young Vic returned to *Doctor Faustus* in April and May 1988 under the direction of Anthony Clark, with Peter Guinness as Faustus, Stephen Jenn as a red-rimmed-eyed and psychopathologically melancholy Mephistopheles, and Jon Strickland as a God-father-like Pope. Faustus was all Bertrand Russell or Thomas Huxley, the sophisticated atheist for whom hell was a fable. The stage was 'surmounted by a circular blue firmament from which hung an hourglass inside a sphere'. The vulgarly madcap comic scenes from the B-text seemed an integral part of the play. Lechery pulled a string that flapped her knees together. When Faustus lost one leg to the Horse-Courser, he sprouted another one, thus terrifying the Horse-Courser, and was tossed a shoe by Mephistopheles – the character who was really pulling the strings.[40]

Court Theatre's production in Chicago in the autumn of 1988, directed by Nicholas Rudall, featured a soulful and tragic Mephistopheles (David Darlowe) and Seven Deadly Sins that were puppets fashioned to strikingly different sizes and operated in Brechtian fashion by stagehands in black leotards. Envy was eight feet tall and spectrally thin; Sloth had trouble staying awake long enough to say his lines; Lechery was a rotund and complacent Miss Piggy who kept crossing and uncrossing her chubby legs. Helen was so evanescent in the brief glimpses of her behind the scenes that one couldn't quite be sure whether one had spotted her or not.

The Oak Park Festival Theatre, just outside Chicago, staged a music-laden production of the play in July and August 1992, directed by Tom Mula.

Phelim McDermott directed a production for the Nottingham Playhouse on 5–21 November 1992.

Philip Frank's production at the Greenwich Theatre took place between 11 November and 11 December 1993.

The American Repertory Theatre Institute for Advanced Theatre Training, at Harvard University, produced the play at the Adams House Pool Theatre in April 1994, as adapted and directed by Adrian Daumas. This lacklustre and mystifying production contained some intriguing and risible touches. Faustus (Swen Miller), lean and sallow, was first seen as cadaver-like on a slab, naked except for a pair of modern-day undershorts. A woman rose from a hole in the floor dressed only in a black robe open down the front. Faustus's first soliloquy was chanted by the chorus as though it were a liturgical prayer. Two actors (Elliot Mandelcorn and Sherri Lee) played Mephistopheles by way of suggesting the male and female sides of his/her diabolical personality. Once he had signed away his soul, Faustus had sex with the female Mephistopheles on the ever-present slab. Eventually Faustus showed himself totally nude to the audience, having dispensed with the underwear. Helen, conversely, was not a naked goddess in a transparent gown but a cross-dressed man in beard and falsies.[41]

Xavier Leret directed a production for the Kaos Theatre Company at Bridewell, London, from 26 July–6 August 1994.

At George Mason University's Centre for the Arts, in Fairfax, Virginia, in November of 1995, Edward Gero, on the theatre faculty, gave a fine performance in the role of Faustus as an arrogant and cynical intellectual. Another faculty member, Timmy Ray James, was Mephistopheles doing his best to please his Mafia-like boss, Lucifer (Hugh Nees). Students were relegated to the lesser roles. The head of the Theatre Fine Arts costume department, Howard Vincent Kurtz, designed spectacular costumes. Rick Davis was director. A postmodern setting provided Faustus with a PowerBook for his volume of magic. His visits with Mephistopheles were to a plantation in the American South (complete with a screening of some choice bits of *Gone with the Wind*), the Vatican at the time of the Holocaust, and America's frontier West of the nineteenth century. Topical bogeymen hinted at included Nazism, genocide, slavery, and capitalist exploitation.[42]

Neil Sissons directed a production for The Compass Theatre Company at the Crucible Studio, Sheffield, as part of a tour, in April 1996. Five actors were on stage throughout in this small-scale, intimate studio performance. Nick Chadwin was Faustus and

Richard Heap was Mephistopheles, 'tall and darkly elegant in evening dress and white spats'. Props were minimal; everything was mimed. 'There was no escape for the audience from the claustrophobic presence of the whole cast and the bare furnishings of the study', writes Lisa Hopkins, so that 'Faustus was, indeed, in hell already, with a strong sense of the whole drama being played out merely within his own, damned, mind'.[43]

Robert Kimbrough, a faculty member at the University of Wisconsin, Madison, adapted and produced a version of the play for Honest Puck Productions in the spring of 1996, with José Rios as Faustus and Ed Maxcy as Mephistopheles. A reviewer found it vibrant, heady, exciting, confident in its professionalism.[44]

Jonathan Best directed the play at The Other Place, Stratford, in July and August 1997, as part of 'On the Edge'.

The English Suitcase Theatre at Simon Fraser University produced the play in late summer and autumn 1997, as one of the best of that year's Fringe Festival in British Columbia. Mephistopheles was cast as a woman, adding to the tone of diabolical sexuality in the spiritual seduction of the protagonist. The show ran for 75 minutes with a cast of three.[45]

Philip Graham and Rob Crouch directed the play for the Bruce Farce Theatre Company at the North Pole Pub, Greenwich in June 1997, and then in August at the Etcetera Theatre, Camden, London, with George Symes as Faustus and Sarah Goddard as Mephistopheles.

Andrew Potter directed the play for the Wycombe Theatre Company at the Wycombe Swan Town Hall Theatre in October 1997, with David Worley as Faustus and Christopher Myles as Mephistopheles.

Simon Bell directed the play for the Galleon Theatre Company at the Prince Theatre, Prince of Orange, Greenwich, in January and February 1998.

Michael Shugg adapted the play for the Valencia Community College Character Company (in Florida) in 1999, in conjunction with Bobbie Bell of Seminole Community College (Sanford, Florida). Mephistopheles was again played by a woman (Barbara Hall), showing up in her second appearance in 'provocative black, with shiny leather boots and a spiky dog collar necklace'. Faustus (Mark March) looked like a student, in his sweater and sport coat, and was. His 'hot whore' shot flames out between her legs. The Seven Deadly Sins staged a nightmare Las Vegas show. Faustus's fate at the end of the play was explained to the audience as follows: 'I think Old Faustus means to kick the bucket'.[46]

The Palatine Theatre Company produced *Doctor Faustus* in early August 2000, at the Old Fire Station in Oxford, with Ross MacDonald as an arrogant and blustering Faustus and Julian Blundell as Mephistopheles. The Prologue entered in billowing smoke. A minimal stage and a cast of seven actors kept the action moving.[47]

The Shifting Sands Theatre Company produced the play at Hoxton Hall, London, in February 2002, to critical acclaim.

Gertrude Stein was the author of *Doctor Faustus Lights the Lights*, staged in March 2003 at the Notery Theater, Stafford. Originally an opera libretto, this piece told of a young boy, a talking dog, and Doctor Faustus, who sold his soul to the devil in exchange for the power of light. The show also played at Simon Fraser University in February and March 2007.

Camenae Theatre Ensemble's all-female production in October 2003, at Side Studio on West Jarvis in Chicago, directed by Sara Keely McGuire, was about the power of greed. An audience capacity of about 15 spectators limited the show to one set and a tiny budget. Bernadine Ann Tippet played Faustus; Tory Leigh was Mephistopheles.[48]

Rebecca Gould and Mervyn Millar directed a production in February 2004 sponsored by the National Theatre Education of London and the Theatre Royal of Plymouth. It took place at the Drum Theatre in Plymouth, the Cottesloe Theatre in London, and the Albany Stage in Deptford. Carl Grose helped with the adaptation, aimed at dumbing the play down for teenagers. Emma Stansfield played Mephistopheles in red tights and a low-cut Elizabethan man's costume. Guy Lewis as Faustus was a weedy young man selling his soul for Helen of Troy, in this case a dressmaker's dummy in a chiffon scarf.[49]

The Wales Actors' Company produced the play at Llanover Hall, Cardiff, Wales, and on tour in February and March 2004, under the direction of Paul Garnault, with Korah Knight as Faustus and Phillip John as Mephistopheles. The show was set in Faustus's study and in his mind. Gernault turned to F. W. Murnau's 1920s silent film *Faust* as inspiration for his prelude using CCTV and video.[50]

At just about the same time in March 2004, the Theatre Arts Department at Castleton State College in Vermont staged the play in a contemporary style, with a student cast including James Lorentz as Faustus and Lauren Martin as Mephistopheles. It was directed by Harry McEnerny IV.

The OFS Theatre in Oxford produced the play in May 2004, with Alex Nicholls as Faustus and Joseph Adams as Mephistopheles, featuring tricksy movie sequences and booming dance music.

A musical adaptation, directed by Marchus Eyre, was staged at the Barons Court Theatre in August and September 2004.

Ben Power adapted a version of the play in which several scenes were set against a plot about the British iconoclastic anti-war artists, Dinos and Jake Chapman, here presented as twin versions of Faust. The show was directed by Rupert Goold at the Theatre Royal, Northampton, in October and November 2004.

A production of the play was staged at the Etcetera Theatre, Camden, in June 2005.

Also in 2005, Adrian Schiller wrote and directed a musical version for Dr Foster: Flipside Productions at the Menier Theatre, London, in October and November.

Richard Keightley as a tormented Faustus and Matt Robinson as a nearly shattered Mephistopheles starred in a production (in tandem with Jonson's *The Devil Is an Ass*) at the tiny White Bear pub theatre in south London, two minutes from the Kennington Tube station, in early 2006. The Left Handed Theatre Company produced; Blanche McIntyre directed.[51]

John Wright directed an 80-minute touring version of the play for Third Party Productions at Tewkesbury, Stamford, Hereford, and the Theatre Royal, Margate, in September and October 2006. Nicholas Collett played Faustus; Anthony Gleave was Mephistopheles. It was extended into a spring tour in 2008.

With Rupert Goold again as director and Ben Power as adapter, Headlong Theatre, formerly the Oxford Stage Company, in association with the Nuffield Theatre of Southampton, updated their 2004 production (see above) at the Hampstead Theatre in October and November 2006, in which Faustus's story was again interwoven with that of the Chapman brothers. Scott Handy played Faustus; Jake Maskell was Mephistopheles. The show was rated as one of *Time Out*'s top ten theatrical events of 2006, and was taken on tour.

In April 2007, the play was staged by the University of North

Carolina (Charlotte) Department of Dance and Theatre at the Anne R. Belk Theatre in Robinson Hall for the Performing Arts. Director Andrew James Hartley chose the A-text for his script, emphasizing the possibility of redemption for Faustus as an aspiring scholar of humble origins until late in the play. A slideshow displayed all the places visited by Faustus and Mephistopheles. The entertainment that Faustus put on for the emperor suggested the spectacles of music, dance, and girls at Las Vegas. The cast, mainly undergraduate, featured James Vesce (a faculty member) as Faustus and Miller McGowan as Alexander. The Old Man was a bag lady.[52]

Maria Bates adapted and directed the play at the Bell Theatre in south London, May 2007, with the assistance of Simon Drake and his House of Magic team.

A production of the play ran for three nights at the University of Warwick in July 2008.

In the autumn of 2008, David Fielding directed the play for the Bristol Old Vic with an ensemble of eight actors.

On 8 December 2008, a staged reading was presented, under the direction of Mark Lamos, at the Red Bull Theatre on West 42nd Street in New York.

* * *

Radio and television productions have also been numerous. See Bakeless, 1.305, for his listing of radio productions down to 1942. Subsequent broadcasts include the following:

22 June 1947: Great Britain, directed by Stephen Harrison with David King-Wood as Faustus and Hugh Griffith as Mephistopheles.

29 February 1958: Great Britain, for schools, directed by Ronald Eyre with William Squire as Faustus and James Maxwell as Mephistopheles.

4 and 7 November 1961: Great Britain, directed by Ronald Eyre with Alan Dobie as Faustus.

2007: 'The Complete Doctor Faustus', directed by Toby Longworth for Lord Strange's Men.

2008, autumn: Great Britain, BBC Radio 3, produced for the Open University for its course, 'The Arts Past and Present'. Based on the A-text, with Toby Jones, Paterson Joseph and Ray Fearon.

Notes

1   This and some other items of information in this chapter make use of my performance history in David Bevington and Eric Rasmussen, eds, '*Doctor Faustus': A- and B-texts (1604, 1616)*, (Manchester: Manchester University Press, 1993). Citations from the text refer to this edition. Also of great value is the essay on 'The Stage-History of the Play', in *Doctor Faustus*, ed. John D. Jump, Revels Plays (London: Methuen, 1962), pp. lviii–xiii; and William Tydeman, '*Doctor Faustus:' Text and Performance* (Basingstoke: Macmillan, 1984).

2   See Eric Rasmussen, '*The Black Book* and the Date of *Doctor Faustus*', *Notes and Queries*, 235, n.s. 37 (1990), pp. 168–70.

3   Barbara Cooper, 'An Ur-Faustus?', *Notes and Queries*, 104, n.s. 6 (1959), pp. 66–68, n. 166.

4   The account is by one J. G. R., in *The Gentleman's Magazine*, 2nd ser., 34 (1850): 234; reprinted in E. K. Chambers, *The Elizabethan Stage*, 4 vols (Oxford: Clarendon, 1923), vol. 3 p. 424. J. G. R. bases his story on a manuscript note on 'the last page of a book in my possession, printed by Vautrollier' in 1585.

5   Aubrey, 1, p. 190, in Chambers, *Elizabethan Stage*, vol. 3, p. 424.

6   G. E. Bentley, *The Jacobean and Caroline Stages*, 5 vols (Oxford: The Clarendon Press, 1941–56), vol. 1, pp. 318–19; and Jump, *Faustus*.

7   John Bakeless, *The Tragicall History of Christopher Marlowe*, 2 vols (Cambridge, MA: Harvard University Press, 1942), vol. 1, p. 296.

8   Edward Phillips, *Theatrum Poeteareum, or, A Complete Collection of the Poets*, 2 vols (London: for Charles Smith, 1675), pp. 11–25; and William Winstanley, *The Lives of the Most Famous English Poets* (London: H. Clark for S. Manship, 1687), p. 134.

9   Quoted in Michael Billington, *The Guardian*, 13 March 2002.

10   Robert Speaight, *William Poel and the Elizabethan Revival* (London: Heinemann, 1954), pp. 113–19. See also Percy Simpson, 'Marlowe's *Tragical History of Doctor Faustus*', *Essays and Studies* 14 (1929), pp. 20–34.

11   Bakeless, 1, pp. 303–6; Jump, p. lxii; and C. L. Barber, 'The Form of Faustus' Fortunes Good or Bad', *Tulane Drama Review* 8.4 (1964), pp. 92–119.

12   Bakeless, 1, pp. 303–5; Jump, p. lxi; Robert H. Fleissner, 'Robert Frost and the Dramatic', *New England Quarterly* 10 (1937), pp. 202–9; and Fleissner, *The Prince and the Professor: The Wittenberg Connection in Marlowe, Shakespeare, Goethe, and Frost* (Heidelberg: Carl Winter, 1986), p. xii.

13   Barber, 'The Form of Faustus' Fortunes Good or Bad', p. 105.

14   Jerzy Grotowski, '*Doctor Faustus* in Poland', trans. Richard Schechter, *Tulane Drama Review* 8.4 (1964), pp. 120–33; Johannes H. Birringer, 'Between Body and Language: "Writing" the Damnation of Faustus', *Theatre Journal* 36 (1984), pp. 335–55.

15   Tydeman, '*Doctor Faustus*', p. 50.

16   See J. C. Trewin, *Birmingham Post*, 15 February 1968, and Irving Wardle, *The Times*, 29 June 1968.

17   H. W. Matalene, III, 'Marlowe's *Faustus* and the Comforts of Academicism', *ELH* 39 (1972), pp. 495–519; J. C. Trewin, '*Dr. Faustus*', *Birmingham Post*, 15 February 1966; and Tydeman, '*Doctor Faustus*', pp. 60ff.

18   Nigel Alexander, 'The Performance of Christopher Marlowe's *Dr. Faustus*', *PMLA* 57 (1971), pp. 331–49.

19   Irving Wardle, *The Times*, 29 June 1968.

20   Maureen O'Farrell, *Evening Press* (Dublin), 11 March 1970; J. C. Trewin, *Birmingham Post*, 25 June 1960; Peter Fiddick, *The Guardian*, 26 June 1970.

21   John Barber, *Daily Telegraph*, 9 September 1974; and Tydeman, '*Doctor Faustus*', pp. 62ff.

22   Michael Billington, *The Guardian*, 7 September 1974.

23   Irving Wardle, *The Times*, 7 September 1974. During their student days in 1960, Ian McKellen, Trevor Nunn and other members of the Marlowe Society had put on a *Doctor Faustus* at the Stratford open-air festival, in a space called The Dell, a natural amphitheatre by the Avon. In an RSC interview on 29 June 2007, as he was directing McKellen in *King Lear*, Nunn recalled how the Marlowe Society then included Derek Jacobi, Corin Redgrave, Mike Burrell, and Margaret Drabble.

24   Russell Jackson, 'Doctor Faustus in Manchester', *Critical Quarterly* 23. 4 (1981), pp. 3–9.

25   Michael Scott, *Renaissance Drama and a Modern Audience* (London: Macmillan, 1982), p. 76. Quoted in Gregory Woods, *A History of Gay Literature: The Male Tradition* (New Haven, CT: Yale University Press, 1998), p. 88; and see Tydeman, 'Doctor Faustus', pp. 50 and 63ff.

26   Michael Schmidt, *Daily Telegraph*, 12 May 1989.

27   Michael Billington, *The Guardian*, 12 May 1989.

28   Simon Trussler, RSC Programme for *Doctor Faustus*, 1989, and his edition of *Doctor Faustus*, Drama Classics Series (London: Nick Hern Books, 1996).

29   Lizzie Loveridge, *Curtain Up*, 4 April 2002.

30   Rob Conkie, *Research Opportunities in Renaissance Drama* 44 (2005), pp. 128–31.

31   Chris Hopkins, *Early Modern Literary Studies* 11.1 (2005), pp. 1–6; Alfred Hickling, *The Guardian*, 10 February 2005.

32   Ruth Lunney, *Marlowe Society of America Newsletter (MSAN)* 25.2 (2005).

33   Alan Armstrong, *Shakespeare Bulletin* 24.1 (2006), pp. 77–80.

34   Ron Huebert, 'Tobacco and Boys and Marlowe', *Sewanee Review* 150 (1984), pp. 206–24.

35   Richard Axton, Christ's College, Cambridge, by personal communication.

36   Rex Gibson, a review, in *Marlowe Society of America Newsletter (MSAN)* 4 (1984), p. 10.

37   Mark Thornton Burnett, *MSAN* 7.2 (1987), p. 6.

38   Vesna Pistotnik, *MSAN* 8.1 (1988), pp. 8–9.

39   Mel Gussow, *New York Times*, arts section, 15 April 1988.

40   Richard F. Hardin, *MSAN* 8.2 (1988), pp. 7–8.

41   Andrew Fingland, *MSAN* 14.2 (1994), pp. 4–5.

42   David Sobelsohn, online, 1995, dcmdva-art.org.

43   Lisa Hopkins, *MSAN* 16. 1 (1996), p. 5.

44   Unsigned, *MSAN* 16. 2 (1996), pp. 7–8.

45   Glen Callendar, *The Peak*, Simon Fraser University's student newspaper, 22 September 1997.

46   Brenda Walton, *MSAN* 19.2 (1999), pp. 6–7.

47   Ruth Alexander, *Daily Info, Oxford*, 2 August 2000.

48   Rick Reed, *Windy City Times*, 8 October 2003.

49   Rhoda Koenig, *The Independent*, 17 February 2004.

50   *Shakespeare Bulletin* 22 (2004).

51   Natalie Bennett, *BC: BlogCritics Magazine*, 1 March 2006; Lois Potter, *Shakespeare Bulletin* 26.1 (2008), pp. 124–31.

52   Lois Potter, *Shakespeare Bulletin*, 2008.

CHAPTER THREE

The State of the Art: Current Critical Research

Robert Logan

No work of Christopher Marlowe has generated the abundance of continuous, widespread responses from scholars and critics that *Doctor Faustus* has. In stirring up controversy, presenting diverse perspectives and articulating emphatic views, the discussions rival those of the most heated Shakespeare studies. Scholars have published editions with the 1604 A-text and the 1616 B-text and filled the pages of journals, book chapters and an entire book with analyses of the authenticity of the two versions and the differences between them; and critics have argued at length over interpretations of Faustus's behaviour and the multiple ambivalences and ambiguities in each of the two texts. Over time, especially among the writings of the critics, controversy has intensified with the result that the only consensus lies in agreeing that there are fewer and fewer reasons for consensus.

The influence of the Faustus story itself has been nothing short of remarkable and extends into the twentieth-first century where, clearly, it qualifies as an archetypal myth. Apart from its power to inspire dramatists, poets and writers of prose fiction down through the centuries, during the twentieth and twenty-first centuries the Faustus story has served as either a direct transcription of an assumed version of Marlowe's text or, in its situational premise of selling one's soul to the devil, as the underpinning of novels, staged plays and operas, radio and television dramas, and educational and commercial films. Along with a renewed interest in Marlowe's biography,[1] *Doctor Faustus* is unquestionably the chief reason for Marlowe's popularity and fame today.

For the purpose of grounding the following discussion, I wish to consider three topics that will enable us to characterize the present state of the art in the scholarship and criticism of *Doctor Faustus*: first, speaking quantitatively, the tendencies reflected in the twenty-first century's scholarship and criticism on the play; second, patterns in the focus and approaches of this scholarship and criticism; and, third, places where I think future scholarship and criticism might profitably dig. I am using the word 'scholarship' to describe the efforts of those who have dealt primarily with the textual matters and print culture of the play; 'criticism' pertains to writings on issues of interpretation. Understandably, at times the two categories overlap and mesh.

Tendencies

In order to establish a larger context for the present state of scholarship and criticism on *Doctor Faustus*, I found it helpful to survey editions, books, articles, notes, chapters in collections and bits and pieces in books published since 1990. When I arrived at 2000, I began to add to the list of published books and essays unpublished material – primarily dissertation abstracts – and, beginning with 2004, conference papers as well. The number of chapters devoted to *Doctor Faustus* in books has increased in the last 25 years or so,[2] but journal articles are still plentiful and usually command the lead in yearly publications. What is perhaps surprising is that, apart from editions and Eric Rasmussen's book of commentary[3] on his and David Bevington's 1993 edition of the A- and B-texts of the play,[4] there is only a single book-length publication devoted exclusively to *Doctor Faustus*.[5] I suspect that the chief reason for this may be the difficulty that scholars and critics have had in resolving the drama's textual and interpretative problems.

From 1997 to 2007, the number of published pieces that touch on either or both of the two texts has never been fewer than six (in 1998) or more than 17 (in 2000). The total number for these ten years adds up to approximately 124, but 104 of them occur after the turn of the century; already, as of January 2009, there are four articles and four books that discuss the tragedy. These figures tell us that the number of publications, whether they treat the drama exclusively or simply include some discussion of it, not only continues to be constant, but, since 2000, the number has been dramatically increasing, and this tendency shows no signs of changing. Conference presentations that include *Doctor Faustus* indicate a similar steady flow of interest into 2009. Their focus appears to be chiefly on the intellectual issues circulating in and around the two texts, as well as on characterization, rather than on scholarly matters.[6]

Patterns

But what about patterns in the focus and the approaches of post-2000 discussions of the play? It almost goes without saying that in any survey of writings on *Doctor Faustus*, one needs to separate the scholarship from the criticism and, in the latter case, traditional from non-traditional perspectives. In the twenty-first century, a clear majority of what has been written has been from a critical rather than from a scholarly perspective and, more often than not, the subjects and approaches have been traditional. Moreover, for most scholars and critics, the 1993 edition of the A- and B-texts by Bevington and Rasmussen has become widely accepted, even if arguments over the authenticity of the two texts are ongoing. For example, Michael Keefer, in his 2006 revised edition of the A-text,[7] takes issue with a conclusion drawn by Bevington and Rasmussen. Although all three agree that 'at some point around 1589 there was indeed a "single underlying text" of *Doctor Faustus*',[8] Keefer believes that the B-text indicates a different originary text of the play from that of the A-text; the other two scholars argue that the A-text is closer to the originary text. Keefer asserts in conclusion that the difference of opinion indicates that 'the early history of the play must be more complex than contemporary textual critics have been willing to acknowledge'.[9] This notion suggests the possibility that further research needs to be done on the origins of the texts and that the efforts of the collaborator(s) and reviser(s) that appear to give rise to the B-text (especially) need to be given more consideration. Such concerns would of necessity involve a broader discussion of sixteenth- and seventeenth-century textual studies and the Tudor-Stuart print culture.

One can easily divide the criticism on *Doctor Faustus* into traditional and non-traditional issues. It is probably no surprise that traditional topics predominate: characterization, genre, religious attitudes, ethical values, the concern with magic and philosophical conflicts. Of course, criticism has sustained the longstanding interest in associating these subjects with Marlowe's personal beliefs. Dramaturgical and poetic techniques have taken a back seat to the substance of the play – to metaphysical considerations in particular. If during the 1990s interest in Marlowe focused with intensity on the

A- and B-texts of *Doctor Faustus*, for the first five years of the new millennium biographies created the greatest buzz. But they did not overshadow the number of treatments of *Doctor Faustus* in books and journals; the play retained its popularity as Marlowe's most written-about work. The notes, articles and discussions in books deal overwhelmingly with traditional topics: in 2000, for example, Robert A. H. Smith in his source study, 'Marlowe and Peele: A Further note on the Final Scholar Scene in the *Doctor Faustus* B-text', wonders whether Marlowe borrowed from Peele's *The Battle of Alcazar* or Peele from Marlowe's play; in 'Calvinist Conceptions of Hell in Marlowe's *Doctor Faustus*', Adrian Streete suggests that the conceptions of hell in both the A- and B-texts have their origins in Calvin; in her essay, 'The Morality Play in *Doctor Faustus*: Faustus as Reprobate Man', Lauren L. Shimman finds the proceedings in Act V akin to those of a morality play, but a morality play lacking a mankind figure for Faustus to identify with and, thereby, assisting in confirming him as a reprobate; Gareth Roberts attributes the unclear sense of magic in the two texts to editorial problems in 'Marlowe and the Metaphysics of Magicians'; in an article entitled 'Marlowe's Literary Double Agency: *Doctor Faustus* as a Subversive Comedy of Error', Suzan Last describes how in the B-text the comic scenes subvert orthodoxy; and in *Christopher Marlowe: A Literary Life*, Lisa Hopkins places her essentially biographical discussion within the literary, theatrical and social milieu that contextualizes Marlowe's life; in doing so, she discusses both Marlowe's plays and poetry.

Interestingly, three offerings attempt to push beyond the conventional limits of *Faustus* criticism. In 'Hell and Hypertext Hath No Limits: Electronic Texts and the Crises in Criticism', Hilary J. Binda examines issues that grow out of reading hypertext through Marlowe in order to illuminate our general understanding of our relationship to texts. Adapting an audience-response approach, in 'Out of Service and in the Playhouse: Richard Norwood, Youth in Transition and Early Response to *Dr. Faustus*', Charles Whitney uses Norwood's 1640 diary to suggest the effect that *Doctor Faustus* might have had on him and others in his younger days. In *Re-Citing Marlowe: Approaches to the Drama*, Clare Harraway invokes poststructuralist theory to promote the notion that writing cannot convey fixed and repeatable meanings; she thus sees Faustus as a victim of a mistaken belief in the power of language. On the whole, this first year of the millennium contains one of the two richest years-to-date of critical work on the play.

In 2001, a similar quantitative pattern obtained but without the same diversity. Criticism dominated over scholarship and, as the titles of the essays indicate, the critics concerned themselves with conventional topics: religion (e.g. ' "Consummatum Est": Calvinist Exegesis, Mimesis and *Doctor Faustus*'), philosophy (e.g. 'Casting Doubt in Marlowe's *Doctor Faustus*'), magic (e.g. 'La imagen del mago en Marlowe y Calderon'), and characterization and theme (e.g. 'The Ambition of Faustus and the Tragic Significance from Subversion' and 'The Four and Twenty Years of Marlowe's Faustus'). There were also some endeavours to grapple with the responses of readers and viewers (e.g. ' "Be Silent Then, for Danger Is in Words": The Wonders of Reading and the Duties of Criticism') and with Marlowe's contemporary relevance (e.g. 'Servant/Master Relationship in Lawrence Durrell's *An Irish Faustus* with Reference To Christopher Marlowe's *The Tragical History of Dr. Faustus*' and 'A "New Deal" and a New Direction: Welles' and Houseman's Depression-Era Productions of *Macbeth*, *Doctor Faustus*, and *Julius Caesar*').

Although 2002 was a banner year for books on Marlowe – four in all[10] – the predominant focus on *Doctor Faustus* occurred in journal articles. The relatively brief sections in the books that directed attention to this particular play talked about the staging of the A- and B-texts, audience response, the ambivalence of the play as an interrogative drama and Faustus as a militaristic figure. The articles reflected a similar diversity. They demonstrated Marlowe's influence on Shakespeare ('Skeptical Moments in *As You Like It* and Their Possible Connection with Marlowe' and 'The Interrogation of the Heavens in *King Lear* and Marlowe's *Doctor Faustus*') and Marlowe's significance in a modern context that considers Sam Shepard's adaptation of *Doctor Faustus* as *Man Fly* ('European Textures: Adapting Christopher Marlowe's *Doctor Faustus*'). Stylometrics ('Faustian Joan'), pedagogy ('Texts That Won't Stand Still' and 'Contextualizing the Demonic: Marlowe's *Doctor Faustus* in the Classroom'), and religion and ambiguity (' "To obtain his soul": Demonic Desire for the Soul in Marlowe and Others') complete the 2002 limning of the Marlovian landscape.

The year 2003 marked the slimmest year of the new millennium for interest in *Doctor Faustus*. A Marlowe collection reprints essays from the twentieth century[11] and in the journal articles for that year, two of the five individual essays move backward in time to take as their subject the Diana and Actaeon myth.[12] Two more articles extend Marlowe's reach into twentieth-century literature and film.[13] The remaining article investigates the similarities between *Love's Labour's Lost* and *Doctor Faustus*. Two of these five articles bear witness to the abiding interest that connections between Marlowe and Shakespeare have long held for both scholars and critics, even when they can only speculate on Marlowe as a source for or an influence on Shakespeare. This tendency has persisted in conferences as well as in publications.

By contrast with 2003, 2004 was rich in Marlowe scholarship and criticism – due in large part to the publication of *The Cambridge Companion to Christopher Marlowe*. The book offers several essays that discuss *Doctor Faustus* in part and one that concentrates exclusively on the play.[14] In reading the essays one readily notices that the perspectives are remarkably varied. Laurie Maguire tells us what we can conclude from the evidence of the composition and printing of the two texts and how our lack of knowledge affects readers; Paul White investigates the anti-Christian sentiment in the play; Richard Wilson links the play with Marlowe's biography; Garrett Sullivan examines Marlowe's use of geography and what it tells us about his geographical knowledge; and Lois Potter surveys the complicated stage history of the play. Thomas Healy's chapter on *Doctor Faustus* examines the popular modern fascination with the play as a metaphysical tragedy attempting to formulate perspectives on heaven, hell and sin, and shows how the play and its subsequent additions work to subvert sixteenth-century moralistic ideas of what drama should do to promote religion. Embedding his argument within the cultural milieu of the 1580s and 1590s, Healy concludes that the play is neither 'in the service of religion' nor ' "the chapel of Satan" ' but, instead, 'celebrates the ascendancy of the theatre's own prerogative as a place for playing'.[15] His conclusion that Marlowe's interest was aesthetic rather than moral (even if the two are not necessarily antithetical) marks a growing tendency in Marlovian scholarship and criticism: to see Marlowe's dominant perspective as that of a man with a strong literary background and artistic interests who managed, without compromising himself, to marshal his talents and accommodate them to the pragmatic and commercial demands of the theatre.

The remaining journal articles and book chapters that treated *Doctor Faustus* in 2004 lend support to the essays in the *Companion* to establish this as an exceptional year, containing as wide a range of critical perspectives as we have seen since 2000. In 'Marlowe's Theater of Night: *Doctor Faustus* and Capital', Richard Halpern invokes theatre history to analyse the play, relating the unvarnished realities of capital exchange in theatrical ventures to the intellectual themes of the play. In a chapter on Marlowe in his book *Shakespeare Minus 'Theory'*, Tom McAlindon rejects poststructuralist and Marxist avenues in favour of a humanistic roadway as he attempts to understand the theatricality of *Faustus*. However, in 'Unpardonable Sins: The Hazards of Performative Language in the Tragic Cases of Francesco Spiera and *Doctor Faustus*', Daniel Gates makes use of poststructuralist theory to capture the power of Marlowe's language, contending that its effectiveness originates in socially constructed responses made inherent in his audiences. David Lucking discusses the figure of the magus in *Doctor Faustus* and *The Tempest*, one more attempt to see links between Marlowe and Shakespeare. James H. Lake interviews Ralph Alan Cohen about his role as director in a Shenandoah Shakespeare production of the play in 2000. In his article, ' "Fairer Than the Evening Air": Marlowe's Gnostic Helen of Troy and the Tropes of Belatedness and Historical Mediation', Michael Keefer rejects a simple, literal reading of Faustus's encounter with Helen of Troy and, instead, views her in the context of her longstanding theological and philosophical heritage. In his book, *The Time is Out of Joint: Skepticism in Shakespeare's England*, Benjamin Bertram includes a chapter on Marlowe, 'Christopher Marlowe's Skepticism', to indicate how *Doctor Faustus* questions early modern forms of Christianity as well as Christianity itself. Finally, in 'Disorder in the House of God: Disrupted Worship in Shakespeare and Others', Bruce Boehrer inquires whether Faustus's disruption of the Pope's meal is motivated by a Protestant anti-Catholic attitude or by something more secular and psychological – namely, the sheer delight of misbehaving.

The following year produced David Scott Kasten's Norton Critical Edition of the two texts of *Doctor Faustus* fleshed out with previous scholarship that includes biographical information and discussions of the composition, publication and early performances of the play, as well as contextual information on the Faust legend, magic and religion. The section on criticism takes into account both early and modern commentary on the play; the modern critics discuss structure and genre, ideas and ideologies, and performance. This volume and Park Honan's biography of Marlowe, *Christopher Marlowe: Poet & Spy*, represent the only two books in 2005 that focus exclusively on Marlowe. Honan offers little new evidence about the play but speculates on Marlowe's patrons, artistic associates and acquaintances.

The articles for 2005 are both scholarly and critical. Thomas Pettitt and Andrew Duxfield wrestle with the texts: Pettitt draws an analogy between the oral transmission of folk tales and the memorial reconstruction of Marlowe's dramas, and Duxfield surveys the problems of editing early modern plays, making use of the two texts of *Doctor Faustus* to indicate the development of textual theory during the twentieth century. Generally speaking, 2005 stands out as a year in which scholars were especially interested in Marlovian textual matters and print culture.

In the critical articles, traditional subjects take the lead. In ' "Faustus . . . for Ever": Marlowe, Bruno, and Infinity', Todd H. J. Pettigrew contends that Faustus's inability to understand the infinite and, therefore, his continual mistaking of the finite for the infinite and vice versa, causes his downfall; and instead of viewing the cosmos from Bruno's perspective, as is conventionally believed, Faustus stands in opposition to Bruno's thinking. In another historical-philosophical article, 'An Age in Love with Wonders: The Philosophical Context of Renaissance Literature', Neil Allan considers the place of Renaissance ideas in the history of philosophical thought, adducing *Doctor Faustus* as an example of a work that raises significant philosophical issues and presents a worldview even as it reflects intellectual thought in transition. Angus Fletcher's '*Doctor Faustus* and the Lutheran Aesthetic' and Mike Pincombe's 'His Master's Voice: The Conjuring of Emperors in *Doctor Faustus* and Its Sources in the German Tradition', in dealing with religion and sources respectively, address familiar topics, whereas Anne B. Darmstätter in 'Le Motif du pact avec le diable chez Rutebeuf et Marlowe' and Daniel Roux in 'Aphanisis of/as the Subject: From Christopher Marlowe to Ruth First' consider Marlowe's significance in other literary traditions. That these last two critics continue to explore Marlowe's reach as several others before them have done reflects the increased popularity of this subject. Significantly, the two critics could not be further apart in their approach; whereas Darmstätter compares the two writers analytically, Roux adapts poststructuralist theory to focus his commentary.

An abundance of journal and book articles in 2006 confirmed the patterns of previous years. Perhaps the most unusual of these offerings are Downing Cless's 'Ecologically Conjuring Doctor Faustus' and Kirsten Shepherd-Barr's *Science on Stage: From 'Doctor Faustus' to 'Copenhagen'*, both of which invoke frames of reference usually considered outside the realm of the humanities. An article by Katharine Lindsay, ' "When thou tookest the book / To view the scriptures, then I turned the leaves / And led thine eye" ' (Marlowe 1986, *Doctor Faustus* V.ii, pp. 89–91): Literary Theory and Hypertext – A Faustian Predicament', employs *Doctor Faustus* to suggest the limitations of hypertext theorizing and to promote experimental evidence over ideology. However, more conventional

philosophical and religious approaches dominated in 2006: Betül
Balkan's 'Free-Will or Society as the Source of Evil in Drama' and
Miguel Martinez López's 'The Philosophy of Death in Christopher
Marlowe's *Dr. Faustus*' demonstrate the philosophical interest and
Lowell Gallagher's 'Faustus's Blood and the (Messianic) Question of
Ethics' and Kristen Poole's 'Dr. Faustus and Reformation Theology'
show the concern with religion. Using only the B-text, Poole probes
the longstanding orthodox-heterodox controversy – i.e. the play as
an affirmation of Christian doctrine vs. the play as anti-Christian.
She concludes that 'an understanding of the English Reformation as
a unified and near universal movement' is fallacious.[16] Moreover,
'Marlowe and his Doctor Faustus were not alone in their conflicted
relationships to free will, predestination, and ultimately, God';[17] the
playwright's contemporary audience also experienced religious
confusion. Two articles treat the appearances of Helen of Troy in
the play: Laurie Maguire's 'Helen of Troy: Representing Absolute
Beauty in Language' and Paul Dean's 'Was this the face?'. Other
articles include David Golz's 'The Four Books of Doctor Faustus'
and Kristen Poole's 'The Devil's in the Archive: *Doctor Faustus* and
Ovidian Physics', and also Michael Mitchell's book chapter in
*Hidden Mutualities: Faustian Themes from Gnostic Origins to the
Postcolonial*. All three of these centre on thematic concerns,
although Poole forcefully historicizes her argument by drawing an
analogy between the devil's trick of shape-shifting and the Ovidian
focus on metamorphosis to indicate that the play 'presents a model
of inhabiting a metamorphic environment',[18] in which reality and
illusion cannot be separated.

Three books were published in 2007 that contained significant
material on *Doctor Faustus*. Michael Keefer published a second
edition of *Doctor Faustus: A 1604 Version Edition* with lengthy
introductory material, an appendix of excerpts from *The English
Faust Book* that are matched with incidents in the play, and a
generous bibliography. In his book, *Shakespeare's Marlowe: The
Influence of Christopher Marlowe on Shakespeare's Artistry*, Robert
A. Logan includes a chapter entitled ' "Glutted with Conceit":
Imprints of *Doctor Faustus* on *Macbeth* and *The Tempest*' in which
he 'focuses on the portion of the legacy of *Doctor Faustus* found in
Shakespeare's last works'.[19] Specifically, the chapter 'explores the
possibilities of the influence of Marlowe's drama in *Macbeth* and
The Tempest, including key metadramatic connections between
Doctor Faustus and Shakespeare's two plays'.[20]

At other points in the book, stressing the impact of *Doctor
Faustus*, Logan establishes links between the drama and *Richard*

II, *Troilus and Cressida* and *King Lear*. David Hawkes examines the Faust myth in Marlowe's play, asserting that the playwright, 'identifiably Lutheran',[21] portrays 'the absurdity'[22] of the protagonist's rebellion against God. John Parker's book, *The Aesthetics of Antichrist: From Christian Drama to Christopher Marlowe*, shows how Marlowe separates secular and sacred drama and yet fuses the two. Claiming that 'the Marlovian revolution in drama revolves around traditional instabilities',[23] Parker demonstrates that Marlowe reconfigures the theatricality he finds in these 'instabilities' in *The Jew of Malta*, *Tamburlaine* and *Doctor Faustus*. In discussing the latter, he investigates just what the portrayal of Doctor Faustus inherits from the tradition of Simon Magus before examining, as the chapter title puts it, 'Marlowe's Sacred Counterfeits'.

The articles in 2007, though fewer in number than in the previous year, continue to display the diversity that we have seen heretofore. Andrew Duxfield in ' "Resolve Me of All Ambiguities": *Doctor Faustus* and the Failure to Unify' presents the case for the ambivalent interpretations of the play as either a warning to the ungodly or a tribute to the spirit of humanism, and our ambiguous response to the protagonist and to the genre of the drama. Because Faustus is seeking, reductively, a unified understanding of the world and his power in it, he is doomed to failure. Arnd Bohm spots a possible source in 'Wise Blood: *Aeneid* 3.22–57 and Marlowe's *Doctor Faustus*', and in 'One Hell of an Ending: Staging Last Judgement in the Towneley Plays and in *Doctor Faustus* A and B', David Bevington ponders the significance of textual variants – specifically, why the B-text finds a parallel in the Towneley Last Judgement but the A-text does not.

In 2008 Lisa Hopkins published a book entitled *Christopher Marlowe, Renaissance Dramatist* that treats some biographical issues and presents introductions to the plays; and David Wootton edited *Doctor Faustus with The English Faust Book*. In a collection of essays, Sara Munson Deats's essay entitled ' "Mark this show": Magic and Theater in Marlowe's *Doctor Faustus*' equates the magician with the playwright, contending that 'the notorious contrariety of the play derives not only from Marlowe's ambivalence toward magic, but from his divided response toward his own medium, the drama'.[24] In the same collection, Deborah Willis's '*Doctor Faustus* and the Early Modern Language of Addiction' examines the B-text to show the complexities of the history of our understanding of addiction. Finally, again in this same volume, Robert A. Logan analyses the two representations of the magus and magic in *Doctor Faustus* and *The Tempest*, concluding that 'both magicians ultimately provide commentary on the two playwrights' views of the imagination and its place in their artistic endeavors'.[25] Four articles also deserve mention. In 'Teaching & Learning Guide for: Modern Problems of Editing: The Two Texts of Marlowe's *Doctor Faustus*', Andrew Duxfield adds to his continuing interest in the theory and practice of editing. In 'Oedipal Marlowe, Mimetic Middleton', Lars Engle compares Marlowe's and Middleton's styles as demystifiers, while noting that, paradoxically, their plays still depict meaningful human action. Invoking Freud's Oedipal and Girard's mimetic modes of demystification, he embeds the two playwrights in theoretical contexts that help explain their portrayals of human agency. As her title indicates, Kay Savage in 'Stage Directions: Valuable Clues in the Exploration of Elizabethan Performance Practice' explores the effect of stage directions on performance practice; although her focus is principally on Greene, the article contains enough information to be helpful to Marlovians eager to discover links with *Doctor Faustus*. Finally, Sarah Wall-Randell in 'Doctor Faustus and the Printer's Devil' investigates the effect that print technology had specifically on Marlowe's understanding of Faustus and magic and more generally on the imagination of the English in early modern times.

What can we conclude from this survey of scholarship and criticism written about *Doctor Faustus* since the advent of the new millennium? During the last five years, a note has been frequently sounded in Marlowe scholarship exhorting scholars and critics to rely on documentary evidence and to accept the limited knowledge we have of the playwright and of the biographical implications in his works. In effect, this is a call to historicize topics, to anchor them within a historical context that relies on documents and is, therefore, as factual as possible. On a more obvious level, the scholarship and criticism on *Doctor Faustus* since the beginning of the new millennium can be characterized in the following ways.

- There is a continued interest in both fresh and traditional topics and approaches, but, clearly, traditional topics and approaches dominate. Poststructuralist methodologies have left only an occasional imprint but an imprint nevertheless.
- Scholars and critics have an increasingly realistic acceptance of what we do not know and cannot know.
- The interest in manuscript and textual studies seems to be slowly accelerating, including what it means to be an author of a playtext.[26]

- The concern with ambivalence and ambiguity in the two texts keeps appearing in essay after essay and, usually, as a chief stumbling block to interpretation.
- We see many attempts to extend the play's range – whether to Marlowe's contemporaries (especially Shakespeare), backward in time to classical writers or forward in time to Marlowe's influence down through the ages.
- Included in the relevance of this tendency is a propensity to fuse traditional methodologies with present-day interests – for example, as we saw above, Deborah Willis's tracing of the complex history of our contemporary understanding of addiction through a close examination of the B-text of *Doctor Faustus*.
- Broadly cultural considerations have become more dominant.
- One finds a stronger reluctance to affirm the validity of an approach that is exclusive or, much less, reductive.

The Future

Given the current state of scholarship and criticism, what new directions might studies of *Doctor Faustus* most profitably pursue? The obvious general answer is that they would do well to enlarge their focus. Here is what I think a wider focus might include.

- More could be done with stagecraft and the pragmatics of dramaturgical strategies.
- Since ambiguity has been widely acknowledged as a major artistic device in *Doctor Faustus*, as well as in Marlowe's other plays and in *Hero and Leander*, is it now time to separate the deliberate from the non-deliberate ambiguity and to attempt a close reading of the two texts, one that takes more into account Marlowe the professional strategist well aware of the effects of dramaturgical and poetic techniques? (Such an examination would of necessity include the efforts of any collaborators and revisers.) For example, would not some discussions that focus on the properties and uses of language in the play considerably enhance our understanding of the two texts?
- Scholarship on the play could benefit from more concentration on audience reception, an area most recently explored by Ruth Lunney and Charles Whitney.
- A tendency that has been granted only slight treatment – *Faustus*'s links with contemporary dramatists and writers apart from Shakespeare – might profitably be expanded.
- Perhaps scholarship has been most lacking in Marlowe's

connection to the wide range of matters pertaining to theatre and stage history.

● Some work has been done on the performance history of the play (by Lois Potter most recently), but this area requires more attention.

At present, the scholarship and criticism on *Doctor Faustus* successfully confer upon readers a wholly salutary benefaction, for they constantly renew themselves and develop interests that reflect a vibrant engagement with the play. But there are, undoubtedly, other illuminating approaches and subjects of focus that could lead to new alternatives, fresh bursts of imagination and innovative analyses. Given the increasing interest in the play since 2000, such undertakings are bound in the coming years to take their place at centre stage.

Reference Works

The following bibliography, although perhaps not exhaustive, is representative and complete enough to depict the present state of the art in scholarship and criticism on *Doctor Faustus*. I have omitted several bits and pieces on the play that are found in a wide-ranging number of individual essays and books.

Biographies

Honan, P., *Christopher Marlowe: Poet & Spy* (Oxford: Oxford University Press, 2005).

Hopkins, L., *Christopher Marlowe: A Literary Life* (Basingstoke: Palgrave, 2000).

Hopkins, L., *Christopher Marlowe, Renaissance Dramatist* (Edinburgh: Edinburgh University Press, 2008).

Kendall, R., *Christopher Marlowe and Richard Baines: Journeys through the Elizabethan Underground* (Madison, NJ: Fairleigh Dickinson University Press; Cranbury, NJ: Associated University Presses, 2003).

Kuriyama, C. B., *Christopher Marlowe: A Renaissance Life* (Ithaca, NY: Cornell University Press, 2002).

Nicholl, C., *The Reckoning: The Murder of Christopher Marlow*, revised edn (London: Vintage, 2002).

Proser, M. N., *The Gift of Fire: Aggression and the Plays of Christopher Marlowe* (New York: Peter Lang, 1995).

Riggs, D., *The World of Christopher Marlowe* (London: Faber & Faber, 2004).

Single Editions (1993–2008)

Bevington, D. and Rasmussen, E., eds, *'Doctor Faustus' A- and B-texts (1604, 1610)* (Manchester: Manchester University Press, 1993).

Kasten, D. S., ed., *Christopher Marlowe: 'Doctor Faustus': A Two-text Edition (A-text, 1604; B-text, 1616), Contexts and Sources, Criticism* (New York: Norton, 2005).

Keefer, M., ed., *'Doctor Faustus': A 1604-Version Edition*, 2nd edn (Ontario: Broadview, 2006).

Wootton, D., ed., *'Doctor Faustus' with 'The English Faust Book* (Indianapolis, IN: Hackett Publishing Company, 2008).

Collections of essays

Bartels, E., ed., *Critical Essays on Christopher Marlowe* (London: Prentice, 1996).

Cheney, P., ed., *The Cambridge Companion to Christopher Marlowe* (Cambridge: Cambridge University Press, 2004).

Deats, S. M. and Logan, R. A., eds., *Marlowe's Empery: Expanding His Critical Contexts* (Newark, DE: University of Delaware Press, 2002).

Deats, S. M. and Logan, R. A., eds., *Placing the Plays of Christopher Marlowe: Fresh Cultural Contexts* (Aldershot: Ashgate, 2008).

Downie, J. A. and Parnell, J. T., eds., *Constructing Christopher Marlowe* (Cambridge: Cambridge University Press, 2000).

Grantley, D. and Roberts, P., eds., *Christopher Marlowe and English Renaissance Culture* (Aldershot: Scolar, 1996).

Oz, A., ed., *Marlowe*, (New York: Palgrave, 2003).

Scott, S. K. and Stapleton, M. L., eds, *Christopher Marlowe the Craftsman: Lives, Stage, and Page* (Aldershot: Ashgate, forthcoming).

White, P. W., ed., *Marlowe, History, and Sexuality: New Critical Essays on Christopher Marlowe* (New York: AMS, 1998).

Wilson, R., ed., *Christopher Marlowe*, (Harlow: Longman, 1999).

2000: individual essays

Binda, H. J., 'Hell and hypertext hath no limits: Electronic texts and the crises in criticism', *Early Modern Literary Studies: A Journal of Sixteenth- and Seventeenth-Century English Literature 5* (2000), pp. 1–29.

Roberts, G., 'Marlowe and the metaphysics of magicians', in *Constructing Christopher Marlowe*, ed. J. A. Downie and J. T. Parnell (Cambridge: Cambridge University Press).

Last, S., 'Marlowe's Literary Double Agency: *Doctor Faustus* as a

Subversive Comedy of Error', *Renaissance and Reformation/ Renaissance et Réforme* 24 (2000) pp. 23–44.

Laroque, F., 'Ovidian v(o)ices in Marlowe and Shakespeare: The Actaeon variations', in *Shakespeare's 'Ovid': The 'Metamorphoses' in the Plays and Poems*, ed. A. B. Taylor (Cambridge: Cambridge University Press, 2000).

Lucking, D., 'Our devils now are ended: A comparative analysis of *The Tempest* and *Doctor Faustus*', *The Dalhousie Review* 80 (2000) pp. 151–67.

Mihailescu, C.-A., *'Les grandes figures de la désillusion: Faust, Hamlet, Don Quichotte'*, in *L'époque de la Renaissance (1400–1600, IV Crises et essors nouveaux 1560–1610)*, ed. E. Kushner, T. Klaniczay and P. Chavy (Amsterdam: Benjamins, 2000).

Shimman, L. L., 'The Morality Play in *Doctor Faustus*: Faustus as Reprobate Man', *Discoveries: South-Central Renaissance Conference News and Notes* 17 (2000) pp. 5–6.

Smith, R. A. H., 'Marlowe and Peele: A Further Note on the Final Scholar Scene in the *Doctor Faustus* B-text', *Notes and Queries* 47 (2001), pp. 40–42.

Streete, A., 'Calvinist Conceptions of Hell in Marlowe's *Doctor Faustus*', *Notes and Queries* 47 (2000), pp.430–32.

Whitney, C., 'Out of Service and in the Playhouse: Richard Norwood, Youth in Transition and Early Response to *Dr. Faustus*', *Medieval and Renaissance Drama in England: An Annual Gathering of Research, Criticism and Reviews* 12 (2000), 166–89.

2000: books

Cox, J. D., *The Devil and the Sacred in English Drama, 1350–1642* (Cambridge: Cambridge University Press, 2000).

Downie, J. A. and Parnell, J. T., eds, *Constructing Christopher Marlowe* (Cambridge: Cambridge University Press, 2000).

Hammill, G. L., *Sexuality and Form: Caravaggio, Marlowe, and Bacon* (Chicago: University of Chicago Press, 2000).

Harraway, C., *Re-Citing Marlowe: Approaches to the Drama* (Aldershot: Ashgate, 2000).

Hopkins, L., *Christopher Marlowe: A Literary Life* (Basingstoke: Palgrave, 2000).

Simkin, S., *A Preface to Marlowe* (White Plains, NY: Longman, 2000).

Wilson, L., *Theaters of Intention: Drama and the Law in Early Modern England* (Stanford, CA: Stanford University Press, 2000)

2001: individual essays

Abdel-Al, N. M., 'Servant/master relationship in Lawrence Durrell's *An Irish Faustus* with reference to Christopher Marlowe's *The Tragical History of Dr. Faustus*', *Gombak Review: A Journal of Language and Literature* 5 (2001) pp. 51–63.

Alcázar, J., 'La imagen del mago en Marlowe y Calderón', in *400 Años de Calderón Coloquio*, ed. A. González (Mexico City, Mexico: Facultad de Filosofía y Letras, Universidad Nacional Autónoma de México, 2001).

Axline, K., 'A "New Deal" and a New Direction: Welles' and Houseman's Depression-era Productions of *Macbeth*, *Doctor Faustus*, and *Julius Caesar*', *Theatre Studies* 45 (2001), pp. 16–49.

Caponi, P., 'The Damnation of the Critic: Faustus' Demoniality and Greg's Intentionality', *Annali di Ca' Foscari: Rivista della Facoltà di Lingue e Letterature Straniere dell'Università di Venezia*, 40 (2001), pp. 57–77.

Coogan, R., 'The Four and Twenty Years of Marlowe's Faustus', *Notes and Queries* 48 (2001), pp. 265–66.

Fehrenback, R. J., 'A Pre-1592 English *Faust Book* and the Date of Marlowe's *Doctor Faustus*', *Library* 2 (2001), pp. 327–35.

Hamlin, W. M., 'Casting Doubt in Marlowe's *Doctor Faustus*', *Studies in English Literature* 41 (2001), pp. 257–75.

Kirchof, E. R., 'As faces do novo mal refletidas pelo Barroco Europeu', *Letras de Hoje: Estudos e Debates de Lingüística, Literatura, e Língua Portuguesa*, 37 (2001), pp. 123–30.

Lunney, R., 'Rewriting the Narrative of Dramatic Character; or, not "Shakespearean" but "Debatable"', *Medieval and Renaissance in England: An Annual Gathering of Research, Criticism and Reviews* 14 (2001), pp. 66–85.

Park, C., 'The ambition of Faustus and the tragic significance from subversion', *Journal of Classic and English Renaissance Literature* 10 (2001), pp. 5–26 (in Korean; English summary).

Pereira, L. F., 'Doutor Fausto: Adrian Leverkühn, a ordem e os donceitos de arte subjetiva e objetiva', *Letras de Hoje: Estudos e Debates de Lingüística, Literatura, e Língua Portuguesa* 36.123 (2001), pp. 193–213.

Pieters, J., ' "Be silent then, for danger is in words": The Wonders of Reading and the Duties of Criticism', *English Studies: A Journal of English Language and Literature* 82 (2001), pp. 106–14.

Streete, A., ' "*Consummatum est*": Calvinist Exegesis, Mimesis and *Doctor Faustus*', *Literature & Theology: An International Journal of Theory, Criticism and Culture* 15 (2001), pp. 140–58.

Wessman, C., ' "I'll play Diana": Christopher Marlowe's *Doctor*

Faustus and the "Actaeon Complex" ', *English Studies: A Journal of English Language and Literature* 82 (2001), pp. 401–19.

2001: books
Simkin, S., *Marlowe: The Plays* (Basingstoke: Palgrave, 2001).
Tromley, F. B., *Playing with Desire: Christopher Marlowe and the Art of Tantalization* (Toronto: University of Toronto Press, 2001).

2002: individual essays
Akstens, T., 'Contextualizing the Demonic: Marlowe's *Doctor Faustus* in the Classroom', in *Approaches to Teaching English Renaissance Drama*, ed. K. Bamford and A. Leggatt (New York: Modern Language Association of America, 2002).
Bevington, D., 'Staging the A- and B-texts of *Doctor Faustus*', in *Marlowe's Empery: Expanding His Critical Contexts*, ed. S. M. Deats and R. A. Logan (Newark, DE: University of Delaware Press, 2002).
Callens, J., 'European Textures: Adapting Christopher Marlowe's *Doctor Faustus*', in *The Cambridge Companion to Sam Shepard*, ed. M. Roudané (Cambridge: Cambridge University Press, 2002).
Cox, J. D., ' "To obtain his soul": Demonic Desire for the Soul in Marlowe and Others', *Early Theatre: A Journal Associated with the Records of Early English Drama* 5 (2002), pp. 29–46.
Edgecombe, R. S., 'Skeptical Moments in *As You Like It* and their Possible Connection with Marlowe', *Shakespeare Bulletin: A Journal of Performance Criticism and Scholarship*, 20 (2002), pp. 45–46.
Kang, S.-J., 'Christopher Marlowe and the Politics of Transgression', *Journal of English Language and Literature/Yongo Yongmunhak* 48 (2002), pp. 639–64 (in Korean; English summary).
Marcus, L. S., 'Texts That Won't Stand Still', in *Approaches to Teaching English Renaissance Drama*, ed. K. Bamford and A. Leggatt (New York: Modern Language Association of America, 2002).
Merriam, T., 'Faustian Joan', *Notes & Queries* 49 (2002), pp. 218–20.
Webb, D., 'The Interrogation of the Heavens in *King Lear* and Marlowe's *Doctor Faustus*', *College English* 61 (2002), pp. 13–29.

2002: books

Deats, S. M. and Logan, R. A., eds., *Marlowe's Empery: Expanding His Critical Contexts* (Newark, DE: University of Delaware Press, 2002).

Kuriyama, C. B., *Christopher Marlowe: A Renaissance Life* (Ithaca, NY: Cornell University Press, 2002).

Lunney, R., *Marlowe and the Popular Tradition: Innovation in the English Drama before 1595* (Manchester: Manchester University Press, 2002).

Shepard, A., *Marlowe's Soldiers: Rhetorics of Masculinity in the Age of the Armada* (Burlington, VT: Ashgate, 2002).

2003: individual essays

Brown, E. C., 'Shakespeare's Anxious Epistemology: *Love's Labor's Lost* and Marlowe's *Doctor Faustus*', *Texas Studies in Literature and Language* 45 (2003), pp. 20–41.

Ellison, J., 'From Fëanor to *Doctor Faustus*: A Creator's Path to Self Destruction', *Mallorn: The Journal of the Tolkien Society*, 41 (2003), pp. 13–21.

Lafont, A., 'Le corps nu de Diane ou les égarements du coeur et de l'esprit dans *Doctor Faustus* et *Edward II*', *Anglophonia* 13 (2003), pp. 69–82.

Laroque, F., 'The Fashioning of Self and Desire: The Metamorphosis of Actaeon in Marlowe and Shakespeare', in *Self-Fashioning and Metamorphosis in Early Modern English Literature*, ed. O. Lausund and S. H. Olsen (Oslo: Novus, 2003).

Torado, J., '*The Matrix* o la literatura errática', *Enfocarte.com: Revista de Arte Y Cultura* 3 (2003) (electronic publication).

2003: books

Kendall, R., *Christopher Marlowe and Richard Baines: Journeys Through the Elizabethan Underground* (Madison, NJ: Fairleigh Dickinson University Press, 2003).

Oz, A, ed., *Marlowe* (New York: Palgrave, 2003).

2004: individual essays

Bertram, B., ' "Religion Hides Many Things from Suspicion": Christopher Marlowe's Skepticism', in *The Time is Out of Joint: Skepticism in Shakespeare's England*, ed. B. Bertram (Newark, DE: University of Delaware Press, 2004).

Boehrer, B., 'Disorder in the House of God: Disrupted Worship in Shakespeare and Others', *Comparative Drama* 38 (2004), pp. 83–103.

Gates, D., 'Unpardonable Sins: The Hazards of Performative Language in the Tragic Cases of Francesco Spiera and *Doctor Faustus*', *Comparative Drama* 38 (2004), pp. 59–81.

Halpern, R., 'Marlowe's Theater of Night: *Doctor Faustus* and Dapital', *English Literary History* 71 (2004), pp. 455–95.

Healy, T., '*Doctor Faustus*', in *The Cambridge Companion to Christopher Marlowe*, ed. P. Cheney (Cambridge: Cambridge University Press, 2004).

Keefer, M., ' "Fairer than the evening air": Marlowe's Gnostic Helen of Troy and the Tropes of Belatedness and Historical Mediation', in *Fantasies of Troy: Classical Tales and the Social Imaginary in Medieval and Early Modern Europe*, ed. A. Shepard and S. D. Powell (Toronto: Centre for Reformation and Renaissance Studies, 2004).

Lake, J. H., 'Ralph Alan Cohen Talks About *Doctor Faustus* 2000', *Shakespeare Newsletter* 54 (2004), pp. 67–68.

Lucking, D., 'Carrying Tempest in his Hand and Voice: The Figure of the Magician in Jonson and Shakespeare', *English Studies: A Journal of English Language and Literature* 85 (2004), pp. 297–310.

Maguire, L., 'Marlovian Texts and Authorship', in *The Cambridge Companion to Christopher Marlowe*, ed. P. Chency (Cambridge: Cambridge University Press, 2004).

McAlindon, T., 'Marlowe Plus and Minus "Theory": The Case of Doctor Faustus', in *Shakespeare Minus 'Theory'*, ed. T. McAlindon (Aldershot: Ashgate, 2004).

Potter, L., 'Marlowe in Theatre and Film', in *The Cambridge Companion to Christopher Marlowe*, ed. P. Cheney (Cambridge: Cambridge University Press, 2004).

Sullivan, Jr., G. A., 'Geography and Identity in Marlowe', in *The Cambridge Companion to Christopher Marlowe* ed. P. Cheney (Cambridge: Cambridge University Press, 2004).

White, P. W., 'Marlowe and the Politics of Religion', in *The Cambridge Companion to Christopher Marlowe*, ed. P. Cheney (Cambridge: Cambridge University Press, 2004).

Wilson, R., 'Tragedy, Patronage, and Power', in *The Cambridge Companion to Christopher Marlowe*, ed. P. Cheney (Cambridge: Cambridge University Press, 2004).

2004: books

Cheney, P., ed., *The Cambridge Companion to Christopher Marlowe* (Cambridge: Cambridge University Press, 2004).

Riggs, D., *The World of Christopher Marlowe* (London: Faber & Faber, 2004).

2005: individual essays

Allan, N., 'An Age in Love with Wonders: The Philosophical Context of Renaissance Literature', *Literature Compass* 2 (2005) (electronic publication).

Darmstätter, A. B., 'Le motif du pact avec le diable chez Rutebeuf et Marlowe', *Colloquium Helveticum: Cahiers Suisses de Littérature Comparée/Schweizer Hefte für Allgemeine und Vergleichende Literaturwissenshaft/Quaderni Svizzeri di Letteratura Generale e Comparata* 36 (2005), pp. 49–66.

Duxfield, A., 'Modern Problems of Editing: The Two Texts of Marlowe's *Doctor Faustus*', *Literature Compass* 2 (2005) (electronic publication).

Fletcher, A., '*Doctor Faustus* and the Lutheran Aesthetic', *English Literary Renaissance* 35 (2005), pp. 187–209.

Pettigrew, T. H. J., ' "Faustus ... for ever": Marlowe Bruno, and Infinity', *Comparative Critical Studies* 2 (2005), pp. 257–69.

Pettitt, T., 'Marlowe's Texts and Oral Transmission: Towards the Zielform', *Comparative Drama* 32 (2005), pp. 213–42.

Pincombe, M., 'His Master's Voice: The Conjuring of Emperors in *Doctor Faustus* and its Sources in the German Tradition', *Hungarian Journal of English and American Studies* 11 (2005), pp. 117–31.

Roux, D., 'Aphanisis of/as the Subject: From Christopher Marlowe to Ruth First', *Shakespeare in Southern Africa: Journal of the Shakespeare Society of Southern Africa, 2005* 17 (2005), pp. 27–33.

2005: books

Honan, P., *Christopher Marlowe: Poet & Spy* (Oxford: Oxford University Press, 2005).

Kasten, D. S., ed., *Christopher Marlowe: 'Doctor Faustus': A Two-Text Edition (A-text, 1604; B-text, 1616), Contexts and Sources, Criticism* (New York: Norton, 2005).

Owens, M. E., *Stages of Dismemberment: The Fragmented Body in Late Medieval and Early Modern Drama* (Newark, DE: University of Delaware Press, 2005).

Szonyi, G., *John Dee's Occultism: Magical Exaltation through Powerful Signs* (Albany: SUNY Press, 2005).

2006: individual essays

Balkan, B., 'Free-will or Society as the Source of Evil in Drama', *Civil Academy: Journal of Social Sciences/Sosyal Bilimler Dergisi* 13 (2006), pp. 64–68.

Cless, D., 'Ecologically Conjuring *Doctor Faustus*', *Journal of Dramatic Theory and Criticism* 20 (2006), pp. 145–67.

Cook, A. and Reynolds, B., 'Comedic Law: Projective Transversality, Deceit Conceits, and the Conjuring of Macbeth, and Doctor Faustus in Jonson's *The Devil is an Ass*', in *Transversal Enterprises in the Drama of Shakespeare and His Contemporaries: Fugitive Explorations*, ed. B. Reynolds (New York: Palgrave Macmillan, 2006).

Dean, P., ' "Was this the face?" ', *English Studies* 87.5 (2006), pp. 539–43.

De Armas, F. A., 'The Ghost of Helen in *Doctor Faustus* and *Don Quixote*', in *Critical Reflections: Essays on Golden Age Spanish Literature in Honor of James A. Parr*, ed. B. Simerka, A. R. Williamsen and S. Polchow (Lewisburg, PA: Bucknell University Press, 2006).

Gallagher, L., 'Faustus's Blood and the (Messianic) Question of Ethics', *English Literary History* 73 (2006), pp. 1–29.

Golz, D., 'The Four Books of Doctor Faustus', *Notes and Queries* 53 (2006), pp. 444–49.

Lindsay, K., ' "When thou tookest the book / To view the scriptures, then I turned the leaves / And led thine eye' (Marlow, 1986, *Doctor Faustus*, V.ii, pp.89–91). Literary Theory and Hypertext – A Faustian Predicament', *Literary and Linguistic Computing* 21.1 (2006), pp. 87–98.

Maguire, L., 'Helen of Troy: Representing Absolute Beauty in Language', *Sederi* 16 (2006), pp. 31–51.

Martinez López, M., 'The Philosophy of Death in Christopher Marlowe's *Dr. Faustus*', in *Spanish Studies in Shakespeare and His Contemporaries*, ed. J. M. González (Newark, DE: University of Delaware Press, 2006).

Poole, K., 'Dr. Faustus and Reformation theology', in *Early Modern English Drama: A Critical Companion*, ed. G. A. Sullivan, P. Cheney and A. Hadfield (Oxford: Oxford University Press, 2006).

Poole, K., 'The Devil's in the Archive: *Doctor Faustus* and Ovidian physics', *Renaissance Drama* 35 (2006), pp. 191–219.

2006: books

Mitchell, M., *Hidden Mutualities: Faustian Themes from Gnostic Origins to the Postcolonial* (Amsterdam: Rodopi, 2006).

Shepherd-Barr, K., *Science on Stage: From 'Doctor Faustus' to 'Copenhagen'* (Princeton, NJ: Princeton University Press, 2006).

Sullivan, G. A., Cheney, P., and Hadfield, A., eds., *Early Modern*

English Drama: A Critical Companion (Oxford: Oxford University Press, 2006).

Whitney, C., *Early Responses to Renaissance Drama* (Cambridge: Cambridge University Press, 2006).

2007: individual essays

Bevington, D., 'One Hell of an Ending: Staging Last Judgment in the Towneley Plays and in *Doctor Faustus* A and B', in *'Bring Furth the Pagants': Essays in Early English Drama Presented to Alexandra F. Johnston*, ed. D. N. Klausner and K. S. Marsalek (Toronto: University of Toronto Press, 2007).

Bohm, A., 'Wise Blood: *Aeneid* 3.22–57 and Marlowe's *Doctor Faustus*', *Notes and Queries* 54 (2007), pp. 248–49.

Duxfield, A., ' "Resolve me of all ambiguities": *Doctor Faustus* and the Failure to Unify', *Early Modern Literary Studies: A Journal of Sixteenth- and Seventeenth-Century English Literature* 16 (2007) (electronic publication).

Huang, A. C. Y., 'Authorial in(ter)ventions: Christopher Marlowe and John Donne', in *Class, Boundary and Social Discourse in the Renaissance*, ed. A. C. Y. Huang, I.-C. Wang and M. Theis (Kaohsiung: Center for Humanities and Social Sciences and College of Liberal Arts, National Sun Yat-sen University, 2007).

2007: books

Hawkes, D., *The Faust Myth: Religion and the Rise of Representation* (New York: Palgrave Macmillan, 2007).

Keefer, M. H., ed., *Doctor Faustus: A 1604 Version Edition*, 2nd edn (Ontario: Broadview, 2007).

Logan, R. A., *Shakespeare's Marlowe: The Influence of Christopher Marlowe on Shakespeare's Artistry* (Aldershot: Ashgate, 2007).

Parker, J., *The Aesthetics of Antichrist: From Christian Drama to Christopher Marlowe* (Ithaca, NY: Cornell University Press, 2007).

2008: individual essays

Duxfield, A., 'Teaching & Learning Guide for Modern Problems of Editing: The Two Texts of Marlowe's *Doctor Faustus*', *Literature Compass* 5.3 (2008), pp. 681–84.

Engle, L., 'Oedipal Marlowe, Mimetic Middleton', *Modern Philology* 105.3 (2008), pp. 417–36.

Savage, K., 'Stage Directions: Valuable Clues in the Exploration of Elizabethan Performance Practice', *Studies in Theatre and Performance* 28 (2008), pp. 161–82.

Wall-Randell, S., 'Doctor Faustus and the Printer's Devil', *Studies in English Literature 1500–1900* 48 (2008), pp. 259–81.

2008: books

Cheney, P., *Marlowe's Republican Authorship: Lucan, Liberty, and the Sublime* (Basingstoke: Palgrave Macmillan, 2008).

Deats, S. M. and Logan, R. A., eds., *Placing the Plays of Christopher Marlowe: Fresh Cultural Contexts* (Aldershot: Ashgate, 2008).

Hopkins, L., *Christopher Marlowe, Renaissance Dramatist* (Edinburgh: Edinburgh University Press, 2008).

Wootton, D., ed., *'Doctor Faustus' with 'The English Faust Book'* (Indianapolis, IN: Hackett Publishing Company, 2008).

2009: books

Cheney, P., *Marlowe's Republican Authorship: Lucan, Liberty, and the Sublime* (Basingstoke: Palgrave Macmillan, 2009).

Notes

1   Book-length biographies of Marlowe appeared in 1992 and 1995; then, another book-length biography was published in 2000, and from 2002 through to 2005 there was at least one book-length biography each year. This burst of scholarly activity has subsided somewhat, although the 1992 biography was revised in 2002, and Lisa Hopkins' *Christopher Marlowe, Renaissance Dramatist* (Edinburgh: Edinburgh University Press, 2008) covers biographical issues as well as Marlowe's works; also several articles dealing with biography have appeared during the past few years, including in 2001 (see under Reference Works).

2   I count ten collections of essays on Marlowe since 1991 (see under Reference Works).

3   Eric Rasmussen, *A Textual Companion to 'Doctor Faustus.'* The Revels Plays Companion Library (Manchester: Manchester University Press, 1993).

4   David Bevington and Eric Rasmussen, eds, *'Doctor Faustus' A- and B-texts (1604, 1616)*; (Manchester: Manchester University Press, 1993).

5   T. McAlindon's *'Doctor Faustus': Divine in Show* (New York: Twayne, 1994).

6   For example, at a 2005 MLA Marlowe session entitled 'Constructing Marlowe' there was a paper entitled 'Marlowe and the World Picture'; at the International Marlowe Conference in 2008, at a session entitled 'Balancing Acts in *Doctor Faustus*', a paper entitled 'Resolving Ambiguity: God's Plot Against Faustus'; and in 2009 at a Renaissance Society of America conference session called 'Reconstructing Marlowe', a paper entitled 'Imagining Death: Ovid's *Elegies*, *Doctor Faustus*, and the Close of *Hero and Leander*'.

7   Michael Keefer, ed., *'Doctor Faustus': A 1604-Version Edition*, 2nd edn (Ontario: Broadview Press, 2006).

8   Keefer, *'Doctor Faustus'*, p. 8.

9   Keefer, *'Doctor Faustus'*, p. 8.

10   Sara Munson Deats and Robert A. Logan, eds, *Marlowe's Empery: Expanding His Critical Contexts* (Newark, DE: University of Delaware Press, 2002); Constance Brown Kuriyama, *Christopher Marlowe: A Renaissance Life* (Ithaca, NY: Cornell University Press, 2002); Ruth Lunney, *Marlowe and the Popular*

Tradition: Innovation in the English Drama before 1595 (Manchester: Manchester University Press, 2002); and Alan Shepard, *Marlowe's Soldiers: Rhetorics of Masculinity in the Age of the Armada* (Burlington: Ashgate, 2002).

11   Avraham Oz, ed., *Marlowe* (New York: Palgrave, 2003).

12   Agnès Lafont, 'Le Corps nu de Diane ou les égarements du coeur et de l'esprit dans *Doctor Faustus* et *Edward II*', *Anglophonia* 13 (2003), pp. 69–82; François Laroque, 'The Fashioning of Self and Desire: The Metamorphosis of Actaeon in Marlowe and Shakespeare', in *Self-Fashioning and Metamorphosis in Early Modern English Literature*, ed. Olav Lausund and Stein Haugom Olsends (Oslo: Novus, 2003), pp. 135–49.

13   John Ellison, 'From Fëanor to *Doctor Faustus*: A Creator's Path to Self Destruction', *Mallorn: The Journal of the Tolkien Society* 41 (July 2003), pp. 13–21; José Torado, '*The Matrix* o la literatura errática', *Enfocarte.com: Revista de Arte Y Cultura* 3 (Feb–Mar. 2003), n.p. (electronic publication).

14   Thomas Healy, 'Doctor Faustus', in *The Cambridge Companion to Christopher Marlowe*, ed. Patrick Cheney (Cambridge: Cambridge University Press, 2004), pp. 174–92.

15   Healy, 'Doctor Faustus', p. 189.

16   Kristen Poole, 'Dr. Faustus and Reformation Theology,' in *Early Modern English Drama: A Critical Companion*, ed. Garrett A. Sullivan, Patrick Cheney and Andrew Hadfield (Oxford: Oxford University Press, 2006), p. 106.

17   Poole, 'Dr. Faustus and Reformation Theology', p. 106.

18   Kristen Poole, 'The Devil's in the Archive: *Doctor Faustus* and Ovidian Physics', *Renaissance Drama* 35 (2006), p. 210.

19   Robert A. Logan, *Shakespeare's Marlowe: The Influence of Christopher Marlowe on Shakespeare's Artistry* (Aldershot: Ashgate, 2007), p. 197.

20   Logan, *Shakespeare's Marlowe*, p. 197.

21   David Hawkes, *The Faust Myth: Religion and the Rise of Representation* (New York: Palgrave Macmillan, 2007), p. 56.

22   Hawkes, *The Faust Myth*, p. 54.

23   John Parker, *The Aesthetics of Antichrist: From Christian Drama to Christopher Marlowe* (Ithaca, NY: Cornell University Press, 2007), p. xi.

24   Sara Munson Deats and Robert A. Logan, eds, *Placing the Plays of Christopher Marlowe: Fresh Cultural Contexts* (Aldershot: Ashgate, 2008), p. 3.

25   Deats and Logan, *Placing the Plays of Christopher Marloew*, p. 8.

26   For example, see Wendy Wall, 'Dramatic Authorship and Print', in *Early Modern English Drama: A Critical Companion*, ed. Garrett A. Sullivan, Patrick Cheney and Andrew Hadfield (Oxford: Oxford University Press, 2006), pp. 3–5.

CHAPTER FOUR

Doctor Faustus and Renaissance Hermeticism

Andrew Duxfield

Doctor Faustus, the most famous of Marlowe's plays, is also arguably the most notorious treatment of magical occult activity in the history of English literature. When Faustus bids divinity adieu, he does so to pursue a career in magic, by which he has been ravished and through which he believes he can become a mighty god. The term 'magic,' however, is decidedly less ambiguous now than it was in Marlowe's time, when it could have been applied to the pursuits of any number of practitioners from neoplatonist philosophers to mathematicians. So what exactly is the magic that Faustus practises, and how does it relate to both his ambition and his fall? These questions have been asked before but have often been approached by equating Marlowe's protagonist with notable Renaissance occultists such as Heinrich Cornelius Agrippa (with whom Faustus explicitly compares himself) and the English magus John Dee. These parallels are undoubtedly important, and I shall discuss them in this chapter, but there is new light to be shed on the play, I suggest, by reading Faustus's plight in the context of the fundamental hermetic ideas from which the philosophy of magi such as Agrippa and Dee arise. Striking parallels, I aim to show, exist between Marlowe's *Faustus* and key passages from the writings of Hermes Trismegistus, the pseudo-historical mystic whose ideas, largely by virtue of their supposed antiquity and apparent compatibility with both Christian doctrine and humanist inquiry, filtered heavily into Renaissance thought. These parallels, I suggest, offer a new perspective on Faustus's intellectual ambition and dissatisfaction with academic learning, and also a potential synthesis between readings of the play as a celebration of an admirably ambitious human being who oversteps his mark, and those that interpret it as a moral tale about the punishment of a foolish and faithless sinner; Faustus's pursuit of knowledge through occult practices can, in the context of hermeticism, be seen paradoxically as an attempt to ascend to a state of divinity. Nonetheless, of course, Faustus is damned, and this chapter will explore his project, and its ultimate failure, in conjunction with the hermetic philosophy to which he appears to adhere, before attempting to place the implications of this failure in their cultural context.

The discovery of the writings of the supposed Egyptian prophet Hermes Trismegistus by agents of the Medici family caused a furore in late fifteenth-century Italy. As Peter French states,

> Their impact might be compared with a modern discovery of Dead Sea scrolls that revealed revolutionary information about Christianity, but even this is not a valid comparison because religion is not the all-embracing concern today that it was during the Renaissance.[1]

The *Corpus Hermeticum*,[2] which was supposed to predate the work of Plato and Pythagoras and be at least contemporary with that of Moses,[3] proposed a philosophy that incorporated a monotheistic religious doctrine bearing a striking resemblance to that of Judeo-Christianity while incorporating an alternative creation myth.[4] The close relationship between some of its ideas and those of the Bible, which it supposedly antedated, although considered astonishing at the time, was deemed less remarkable in 1614 by the work of the philologist Isaac Casaubon, whose analysis of the texts showed them, in fact, to date from early Christian times. However, such was the excitement at the time of their discovery that Marsilio Ficino was ordered to postpone his ongoing translation of the works of Plato in order to prepare them for western consumption. Indeed, the fact that Ficino was absorbed in these two projects at the same time may have been significant, as he incorporated hermetic ideas into his neoplatonic philosophy, which was to prove influential across Europe and throughout the Renaissance. The *Corpus* is a series of dialogues, predominantly between Hermes Trismegistus and 'Mind,' or Pimander – an articulation of the intellect of God – and between Hermes and his son Tat, and altogether represents a kind of religious philosophy which instructs man on how to regain his lost divinity and achieve oneness with God. Throughout the careers of subsequent philosophers such as Giovanni Pico Della Mirandola,

Francesco Giorgi and Heinreich Cornelius Agrippa, occult thought became a fusion of hermeticism, Christian doctrine, neoplatonism and a Christianized version of the mystical Hebrew practice of cabala, which applied divine numerological significance to letters of the Hebrew alphabet, facilitating the search for esoteric wisdom embedded in the Torah (Christian cabalists used it to find evidence in the Old Testament of the divinity of Christ).[5] Despite the apparently esoteric and eccentric nature of this movement, hermetic and cabalistic ideas were initially well received across Renaissance Europe, and influential enough for the great historian Frances Yates to contend that they formed the central driving force behind the Renaissance itself.[6]

Doctor Faustus explicitly invites the association of its protagonist with controversial occultist thinkers. Upon agreeing to learn the secrets of conjuring from Valdes and Cornelius, Faustus is advised by his new patrons to

> haste thee to some solitary grove,
> And bear wise Bacon's and Albanus' works,
> The Hebrew Psalter, and New Testament;
> And whatsoever else is requisite
> We will inform thee ere our conference cease.
>
> (I.i.155–59)[7]

The Bacon referred to here is Roger Bacon, the thirteenth-century English philosopher with an interest in astrology and mathematics whose notoriety as a conjurer was revitalized, possibly around the time that *Doctor Faustus* was first being performed, by Robert Greene's *Friar Bacon and Friar Bungay*,[8] while Albanus probably refers to the Italian philosopher Pietro d'Albano, whose posthumous reputation was similarly infamous.[9] The inclusion of the Hebrew Psalter and the New Testament in this occult reading list suggests a Christian cabalist element in the conjuring of Faustus, who only a few lines earlier has overtly aligned himself with a more recent cabalist and hermetic philosopher by boasting that he 'Will be as cunning as Agrippa was' (I.i.119), and who will later, during his conjuration, draw attention to the cabalist elements of his magic by announcing that 'Within this circle is Jehovah's name, | Forward and backward anagrammatised' (I.iii.8–9).

Besides these internal references, Faustus has often been equated with John Dee, most forcibly by Frances Yates, who argues that 'audiences would inevitably have recognised Faustus as an unfavourable reference to Dee'. Since she sees occult philosophy as the central system of thought behind the Renaissance movement and Dee as its chief exponent in Elizabethan England, Yates suggests that 'we are in fact witnessing in this play a reaction against the Renaissance'.[10] To whatever extent one accepts this reading, and, as I hope will become clear, I think it underestimates the complexity and ambiguity of the play, there is merit in the association of Faustus with the Elizabethan magus. Dee was certainly the most notorious practitioner of anything close to Faustus's magic in England, and, like Faustus (and like Giordano Bruno, another hermetic magus who has been compared to Marlowe's protagonist),[11] he took his magic on a momentous European tour and briefly enjoyed the patronage of the Holy Roman Emperor.[12] The 'Lines, circles, signs, letters and characters' that Faustus 'most desires' (I.i.53–54), as well as being 'illustrated in some profusion' among the pages of the 1567 edition of Agrippa's *De Occulta Philosophia*,[13] can also be found liberally distributed throughout the 1570 English edition of Euclid's *Elements*, to which Dee appended his *Mathematical Preface* (a document in which he advises the reader to 'Looke in the 27. and 28. Chapters, of the second booke, *De Occulta Philosophia*').[14] Most obviously, of course, the conjuring of Mephistopheles could be seen as a parody of the angel summoning for which Dee (like Agrippa before him) was so infamous. Given the clear parallels between the protagonist and some of the more notorious magi of the Renaissance period, the play undoubtedly invites analysis in the light of the ideas to which they adhered.

Before treating the play in detail, however, I will briefly illustrate some of the core ideas of the *Corpus*'s theology. As mentioned earlier, the *Corpus* shares a number of familiar ideas with Christianity: human beings are created by a god who, it is stressed, is the only god (although, as is characteristic of this obscure text, a small number of passages seem to refer to more than one), and live in a fallen state, divine souls mired in corrupt material bodies. Eventually, as in the Christian tradition, humanity can achieve salvation, but the means by which this can happen are crucially different, indeed apparently opposed; rather than through faith, human beings regain their divine state through knowledge. The *Corpus* valorizes knowledge to the extent that ignorance becomes synonymous with the Christian idea of sin. Book Eight, entitled 'That the greatest Evil in Man, is, The not knowing God,' makes this clear:

> Whither are you carried, O men, drunken with drinking up the strong wine of ignorance? which seeing you cannot bear: why do you not vomit it up again?

2. Stand, and be sober, and look up again with the eyes of your heart; and if you cannot all do so, yet do as many as you can.
3. For the malice of Ignorance surroundeth all the Earth, and corrupteth the Soul, shut up in the Body, not suffering it to arrive at the Havens of Salvation.[15]

Crucial to this concept of understanding God as the key to divine ascension is the notion of unity. God created the world through his intellect, and, as such, the world is contained within the mind. As human beings have been blessed, as in Judeo-Christian tradition, above all other animals, they have the potential to understand God and share his intellect – the *Corpus* states that 'an earthly man, is a mortall God; and that the heavenly God, is an immortall man'[16] – but to do so they must understand *everything*, as everything is the mind of God, and vice versa:

116. Or art thou ignorant, that as the parts of the World, are Heaven, and Earth, and Water, and Air; after the same manner the Members of God, are Life and Immortality, and Eternity and Spirit, and Necessity, and Providence, and Nature, and Soul, and Minde, and the Continuance or perseverance of all these which is called Good.
117. And there is not any thing of all that hath been, and all that is, where God is not.[17]

In this spirit occult philosophers such as Pico della Mirandola and Agrippa attempted to develop philosophies that assimilate hermetic, Hebrew, and classical wisdom and achieve a union between this fusion of thought and Christian theology. Of Francesco Giorgi, for example, Yates remarks:

The word One, or Monas, falls constantly from Giorgi's pen, usually accompanied by a cluster of names of the authorities from whom he drives [*sic*] this concept. As Vasoli puts it, Giorgi wishes to be the carrier of a wisdom capable of including Hermes Trismegistus, Orpheus, Francis of Assisi, Plato and the Cabalists, Plotinus and Augustine, in the common understanding of the arcane mundi, and of the spiritual destiny of man in the return to the inaccessible One.[18]

It is in this same spirit that Dee creates his *monad* or 'London Seal of Hermes', the symbol that adorned the frontispiece of his *Monas Hieroglyphica*, which apparently constituted 'a unified construction of significant astro-chemical symbols that embodied the underlying unity, or *monas*, of the universe',[19] and, I suggest, in which Doctor Faustus announces his dissatisfaction with disparate academic disciplines and turns to magic in order to achieve an all encompassing understanding of the world.

When, at the beginning of the play, Faustus asks the question 'Is to dispute well logic's chiefest end?' (I.i.8), he raises an essential problem that a hermetic thinker is likely to have had with the established academic system. The arts courses at the universities focused heavily on disputation in Marlowe's time; Marlowe himself would have been well versed in the art, having graduated with an MA from Cambridge. The student of logic, or dialectic as it is also known, was judged on the ability to defend or attack a position rather than on the capacity to uncover truth; emphasis was placed on the ability to win an argument rather than on being right. This practice by definition requires opposing stances and has no capacity to satisfy the mind of one who wishes to understand the world in its unity, and hence to know God. Similarly, the sequential dismissal of the discrete university disciplines of logic, medicine, law and theology seems to suggest a rejection of compartmentalized knowledge altogether, an idea reflected in more political language later in the same speech, when Faustus has moved on to contemplation of magic:

> Emperors and kings
> Are but obeyed in their several provinces,
> Nor can they raise the wind or rend the clouds;
> But his dominion that exceeds in this
> Stretcheth as far as doth the mind of man.
> A sound magician is a mighty god.
>
> (I.i.59–64)

It is the mind that human beings share with God, and as such it is fitting that Faustus selects the mind as an image to represent the potential of magic; the successful hermetic thinker – the sound magician – does indeed become a mighty god, providing that he can first know God, and to do so his intellect cannot be allowed to restrict its dominion to several provinces; as the *Corpus* states:

> 125. After this manner therefore contemplate God to have all the whole world to himself, as it were all thoughts, or intellections.
> 126. If therefore thou wilt not equall thy self to God, thou canst not understand God.

127. For the like are intelligible by the like.[20]

Faustus manifests this desire when he begins to demand that Mephistopheles supply him with knowledge of the workings of the world, including the motions of the planets and the nature and location of hell. Perhaps the most apt reflection of the hermetic spirit of universal learning occurs in the following passage in which, having just been presented with a book of incantations, Faustus asks Mephistopheles to provide him with a variety of further learned texts:

> MEPHISTOPHELES: Hold, take this book. Peruse it thoroughly.
> The iterating of these lines brings gold;
> The framing of this circle on the ground
> Brings whirlwinds, tempests, thunder, and lightning.
> Pronounce this thrice devoutly to thyself,
> And men in armour shall appear to thee,
> Ready to execute what thou desir'st.
> FAUSTUS: Thanks, Mephistopheles. Yet fain would I have a book wherein I might behold all spells and incantations, that I might raise up spirits when I please.
> MEPHISTOPHELES: Here they are in this book. *There turn to them.*
> FAUSTUS: Now would I have a book where I might see all characters and planets of the heavens, that I might know their motions and dispositions.
> MEPHISTOPHELES: Here they are too. *Turn to them.*
> FAUSTUS: Nay, let me have one book more – and then I have done – wherein I might see all plants, herbs, and trees that grow upon the earth.
> MEPHISTOPHELES: Here they be. *Turn to them.*
> FAUSTUS: O, thou art deceived.
> MEPHISTOPHELES: Tut, I warrant thee.
>
> (II.i.162–82)

At every stage, Faustus's request for a book on a particular discipline (each request is for a book that covers *all* of the knowledge in its specific area) is met with the revelation, the stage directions would seem to suggest, that the information required is in the book that Mephistopheles has already presented him with. Like the *Corpus Hermeticum*, or John Dee's *Monas Hieroglyphica*, this would seem to be a book containing the entire knowledge of the universe, providing one knows how to read it. This kind of learning, the

Corpus makes clear, is essential to anyone who would achieve ascension:

> 128. Increase thyself unto an immeasurable greatnesse, leaping beyond every Body, and transcending all Time; become Eternity, and thou shall understand God: If thou believe in thyself, that nothing is impossible, but accountest thyself immortall, and that thou canst understand all things, every Art every Science, and the manner and custom of every living thing.[21]

This passage resonates with the ambitions of Faustus in its insistence that one must assert one's ability to understand every art, every science and the workings of all nature. Furthermore, it calls to mind the element of Faustus's character often cited as an obstacle to audience sympathy, namely his arrogance. How could Faustus possibly have expected his pact with Lucifer to meet with anything other than disaster? Why does he embark on his project with the apparent opinion that he is beyond damnation and that 'Hell's a fable' (II.i.130)? The advice given here by Pimander provides a context for Faustus's boastfulness; he believes in himself and his actions lead one to suspect that he may well account himself immortal. Indeed, the *Corpus* does not stop at recommending the maintenance of a healthy sense of self-esteem; we are in fact told that a lack of self-belief is evil:

> 131. But if thou shut up thy Soul in the Body, and abuse it, and say, I understand nothing, I can do nothing, I am afraid of the Sea, I cannot climb up into Heaven, I know not who I am, I cannot tell what I shall be; what hast thou to do with God? for thou canst understand none of those Fair and Good things; be a lover of the Body, and Evil.
> 132. For it is the greatest evil, not to know God.[22]

Viewed through the lens of Hermeticism, Faustus's arrogance might be seen as a sign of piety rather than a hubristic flaw; a dogged determination to avoid the evil of submission to ignorance rather than a pig-headed obstinacy.

Yet, of course, it must be remembered that Faustus clearly fails in his project and is damned at the play's close. If we are to continue to read the play in the context of hermeticism, it is important to ask why this happens. While Faustus adopts the appropriate posture for the Hermetic magus in appearing to have total belief in his ability to understand everything, one might question the extent to which he respects or even understands the ends to which this knowledge should be directed. We encounter a striking example of this negligence when Faustus muses on the uses that his new powers will be put to:

> I'll have them fly to India for gold,
> Ransack the ocean for orient pearl,
> And search all corners of the new-found world
> For pleasant fruits and princely delicates.

>   (I.i.84–87)

Book Ten of the *Corpus* contains a passage highly reminiscent of Faustus's statement:

> 120. And judge of this by thy self, command thy Soul to go into *India*, and sooner then thou canst bid it, it will be there.
> 121. Bid it likewise passe over the *Ocean*, and suddenly it will be there; Not as passing from place to place, but suddenly it will be there.
> 122. Command it to flie into Heaven, and it will need no Wings, neither shall any thing hinder it; not the fire of the Sun, not the *Aether*, nor the turning of the Spheres, not the bodies of any of the other Stars, but cutting through all, it will flie up to the last, and furthest Body.[23]

This passage in the *Corpus*, which employs its sense of scale and exoticism to illustrate the limitlessness of the potential of the liberated soul, is grossly parodied by Faustus's musings; in place of the soul are diabolical spirits, and rather than representing the process of coming to know God, India and the ocean become ends in themselves, serving to supply Faustus's material desires. Nor is the material nature of Faustus's desire here expressed entirely inconsistent with his priorities elsewhere; as has long been observed, Faustus makes less than profound use of his 24 years of earthly power. As is evident from passages already quoted from the *Corpus*, the goal of the magus is essentially spiritual: the liberation of the divine soul from the trappings of the mortal body, achieved through contemplation. Yet Faustus spends his allotted time indulging in banal pleasures of the flesh, satisfying his diminished ambition by acting as a court performer for European potentates or garnering cheap laughter by conducting japes at the expense of victims ranging from the Pope to a humble Horse-Courser.

The *Corpus Hermeticum*'s privileging of the soul over the body is similar to that of the Christian tradition, and Faustus's fleshly indulgences are as sinful or evil, to use the term from the *Corpus*, in a hermetic context as they are in a Christian one. In this sense the crucial passage in Act V in which Faustus chooses the indulgence of the flesh (as represented by Helen of Troy) over the pious protestations of the Old Man constitutes as much a rejection of knowledge as it does a rejection of faith, since the *Corpus* explicitly equates the indulgence of the body with ignorance. Clearly, then, despite the hermetic emphasis on knowledge as opposed to faith, there are a number of parallels between hermeticism and Christianity, and a number of ways in which Faustus offends the tenets of both. Yet it is worth examining the extent to which the focus of hermeticism on knowledge represents a departure from Christian ethics. What, for example, is meant by 'knowledge' in the *Corpus Hermeticum*? The following passage implies a formulation that equates it firmly with belief:

> 50. When I say the things that are, I mean God; for the things that are, God hath; and neither is there any thing without him, nor he without any thing.
> 51. These things, O *Asclepius*, will appear to be true, if thou understand them; but if thou understand them not, incredible.
> 52. For to understand is to beleeve; but not to beleeve, is not to understand.[24]

Knowledge, or understanding, appears here not to be something acquired by learning, but the instantaneous product of an act of faith; before one can understand one must believe. In this context, lack of understanding begins to look a lot like religious despair, the sin to which the downfall of Faustus has often been attributed by critics.[25] When, in the final soliloquy, Faustus desperately cries 'O, I'll leap up to my God! Who pulls me down?' (V.ii.77), he reveals himself not only to be despairing of God's mercy but also to be the 'lover of the body, and Evil', who 'cannot climb up into Heaven' that Pimander describes in the passage quoted earlier. Faustus proves incapable of mastering the art of the magus. Rather than coming to know God, he must ask Mephistopheles who made the world, a question which, to add insult to injury, the devil is not able to answer. Furthermore, he never attains the unity of understanding the *Corpus* prescribes as necessary, a unity that requires the synthesis of polar opposites:

129. Become higher than all heighth, lower than all depths, comprehend in thy self, the qualities of all the Creatures, of the Fire, the Water, the Dry, and Moyst; and conceive likewise, that thou canst at once be every where in the Sea, in the Earth. 130. Thou shalt at once understand thyself, not yet begotten in the Womb, young, old, to be dead, the things after death, and all these together; as also, times, places, deeds, qualities, quantities, or else thou canst not yet understand God.[26]

The concept of uniting ostensibly polar opposites in a superhuman understanding relates directly to Faustus, who asks himself excitedly, having arranged his deal with Lucifer,

Shall I make spirits fetch me what I please,
Resolve me of all ambiguities [...] ?

(I.i.81–82)

As has already been discussed, Faustus does attempt a resolution of ambiguities through the perusal of books that contain exhaustive knowledge, but the resolution of ambiguities appears to be a lost cause in a play structured around dichotomies. In the tradition of the *psychomachia*, Faustus's inner turmoil is represented visually by the presence of the Good and Evil Angels, while other forces of good and evil strike balances throughout the play: Faustus's loyal students oppose the forbidden learning of Valdes and Cornelius; and the pious Old Man, who offers Faustus the true path, constitutes the counterpoise to the temptation of the succubus Helen of Troy. Jonathan Dollimore observes this polarity to the play, stating that 'not only heaven and hell but God and Lucifer, the Good Angel and the Evil Angel, are polar opposites whose axes pass through and constitute human consciousness'.[27] This concept of constitution of consciousness through unresolved dichotomies is borne out by the fact that Faustus seems to be possessed of a fissured identity; throughout the play he refers to himself in the third person as if he were in some way alienated from himself; we see visual images of this fracture when he allows himself to be dismembered by the Horse-Courser in the interests of a confidence trick (IV.i.169–85), and when, in the B-text, he is torn apart by devils at the point of his damnation (V.iii).

Equally as bifurcated is the generic structure of the play itself, which seems simultaneously to make it both a tragedy and a medieval morality play, despite the fact that these two genres would promote mutually incompatible views of the protagonist. Is this play meant to be a cautionary tale about a foolish gull of Lucifer who is justly punished for his lack of faith, or is it the tragedy of a man who errs fatally but demonstrates the determined spirit of Renaissance humanism?[28] The effect is described eloquently by Kristen Poole:

> Instead of Everyman, the generalized representative of humanity, we have in Faustus a highly individualized, complex, and modern character, one whom in many respects epitomizes the ideals of his age. The interaction of this man with the allegorical angels thus presents an encounter that is not only anachronistic, but one that intersplices characters from wildly divergent genres, as if a cowboy from a John Wayne western wandered into a James Bond spy thriller. The result of this generic intermingling is a world that is morally ambiguous, as both the old and the new, the angels and Faustus, seem alternately – or simultaneously – to be the subject of valorization and critique.[29]

The two conflicting genres of the play reflect the conflict of ideas commonly perceived to be taking place within it; to generalize somewhat, Faustus is the victim of living on the fault line between a medieval scholastic world that promotes faith and piety and a Renaissance humanist world that demands individualist endeavour and the widespread pursuit of knowledge. With this in mind, a reading of the play in the context of hermetic philosophy provides an interesting perspective, as hermeticism attempts to reconcile the pursuit of knowledge with faith. Like the unity that Faustus tries to achieve in Marlowe's play, the unity foregrounded in hermeticism between religion and the pursuit of knowledge, and the more comprehensive unity that Renaissance occult philosophers attempted to establish between versions of hermeticism, cabala and Christian faith, is an uneasy one. Indeed, the internal tension evident in the work of Agrippa illustrates this; his *De Occulta Philosophia*, the 'indispensable handbook of Renaissance "Magia" and "Cabala"',[30] shared a place in his oeuvre with *De Vanitate Scientiarum*, a work which displayed a great deal of scepticism and which claimed that all wisdom was vanity save for that of the Scriptures.[31] The apparent contradiction between these two works is mirrored by Faustus's oscillation from bombast to repentance. No middle ground, it seems, is possible for him; he routinely changes allegiance from magic to Christ and back again. It also reflects, as Gareth Roberts astutely observes, the divergence of critical responses to the play:

The question of the interrelationship of these two Agrippan works, and the difficulty of finding a consistent reading of Agrippa, when these two important works seem to gesture in opposite directions, is illuminatingly analogous to the balance of two antithetical critical views of Marlowe's *Faustus*.[32]

The ambivalent world of Marlowe's play reflects the atmosphere of religious and political disharmony in which late sixteenth-century Elizabethans, and Europeans in general, lived. It is perhaps no surprise that occult philosophy, which places such value on unity, should have become popular during the age of the Reformation and the Renaissance, a period of profound ideological seismic shift in Europe; perhaps a form of wisdom that united aspects of thought from sources as widely diverse as classical wisdom, magic, Hebrew cabala and Christianity could potentially provide a solution to the religio-political schism of the time. The world which Marlowe creates, however, is more cynical than that; here fracture is too profound, ideologies too incompatible, for any encompassing system of thought to reconcile them. Faustus attempts to live on either side of a divide that cannot be bridged, and suffers accordingly.

Marlowe was right to be cynical. By the late sixteenth century Christian magi such as Agrippa and Dee faced constant suspicion due to their angel-summoning, which they insisted was totally benign.[33] During the time Marlowe was writing, a groundswell of opinion was building against occultist philosophy, as Yates writes:

It is important to bear in mind the late date of the Elizabethan Renaissance. It begins to flourish at a time when, on the continent, the reaction against Renaissance Neoplatonism and its associated occultisms was growing greatly in intensity as part of the Counter-Reformation effort to apply a restrictive attitude towards Renaissance Neoplatonism.[34]

The Christian cabalism that had previously been a legitimizing element of occult thought was now seen as degraded by its association with the occult, and its practitioners increasingly derided as sorcerers. As a result, its potential efficacy as a unifying concept suffered. After Marlowe's death, John Dee would live the last years of his life ostracized in abject poverty,[35] and in 1600 Giordano Bruno would be burnt at the stake in Rome, both suffering ignominy as a result of their occultism. Beyond the obvious resonances that exist between the play's protagonist and notorious contemporary practitioners of 'magic', the parallels between Faustus's project and that of hermetic thought, particularly as delineated in the *Corpus Hermeticum*, are illuminating; the intellectual optimism of the hermetic writings, with their emphasis on the importance of universal knowledge, bears remarkable resemblance to the far reaching and all encompassing ambitions that Faustus declares in the opening parts of the play. Those ambitions soon fade in the face of the reality of the ambivalent world that Faustus inhabits; no unifying philosophy or ideology is sufficient to reconcile the moral and generic ambiguity of *Doctor Faustus*, as exemplified by the stubborn resistance that the play still offers to any unilateral interpretation.

Notes

1   Peter French, *John Dee: The Life of an Elizabethan Magus* (London: Routledge & Kegan Paul, 1972), p. 68.

2   The text is sometimes referred to as the *Pimander*, after its first book. I shall refer to it here as the *Corpus Hermeticum*, or *Corpus*.

3   The author of the preface to an early edition of the first English translation of the *Corpus Hermeticum* named only as I. F., contends, despite there being strong evidence to the contrary by this point, that 'This Book may justly challenge the first place for antiquity, from all the Books in the World, being written some hundreds of yeers before *Moses* his time, as I shall endeavour to make good'. Hermes Trismegistus, *Hermes Mercurius Trismegistus his Divine Pymander in Seventeen Books* (London, 1657), Wing/H1566, Sig. A3. I shall quote from this edition throughout the chapter. The *Corpus* was not available in English during Marlowe's lifetime, but Latin translations of it circulated widely; Ficino's translation had gone through 16 editions by the time the A-text of *Doctor Faustus* was published.

4   For a useful summary of the ideas expressed in the hermetic texts, see Peter French, *John Dee*, pp. 62–88. This chapter will go on to discuss some of these ideas in greater detail.

5   For concise accounts of the careers and legacies of these and other key figures in the development of Renaissance occult philosophy, see Frances A. Yates, *The Occult Philosophy in the Elizabethan Age* (London: Routledge & Kegan Paul, 1979), pp. 9–59, and John S. Mebane, *Renaissance Magic & the Return of the Golden Age: The Occult Tradition in Marlowe, Jonson, and Shakespeare* (Lincoln. NE: University of Nebraska Press, 1989), pp. 22–72.

6   See Yates, *The Occult Philosophy*.

7   Christopher Marlowe, *'Doctor Faustus': A- and B-texts (1604, 1616)*, ed. David Bevington and Eric Rasmussen (Manchester: Manchester University Press, 1993). This quotation, and all subsequent quotations from the play, are taken from the A-text of this edition unless stated otherwise.

8   Opinion on the date of *Dr Faustus*'s composition and earliest performances is divided, with critics generally preferring either a date at the early stages of Marlowe's professional career (1588–89) or in the vicinity of his death (1592–93). See R. J. Fehrenbach, 'A Pre-1592 *English Faust Book* and the Date of *Doctor Faustus*', *Library: The Transactions of the Bibliographical Society* 2.4 (2001), pp. 327–35. Greene's *Friar Bacon and Friar Bungay* was written in 1589.

9   On the identity of 'Albano', see Bevington and Rasmussen, A-text, I.i.156, note.

10 Yates, *The Occult Philosophy*, pp. 120, 119.

11 See, for example, Hilary Gatti, 'Bruno and Marlowe: *Doctor Faustus*', in *Christopher Marlowe*, ed. Richard Wilson (London: Longman, 1999), pp. 246–65.

12 See Yates, *The Occult Philosophy*, pp. 87–89, and Benjamin Woolley, *The Queen's Conjuror: The Life and Magic of Dr Dee* (London: Flamingo, 2002), pp. 243–71.

13 See Gareth Roberts, 'Marlowe and the Metaphysics of Magicians', in *Constructing Christopher Marlowe*, ed. J. A. Downie and J. T. Parnell (Cambridge: Cambridge University Press, 2000), pp. 57–58.

14 Euclid, *The Elements of Geomotrie* (London, 1570), STC, 2nd edn/10560, sig. C4.

15 Hermes Trismegistus, *Hermes Mercurius Trismegistus*, p. 115.

16 Trismegistus, *Hermes Mercurius Trismegistus*, p. 71.

17 Trismegistus, *Hermes Mercurius Trismegistus*, p. 180.

18 Yates, *The Occult Philosophy*, p. 33.

19 Peter French, *John Dee*, p. 78. I. F., in his preface to the *Corpus Hermeticum*, attributes a similarly universal profundity to Hermes Trismegistus's work itself, stating, with a judicious caveat, that 'he attained to, and transmitted to Posterity (although in an Ænigmaticall, and obscure style) the Knowledge of the Quintessence of the whole Universe', Hermes Trismegistus, *Hermes Mercurius Trismegistus*, sig. A4v.

20 Trismegistus, *Hermes Mercurius Trismegistus*, p. 155.

21 Trismegistus, *Hermes Mercurius Trismegistus*, p. 155.

22 Trismegistus, *Hermes Mercurius Trismegistus*, p. 156.

23 Trismegistus, *Hermes Mercurius Trismegistus*, pp. 153–54.

24 Trismegistus, *Hermes Mercurius Trismegistus*, p. 204.

25 See, for example, Arieh Sachs, 'The Religious Despair of Doctor Faustus', *Journal of English and Germanic Philology* 63 (1964), pp. 625–47.

26 Trismegistus, *Hermes Mercurius Trismegistus*, pp. 155–56.

27 Jonathan Dollimore, '*Doctor Faustus*: Subversion through Transgression', in *Christopher Marlowe*, ed. Richard Wilson (London: Longman, 1999), p. 237.

28 For a detailed discussion of the significance of the generic ambiguity of the play, see Andrew Duxfield, ' "Resolve me of all abiguities": *Doctor Faustus* and the Failure to Unify', *Early Modern Literary Studies*, Special Issue 16 (2007): 7.

29 Kristen Poole, '*Dr. Faustus* and Reformation Theology', in *Early Modern English Drama: A Critical Companion*, ed. Garrett A. Sullivan, Patrick Cheney and Andrew Hadfield (Oxford: Oxford University Press, 2005), pp. 102–3. John Mebane, while asserting the play's status as a tragedy, makes a similar point: '*Dr. Faustus* is neither a morality play nor an unambivalent celebration of radical humanism; it is a tragedy which dramatizes a conflict between two irreconcilable systems of value, each of which, we may feel, has at least partial validity and a genuine claim to our allegiance' (*Renaissance Magic*, p. 118).

30 Yates, *The Occult Philosophy*, p. 37.

31 Yates, *The Occult Philosophy*, pp. 41–44.

32 Gareth Roberts, 'Necromantic Books: Christopher Marlowe, Doctor Faustus and Agrippa of Nettesheim', in *Christopher Marlowe and English Renaissance Culture*, ed. Daryll Grantley and Peter Roberts (Aldershot: Scolar Press, 1996), p. 158.

33 Sara Munson Deats describes the distinction that Renaissance magi made between the magic they practised and the magic they were sometimes accused of practising: 'Devotees of white magic – like Cornelius Agrippa, John Dee, and Giovanni Pico della Mirandola – distinguish between natural or beneficial magic and black magic, embracing the occult aspiration that through natural magic, such as the study of Hermetic science and Christian Cabalism, the individual might achieve godlike wisdom and stature, while rejecting black magic as a perversion of nature and thus deleterious'; see ' "Mark this show": Magic and Theater in Marlowe's *Doctor Faustus*,' in *Placing the Plays of Christopher Marlowe: Fresh Cultural Contexts*, ed. Sara Munson Deats and Robert A. Logan (Aldershot: Ashgate, 2008), p. 15.

34 Yates, *The Occult Philosophy*, p. 76.

35 Yates, *The Occult Philosophy*, pp. 89–93.

CHAPTER FIVE

Imperialism as Devilry: A Postcolonial Reading of *Doctor Faustus*

Toni Francis

In his most popular and oft-performed play, *Doctor Faustus*, Christopher Marlowe reconstructs both the English mystery play and English tragedy to focus on the emerging issues of the early modern context. In order to achieve this innovative goal, Marlowe complicates conceptions of evil, conflates the identity of the hero and Everyman, and stretches the 'deal with the devil' topos beyond the scale of the clerical genre from which it emerged. Adapting his morality format to more contemporary issues, in *Doctor Faustus* Marlowe establishes a direct relationship between Faustus's surrender of his soul to Lucifer and England's pursuit of imperialist power through the mechanism of colonialism. Marlowe's multiple allusions to colonialism and imperialism in this play suggest a subtle – and sometimes not so subtle – critique of the discourses of imperialism and colonialism emerging in the early modern period. In *Doctor Faustus*, 'the devil' indeed wears many hats.

Colonial Expansion in the Elizabethan Era

While the British Empire had not yet reached its height in 1588 – the year that contemporary scholars date the composition of *Doctor Faustus* – colonial expansion was still a major issue in the discourses of the day. The following two decades witnessed the first organized English settlements in the Americas. The late-1500s were rife with sea wars between England – a leader in the Protestant Alliance – and Spain's Catholic Empire. According to John C. Appleby, 'the sea wars of the 1580s and 1590s helped to forge and fashion the tools of

Empire, developing the ships, men, and capital needed for seaborne expansion'.[1]In addition, I would argue that Elizabeth's strategic handling of these sea wars also helped to forge the ideology of empire.

Elizabeth's war with Spain introduced new maritime innovations in the art of war. Specifically, as Appleby notes, 'Queen Elizabeth's war with Spain marked the unequivocal triumph of the new technology of the sailing ship, armed with heavy guns and mounted on the broadside, over the obsolete galley'. Elizabeth's martial tactics were also distinctive in their attention to maritime expansion. Increasingly concerned with impeding Spanish forces in Europe – particularly in the Netherlands and France – Elizabeth shied away from heavy state investment in colonization and worldwide imperialism and instead encouraged private investment and what – at least in hindsight – can only be considered piracy. According to Appleby, advocates for colonial expansion, such as Richard Hakluyt, pleaded the case that 'the creation of an English Empire in America [would] rival and eventually supersede Spain's', but Elizabeth preferred to fund the domestic war against Spain in Europe and leave the international war with Spain to the privateers and pirates.[2]

As the principal vehicle of English colonial expansion and the most rewarded approach to maritime war in the colonies, the practice of piracy became the primary metaphor for early modern colonialism and imperialism. In the discourse of colonial expansion, piracy served as both a means by which to attain private and state capital, and a means by which to defeat the growing Catholic Empire and expand the power and privilege of the Protestant Church. In 1585, Elizabeth sponsored Francis Drake's expedition to the Caribbean but provided only two of the 30 ships in the fleet and roughly a third of the invested funds.[3] From 1585 into the seventeenth century, privatizing was the major engine of colonial expansion; the annual estimate of the prizes of these ventures totalled about £200,000.[4]

According to Clinton Black, piracy increased rapidly during the Tudor reign. Black notes that the 'adventurous years of Queen Elizabeth I' sparked many Englishmen of position and birth to sail the Spanish Main to the tropics in search of fortune. These same 'semi-private adventurers' later 'evolved into the buccaneers, themselves forerunners of the West Indian pirates'. This evolution is hardly linear, however, due to the intricacies of Elizabethan diplomacy in relation to the war with Spain, the economic lure of piracy and the emerging idea of empire. As Black observes, 'anomalies of practice often clouded the nice distinctions since in many cases the same men were at different times buccaneers, privateers, and pirates'.[5] Elizabeth's semi-private adventurers shifted between the roles of pirate and privateer, buccaneer and colonizer, as appropriate to their positions both in the Old World of England and its new emerging empire. Elizabeth's private investment in piracy served as the primary approach to English colonization and later fuelled the large-scale approach to global colonization that would follow. John H. Bodley remarks that 'from 1500 to 1900 the capitalist world system assumed its essentially modern form propelled by colonialism and economic growth funded by a frenzy of investment by a wealthy few economic elites', adding that 'In the process, some 590 million tribal peoples died'.[6]

Elizabeth's strategic employment of piracy as a tactical man-oeuvre against Spain served, possibly inadvertently, to produce an indelible English power in the New World, while maintaining the queen's ostensible innocence in terms of empire building. As Jeremy Black points out, 'the relationship between public and private was important to the English transoceanic activity, as an unwillingness by the Crown to confront directly imperial interests of Portugal and Spain encouraged a reliance on unofficial or semi-unofficial action such as privateering'. Black cites as an example the case in 1562–63 of Ambrose, Earl of Warwick, governor of Le Havre, then under English occupation, who had granted letters of marque to privateers, which were unquestionable and eagerly accepted. Such examples serve for Black as 'a reminder of the need not to separate public and private, official and unofficial, too clearly in accounts of empire'.[7] Black's history of Drake's exploits also illustrates the shifting positions of the semi-private adventurer between pirate, privateer and colonizer. After circumnavigating the globe in 1577–80, Drake, the first Englishman to do so and the second sailor to pass the Straits of Magellan, 'yielded an excellent return to his investors, particularly to Elizabeth'. Drake managed to boost the coffers of the English crown by attacking unsuspecting Spanish ships and positions in the Pacific. As a result, 'Drake made a number of profitable seizures'. Interestingly, Drake's primary goal was not land and empire, but rather plunder. Black comments that Drake 'did not further the cause of English settlement, although he sailed up the Californian coast and claimed it as "Nova Albion" for Elizabeth'. However, Elizabeth rewarded Drake for his exploits. 'In April 1581, she knighted him on board his ship, the *Golden Hind*, at Deptford', a validation that Black argues was 'an important display of approval, and one that was subsequently to be seen as an important symbolic moment in English imperialism, one that linked personal heroism, enterprise, and bellicosity with monarchy and Protestantism'.[8]

By 1608, following the signing of the Treaty of London, 'the English maritime enterprise had assumed a global character, paving the way for the establishment of colonial settlements in North America and the Caribbean, and a scattering of trading posts in Africa, Asia, South America, and the Mediterranean'.[9] The settlement of these nations was greatly heightened by the influence of piracy; the lure of prize and plunder, coupled with the missionary drive to build a Christianized world and a Protestant Empire, would prove devastating to the indigenous peoples of the New World. According to Appleby, the Treaty of London 'enabled the English to claim that where land was not effectively occupied by a Christian nation, it was open for others to settle'.[10] Similarly, Anthony Pagden also asserts that, 'like the Spanish, the English first saw themselves as conquerors, and like the Spanish, they sought to legitimize their Imperial ambitions in the name of an obligation to convert the heathen Americas to a Christian faith'.[11] Connecting the world of trade with the word of God, Pagden cites Richard Hakluyt's *Pamphlet for the Virginia Enterprise* which 'set out the threefold objectives of the new colony as: "to plant Christian religion, to traffic, to conquer"'.[12] These agendas, along with the methods of piracy, provide the building blocks for the discourse and practice of colonialism.

Faustus and Signification

The majority of critical analyses of necromancy and witchcraft in Marlowe's *Doctor Faustus* have remained focused on religious or philosophical issues, with few alternative treatments of the metaphorical significance of Faustus's decision. Exceptions to this dominant orientation include a number of studies that focus on the metadramatic nuances of the play, interpreting Faustus as a type of playwright. Critics adopting this orientation include, among others, Alvin B. Kernan, Joel B. Altman, Barbara Howard Traister, John Mebane, Darryll Grantley, Patrick Cheney, Huston Diehl and Ian McAdam.[13] More recently, Sara Munson Deats has developed this metadramatic interpretation to posit a parallel in the play between magic and theatre.[14] Despite the contemporary popularity of this metadramatic approach, however, the theological interpretation of magic and witchcraft in the play still remains dominant in Marlowe criticism. While for most commentators, Faustus's turn to the 'dark side' creates a battleground between good and evil, as represented in Marlowe's wrestling angels, for some critics the construction of devilry itself in the play deserves further examination. Adrian Streete remarks that Marlowe's construction of hell in the tragedy differs from that presented in the *Faustbooks*, arguing that Mephistopheles's statement 'Why, this is hell, nor am I out of it' presents a specifically Calvinist rather than Catholic or Anglican notion of hell.[15] Streete contends that in *Doctor Faustus*, Mephistopheles defines hell in a less literal and more subjective sense than traditionally depicted, signifying solipsism, or the eternal separation from God.

Paul Kocher provides one of the few early treatments of the play that departs from the religious debate to focus solely on the presentation of witchcraft.[16] Kocher discovers in Marlowe's witchcraft a palimpsest of witch lore derived largely from English and continental texts, rather than from actual experiences with English pagan practices. Kocher's treatment of what kind of witch or devil Faustus represents, while historically interesting, reveals far more about Marlowe than it does about Faustus and even less about the play itself. While Kocher debates whether or not Faustus ever actually becomes a witch, I would insist that witchcraft in the play can be read as figurative as well as literal. A figurative reading thus interprets the witch as a central metaphor of the play rather than as a two-dimensional portrait of sixteenth-century paganism. This interpretation suggests that an even more palpable and topical evil serves as the basis for Faustus's necromancer, that of the emerging English imperialist.

Doctor Faustus has not yet been thoroughly examined as a critique of British imperialist discourse, although William Tate does investigate the references to imperialism in the play, identifying both Faustus and Elizabeth as Solomonic figures, while asserting that Marlowe 'explicitly associates [King] Solomon's negative characteristics with imperialism' in order to suggest that 'instead of confirming an appropriately masculine rule, colonialism offers a demonic temptation that eventually emasculates rulership'.[17] However, Tate is primarily interested in connections between Solomon, Sheba and Elizabeth, and, in his search for overt allusions to Solomon, draws little attention to Marlowe's explicit references to colonialism.

Tate's analysis of empire aside, a large number of the critical discourses circulating around *Doctor Faustus* centre on the secular or sacred ethos of this play, attempting to ascertain whether Marlowe's work is a defence of Christian faith in the face of doubt or a defence of the intellectual's Promethean endeavour to transcend the paradigms of the time. For David Bevington and Eric Rasmussen, each interpretation depends upon 'how we are to "read" the orthodoxy that governs the plot of *Doctor Faustus*'.[18] The two critics can find no definitive answer to the question of Christian orthodoxy in Marlowe's play; in their judgement, 'the very persistence of rival interpretations of *Doctor Faustus* as orthodox and heterodox would seem to suggest that neither can wholly invalidate the other, and that both are to an important extent "true"'.[19] Deats closely examines the interesting ambiguity in Marlowe's plays that allows for multiple and seemingly contradictory interpretations, attributing this ambiguity to the production of interrogative dramas during the early modern period in response to the censorship laws of the 1590s.[20] Citing Annabel Patterson, Deats explores the need for playwrights of the period to 'obscure the subversive material of their texts beneath the cloak of indirection and to craft plays that they intended to be experienced differently by diverse audiences'.[21] She suggests that Marlowe's plays, like those of Shakespeare, are interrogative dramas that intend to tease out the prevailing and contradictory arguments of the day and present them both simultaneously, 'arguing on both sides of the question'.[22] For Deats, therefore, *Doctor Faustus* is neither a Christian play nor a heroic tragedy, but both at once; what critics or audience members glean from the play depends on whether the critical lens with which they view the tragedy will permit them to see one side, the other side, or, in the best case scenario, both at the same time.

Simultaneously seeing both sides of the issue enables critics to view the play as an intervention into the prevailing discourses of the period. Breaking away from the sacred/secular, Christian/satanic dichotomy in the play also enables critics to analyse the additional issue of colonialism and imperialism that Marlowe vividly introduces in the language and imagery. Standing back from the anamorphic structure of *Doctor Faustus* and viewing the play 'awry', from a non-traditional poststructuralist perspective, I can see not only the attempt to question the religious control of the imagination and the immoral applications of the new science, but also an attempt by Marlowe to place this debate within the larger context of colonial expansion and British imperialism in order to reveal the connection between necromancy and new innovative forms of immorality. In this interpretation, therefore, necromancy becomes associated with imperialism and Faustus with the colonialist pirate/privateer who sells his soul for the power and control intrinsic to the imperialist enterprise.

Faustus as Imperialist

Marlowe's critique of the discourse of imperialism becomes more apparent when applied to the concept of necromancy presented but not fully practised in the play. Necromancy, often defined as witchcraft or sorcery, can denote not only the raising or conjuring of the dead, but also the satanic dark arts or devil worship. Through Faustus, Marlowe begins the drama with a vigorous defence of necromancy as the only remaining challenge for the genius. Once Mephistopheles enters the stage, however, the practice of necromancy is quickly abandoned or reduced to vague references. This play, although centred on 'dark magic', presents no cackling witches with boiling cauldrons, no grandiose feats of voodoo magic, but rather the recitation of biblical Latin from ancient books in a ceremony that almost mimics a Mass. In fact, Faustus lacks the overt emblematic character of the devil conjurer. He calls on Mephistopheles who arrives on cue, ostensibly as a result of Faustus's conjuring tricks. Yet when Faustus queries, 'Did not my conjuring speeches draw thee, speak?', Mephistopheles replies,

> That was the cause, but yet *per accidens*.
> For when we hear one rack the name of God,
> Abjure the Scriptures and his Saviour Christ,
> We fly in hope to get his glorious soul,
> Nor will we come unless he use such means
> Whereby he is in danger to be damned.
> Therefore, the shortest cut for conjuring
> Is stoutly to abjure the Trinity
> And pray devoutly to the prince of hell
>
> (I.iii.47–55)[23]

Here, Mephistopheles makes it clear that although Faustus's spell was the efficient cause, it was not the final cause of Mephistopheles's appearance and that the demon was summoned not by Faustus's conjuring powers but by his blasphemy. Later, Mephistopheles provides what magic he can – playing practical jokes on Popes, Horse-Coursers and clowns; however, Faustus's conjuring power is undercut by Wagner's and Robin's abilities to accomplish similar feats with little power save literacy (I.iv.44–53; III.ii.25–28). In attempting to ascertain the place of magic and necromancy in *Doctor Faustus*, I question whether this play was ever meant to probe the actual practice of dark magic, or whether necromancy – and more specifically, selling one's soul to the devil – can be interpreted as a metaphor for a more contemporary form of soul-selling – that is, England's violent and gluttonous domination of the indigenous peoples of Africa, India and the New World represented in the play as England's descent into Hades.

In the first act of the play, Faustus is lured to necromancy by the rewards that he believes it will bring:

> Oh, what a world of profit and delight,
> Of power, of honor, of omnipotence
> Is promised to the studious artisan!
> All things that move between the quiet poles
> Shall be at my command. Emperors and kings
> Are but obeyed in their several provinces,
> Nor can they raise the wind or rend the clouds;
> But his dominion that exceeds in this
> Stretcheth as far as doth the mind of man.
> A sound magician is a mighty god.
> Here, Faustus, try thy brains to gain a deity.
>
> (I.i.55–65)

Although traditional criticism has characterized Faustus as a seeker after forbidden knowledge, a close reading of the text clearly identifies his *summum bonum* as power and wealth, not prohibited knowledge and the language that he uses in this passage and throughout the play to clarify the rewards of necromancy can be read as alluding specifically to the power gained through the colonial enterprise. Faustus wants imperialistic power; he wants to control the world and all of its inhabitants. As Bevington and Rasmussen state, ' "Power" is a resonant word in Marlowe', and Faustus 'pictures human destiny in the language of subversion and control'.[24] Marlowe continues to combine colonialist imagery with Faustus's idealization of necromancy throughout Act I. 'Glutted with conceit' of his imagined rewards, Faustus expresses his yearnings:

> Shall I make spirits fetch me what I please,
> Resolve me of all ambiguities,
> Perform what desperate enterprise I will?
> I'll have them fly to India for gold,
> Ransack the ocean for orient pearl,
> And search all corners of the newfound world
> For pleasant fruits and princely delicates.
>
> (I.i.85–87)

Faustus's mind drifts as well to Africa, where, imagining himself the great imperialist, his plans for the world anticipate the British empire, on whose land, in its time, the sun never set:

> Had I as many souls as there be stars,
> I'd give them all for Mephistopheles.
> By him I'll be great emperor of the world
> And make a bridge through the moving air
> To pass the ocean with a band of men;
> I'll join the hills that bind the Afric shore
> And make that land continent to Spain,
> And both contributory to my crown.
>
> (I.iii.104–111)

Faustus's compensation for his soul is empire – interestingly, one that includes power over Spain and her treasury. The justifications offered by Valdes and Cornelius for practising necromancy are similarly replete with colonial references. Introducing the discourse of imperialism, Valdes lauds the magician, stating,

> Faustus, these books, thy wit, and our experience
> Shall make all nations to canonize us.
> As Indian Moors obey their Spanish lords,
> So shall the subjects of every element
> Be always serviceable to us three.
>
> (I.i.121–25)

Valdes continues by depicting these subjects as protecting lions, faithful horses and willing women, and by describing the spoils of their pursuits:

> From Venice shall they drag huge argosies,
> And from America the golden fleece
> That yearly stuffs old Philip's treasury
> If learned Faustus will be resolute.
>
> (I.i.132–35)

In prophetic words that anticipate not only the exploitation of colonial lands but also the despoiling of the environment that would occur in the following years, Cornelius adds,

> The spirits tell me they can dry the sea
> And fetch the treasure of all foreign wrecks –

> Ay, all the wealth that our forefathers hid
> Within the massy entrails of the earth.
>
> (I.i.146–49)

Boasting of his imperial power and dominion over the earth while offering grapes out of season to the duchess, Faustus proclaims,

> If it like your Grace, the year is divided into two circles over the world, that when it is here winter with us, in the contrary circle it is summer with them, as in India, Saba, and farther countries in the East; and by means of a swift spirit that I have, I had them brought hither
>
> (IV.ii.20–24)

Throughout the first act of the play, necromancy is continually associated with the ravishing of the colonized lands for treasure so characteristic of the imperialist endeavour.

Faustus's deal with Mephistopheles is also closely linked to colonization in the play. Lucifer, a colonizer of souls, constantly attempts to 'enlarge his kingdom'. After the signing of the contract, Mephistopheles asks Faustus, 'shall I have thy soul?' adding, 'And I will be thy slave', thereby suggesting that Faustus, in selling his soul, assumes the role of the slaver (II.i.44–45). This discourse of imperialism and the direct references to colonialism that serve to define the rewards of necromancy in the play gain resonance when understood as a literary device that Marlowe employs to illumine at least one of the most important issues explored in *Doctor Faustus*; throughout the play, the characters use the language of power and control to associate necromancy with colonialism and imperialism.

Moreover, Marlowe's Lucifer emerges as a more complex devil than the emblematic model presented in the English mystery play; this Lucifer is a multi-faceted figure, represented by various demons, devils and spirits that Mephistopheles explains are 'forever damned *with* Lucifer' (I.iii.74; emphasis added).[25] But neither is Lucifer's multiple identity exactly illusionist. The overarching concept of evil that the devil trope provides, combined with its varying representations in *Doctor Faustus,* suggest that, in this play, Lucifer may stand not for evil in general, but rather for an emerging evil that pervades the tragedy. This new evil, not yet fixed or emblematically signifiable, is the discourse of imperialism and, in my reading, it is this particular evil that consumes Faustus's soul.

In my interpretation, therefore, Christianity and the devil are consistently conflated in *Doctor Faustus*. When Faustus conjures

Mephistopheles, he asks him to leave and return dressed as a Franciscan friar, stating, 'That holy shape becomes a devil best' (I.iii.27). This could be interpreted as a satire of Catholicism, but it could also be read as conflating Christianity with black magic. The possible connection that Marlowe draws here between Christianity and necromancy could serve to extend the metaphor of imperialism to include the agenda of Christianization infused into the discourse of colonialism, as Hakluyt's *Pamphlet* strongly suggests. A notable cause for Faustus's despair at the end of his life and for his refusal to believe that salvation is possible can thus be attributed to the fact that Faustus – and indeed Marlowe's audience – is never certain who 'the devil' is; to extend the metaphor, Marlowe seems to imply that within the discourse of imperialism – and particularly within the Christian argument for colonization – it is difficult to ascertain exactly who the 'good' or 'evil' are since demonic spirits, damned souls, Lucifer and perhaps even Christ are all conflated in the play. For example, Faustus uses an inverted Christian discourse to conjure Mephistopheles; Mephistopheles, a damned soul, explains to Faustus that, technically, he has not left hell because 'this is hell, nor am I out of it' (I.iii.78). In an effort to save his soul, Faustus calls upon Christ and Lucifer appears (II.iii.83). At the end of his life, Faustus again attempts to save his soul, but his pleas for salvation are contradictory, as he calls upon Christ and the devil in the same breath: 'Ah, my Christ! | Ah, rend not my heart for naming of my Christ! | Yet will I call on him. O, spare me, Lucifer!' (V.ii.76–78). As Faustus appeals to one, he appeals to the other; it is as if the two are finally inseparable.

Just as the Church and God were so central to the practice of imperialism, so Christ is central to necromancy. In both cases, Christianity is polarized and set against the very thing upon which it depends. God needs the evil devil against which to represent goodness; Christianity needs the beastly heathen against which to represent the saved soul. And in both cases, the spoils are not half bad. Marlowe expresses this final point in the comic scene in which Faustus steals from the Pope the gifts that the prelate has received from foreign cities (III.i.60–73), perhaps indicating Faustus's scorn of the Church for its investment in colonialism and imperialism. Unable to come to terms with the good and godly enterprise of world domination, Faustus offers a lacklustre and faithless repentance that utterly fails. It can then be said that Marlowe's Faustus ultimately battles with the binary opposition of good and evil presented in Christian ideology and with the living contradiction that this ideology becomes within the discourse of imperialism and colonialism. For Faustus, after imperialism, there is no good without evil.

Notes

1   John C. Appleby, 'War, Politics, and Colonization, 1558–1625', in *The Oxford History of the British Empire: Volume I: The Origins of Empire: British Overseas Enterprise to the Close of the Seventeenth Century*, ed. Nicholas Canny (Oxford: Oxford University Press, 1998), p. 68.

2   Quoted in Appleby, 'War, Politics, and Colonization', p. 80.

3   Appleby, 'War, Politics, and Colonization', p. 66.

4   Appleby, 'War, Politics, and Colonization', p. 67.

5   Clinton V. Black, *Pirates of the West Indies* (Cambridge: Cambridge University Press, 1989), pp. 2–3.

6   John H. Bodley, *The Power of Scale: A Global History Approach* (Armonk, NY: M.E. Sharpe, 2003), p. 117.

7   Jeremy Black, *The British Seaborne Empire* (New Haven, CT: Yale University Press, 2004), p. 35.

8   Black, *The British Seaborne Empire*, p. 36.

9   Appleby, 'War, Politics, and Colonization', p. 55.

10 Appleby, 'War, Politics, and Colonization', p. 70.

11 Anthony Pagden, 'The Struggle for Legitimacy and the Image of Empire in the Atlantic to c. 1700', in *The Oxford History of the British Empire: Volume I: The Origins of Empire: British Overseas Enterprise to the Close of the Seventeenth Century*, ed. Nicholas Canny (Oxford: Oxford University Press, 1998), pp. 34–54.

12 Pagden, 'The Struggle for Legitimacy', p. 36.

13 Alvin B. Kernan, *The Playwright as Magician: Shakespeare's Image of the Poet in the English Public Theater* (New Haven, CT: Yale University Press, 1979), p. 157; Joel B. Altman, *The Tudor Play of Mind: Rhetorical Inquiry and the Development of English Drama* (Berkeley, CA: University of California Press, 1978), pp. 321–88; Barbara Howard Traister, *Heavenly Necromancers: The Magician in English Renaissance Drama* (Columbia, MO: University of Missouri Press, 1984), pp. 89–107; John Mebane, *Renaissance Magic and the Return of the Golden Age* (Lincoln, NE: University of Nebraska Press, 1989), pp. 113–36; Darryll Grantley, ' "What means this shew?": Theatricalism, Camp, and Subversion in *Doctor Faustus* and *The Jew of Malta*', in *Christopher Marlowe and English Renaissance Culture*, ed. Darryll Grantley and Peter Roberts (Aldershot: Scolar Press, 1996), pp. 224–38; Patrick Cheney, *Marlowe's Counterfeit Profession: Ovid, Spenser, Counter-Nationhood* (Toronto: Toronto University Press, 1997), pp. 190–220; Huston Diehl, *Staging Reform, Reforming the Stage: Protestantism and Popular Theatre in Early Modern England* (Ithaca, NY: Cornell University Press, 1997), pp. 67–81; Ian McAdam, *The Irony of Identity: Self and Imagination in the Drama of Christopher Marlowe* (Newark, DE: University of Delaware Press, 1999), pp. 112–45.

14 Sara Munson Deats, ' "Mark this show": Magic and Theatre in Marlowe's *Doctor Faustus*', in *Placing the Plays of Christopher Marlowe: Fresh Cultural Contexts*, ed. Sara Munson Deats and Robert A. Logan (Aldershot: Ashgate, 2008), pp. 13–24.

15 Adrian Streete, 'Calvinist Conceptions of Hell in Marlowe's *Doctor Faustus*', *Notes and Queries* 47 (2000), p. 431.

16 Paul Kocher, 'The Witchcraft Basis in Marlowe's *Doctor Faustus*', *Modern Philology* 38 (1940), pp. 9–36.

17 William Tate, 'Solomon, Gender, and Empire in Marlowe's *Doctor Faustus*', *Studies in English Literature* 37 (1997), p. 257.

18 David Bevington and Eric Rasmussen, eds., *'Doctor Faustus': A- and B- texts (1604, 1616)* (Manchester: Manchester University Press, 1993).

19 Bevington and Rasmussen, 'Doctor Faustus', p. 31.
20 Sara Munson Deats, 'Marlowe's Interrogative Drama: *Dido, Tamburlaine, Doctor Faustus*, and *Edward II*', in *Marlowe's Empery: Expanding his Critical Contexts*, ed. Sara Munson Deats and Robert A. Logan (Newark, DE: University of Delaware Press, 2002), pp. 107–30.
21 Deats, 'Marlowe's Interrogative Drama', p. 108.
22 Deats, 'Marlowe's Interrogative Drama', p. 117.
23 The text of *Doctor Faustus* cited here is the A-text reprinted in *English Renaissance Drama*, ed. David Bevington, Lars Engle, Katherine Eisaman Maus and Eric Rasmussen (New York: Norton, 2002), pp. 245–86.
24 Bevington and Rasmussen, 'Doctor Faustus', p. 16.
25 Catherine Belsey uses the terms 'illusionist' and 'emblematic' to distinguish between the tropic figures employed in early modern drama. While emblematic characters borrow more from the morality plays of the previous centuries and are hence more two-dimensional and representative of ideas, illusionist characters are proto-realistic constructs which appear more rounded and hence offer more interpretative complexity; for a full discussion of the difference between the 'illusionist' and 'emblematic' modes, see Belsey, *The Subject of Tragedy; Identity and Difference in Renaissance Drama* (New York: Routledge, 1985), pp. 13–33.

CHAPTER SIX

'What means this show?' Staging Faustus on Campus

Andrew James Hartley

I directed *The Tragical History of Doctor Faustus* in April 2007 on the main stage at the University of North Carolina, Charlotte – a 320-seat modified proscenium theatre – as the climax of the theatre department's spring season. As such, its cast and its audience were dominated by undergraduates, few of whom had any real experience with Marlowe as text, and less with Marlowe on stage.

Faustus is a difficult play with a vexed textual history. I chose the A-text as the core of my script, partly because it is shorter, and partly because some of the more Calvinist pronouncements of the B-text's ending seemed to me too limiting for the central character as I was envisaging him. While it was interesting to think that Faustus never had any real choice in his damnation, I felt that we had a hard enough time as it was finding character arcs and story structure in the sense most familiar to contemporary audiences without stripping Faustus of any real agency as well. Modern audiences and actors expect to see a protagonist learn and change through experience, experience which is at least partly shaped by his actions. A modern hero – even a tragic hero – generally has to be less acted upon than he is acting in ways shaping his destiny. The pursuit of practical theatre is not a quest for a perfect or definitive production, but an attempt to create a new art object from that play. The choice of text was based on what I thought best suited to the goals of the production. That choice made, I cut a little and clarified the odd word, rolled a couple of characters together to try to work against the script's inherent bittyness, but left the text largely intact.

Such a decision posed problems that the production solved only partially. Shakespeare's sense of language, character and structure are much more familiar to actors, if only because they have shaped our modern notion of language, character and story. Marlowe's text, dotted as it is with classicism, arcane theology, Latin tags, contemporary slang, obscure verbal humour, grandiloquence, formal rhetorical devices and all the trappings of the mighty line itself, is harder. American students are trained in little of what makes Marlowe *Marlowe* (not Shakespeare), and the struggles they face when tackling blank verse and unfamiliar diction in Shakespeare are compounded by a more marked sense of cultural and theatrical alienation in a Marlowe text. While the technical difficulties of this large-scale production occasionally made me wish that I was staging the play as I had originally intended – in a black box with half a dozen actors – it quickly became apparent that, like most directors tackling Marlowe, I did not have the cast to rely on delivery of that mighty line. This was not fixable, because while actors can be trained during or before the rehearsal period, audiences cannot, except in the most ham-fisted fashion.

Part of the problem is inherent in doing Renaissance 'Not Shakespeare' plays. I have directed and been a dramaturg for numerous Shakespearean productions, but I have also directed Kyd (once), Jonson (twice) and Middleton (three times). Each playwright poses particular issues and challenges for the director who knows his audience will always be viewing the production through the gauze of Shakespeare – if they have any period reference at all. Marlowe is, I suspect, the most difficult to stage today, largely because of the plays' reliance on linguistic spectacle.

This is hardly news, of course. Marlowe has a different notion of tragedy and plays by different rules. The problem is that most other Renaissance writers (meaning, of course, Shakespeare) lend themselves much better to these expectations of character and plot, so that Marlowe seems alien to a modern audience, even by Shakespearean standards. The core story of Faustus does not help, because most general audience members – particularly those in the Carolinas – either find the pact with the devil wholly unbelievable, or they find it plausible enough to want to treat the play simply as a sermon on the dangers of turning from God. Faustus himself experiences that essential component of drama – conflict – but for the play to work on stage, that conflict must be something in which the audience can share. When it comes to tales of selling one's soul, the American South has largely made up its mind what it thinks about that, and for most of our audience there was not a lot of grey area.

In *Faustus* – at least in the texts that we have to work with – the verbal pyrotechnics also stand in for what modern audiences most expect: plot and character. In movie terms, *The Tragical History of Doctor Faustus* has no second act. It begins and ends well, but while the engine of the story gets going quickly and ends with resonance, the bulk of the main action consists of a series of repetitive conversations about whether or not Faustus should pursue his current course, and a series of set-piece distractions, some comic, some spectacular. This comparative lack of plot has repercussions for character as well, since the protagonist reaches his decision to enter the demonic pact relatively quickly and then stays that course until he is finally damned. Conventional wisdom suggests that a reading has to get pretty subtle and inventive to find what theatre practitioners would term a 'character arc', Stanislavskian objectives, the barriers that character have to overcome to reach those objectives and the needs which actors are accustomed to discovering within the character's more conscious goals. But theatre is not finally about reading alone, and the process by which a playtext becomes a performance event is necessarily adaptive and constructive as well as interpretative. For a director, not all of the answers will come from the words on the page, and part of his or her task is seeing beyond what *is* there in the words, to what *might* be there on the stage. So long as this transformative building through script preparation, design and rehearsal does not create obvious and counterproductive contradiction with the script, there is no problem: it is, indeed, what theatre is supposed to do.

I entered the process with a set of basic assumptions, then: assumptions that were crucial to the way that I wanted to tell the story on the stage. The first of these was that the production – although stylized in effect – would be seeking to present Faustus in broadly naturalistic and contemporary terms. This meant that he would be a character in the modern sense, with an intellectual and emotional through-line, and that he would have a degree of agency concerning what befell him.[1] Theologically, this meant that redemption had to be a real possibility until very late in the story, so we took the words of the Good Angel and the Old Man (played as a bag lady in our production) at face value. It also meant that redemption and damnation were crucially tied to self-awareness as much as they were to cosmic/theological power structures. I had no interest in presenting the story simply as a moral lesson and rejected that reading of the play as being deaf to its ironies. The key question for me in character terms was not 'what will happen', but 'why will it happen?'. With hell so clearly real in the play, and with redemption apparently always a real possibility (at least until his communion with 'Helen' and possibly even into his final speech), why does Faustus persist in what is clearly self-destructive? If I could not answer that question, I knew that the audience would merely find him absurd and repulsive. There had to be a logic to it.

My first impulse was to draw on some of his language of contempt for what he considered 'servile', reading his self-destruction as a reluctance to give God his due, a refusal to bow down before anything, thereby enacting Lucifer's own *'non serviam'*. Exploring the text in the approach to the rehearsals proper, however, made this – to my mind, interesting – reading less and less fruitful. The defiance and rebelliousness never became sufficiently explicit that I felt it was playable, and however nicely it might read as irony, Faustus's subsequent subservience to Lucifer prior to the Seven Deadly Sins pageant seemed to seriously undermine this reading. But if actual defiance of authority would not work, there was something in the manner of Faustus's defiance and the way that it tended to collapse in on itself that struck me as both playable and immediate in a contemporary sense.

It always struck me as significant that the Prologue goes out of its way to tell us about Faustus's pre-history, spelling out his humble origins, 'his parents base of stock' (Prologue 11).[2] With this in mind I began to consider his necromantic career an extension of what had gone before: a process of self-betterment, of aspiration of an expressly social kind. Lawrence Stone and others have made a fine case for the way that the upwardly mobile of the early modern period adopted the trappings of their erstwhile superiors because these were what defined success: the townsman whose trade raised him to the income levels of the peerage bought the titles, clothes, houses and so on of the peerage because there was no other standard of success. Faustus – like Tamburlaine – rises from the bottom, but that movement does not put him outside the structures of social hierarchy and his success is framed accordingly. While Tamburlaine gathers and distributes crowns, Faustus – for all his early talk of becoming emperor of all the world – cannot stop thinking of himself as needing the validation of his superiors. Whatever his magical power, Faustus is a dutiful subject whose most public successes are as a kind of entertainer for the rich and famous.

This idea provided a bridge from the play to the culture of our audience, who fully understand the lure not simply of wealth and power, but of fame. Faustus's rebellion against God is not a real rebellion, not simply satanic defiance, and is therefore more about what he is getting – or thinks that he is getting – out of the demonic pact. The power and knowledge delivered to him by Mephistopheles are – in my reading – limited, circumscribed by other rules that he has not anticipated or that are simply less exciting or novel than he assumes (even the answers to his questions on cosmology turn out to be 'slender trifles' [II.iii.49] that even Wagner knows). What keeps him on the straight and narrow (or its demonic equivalent) and prevents him from turning to God is the promise of indulgence wrapped in the glamour of celebrity. Like Jonson's Epicure Mammon, his hedonism is built around an excess which presumes a jealous observer. Our Faustus, then, was one who thought of himself in the third person (a mode he adopted throughout the play), someone always watching himself in a mirror and choosing what he thinks will impress others.

To balance the various foreign elements of the play for a general audience (many of whom would be students and their families), I had opted to go for a stylized contemporary look, and my ideas about who Faustus was crystallized when James Vesce was inserted into the role.[3] Vesce is the primary teacher of directing in the theatre department, a former Jesuit seminarian in his late fifties, a bachelor, intelligent, interested in philosophy but also irascible and famously exasperated by student apathy. He is fascinated by ideas of celebrity (and taught a cultural studies course called 'Paris Hilton's America' a year after the show closed) and is also a gifted musician and songwriter who works extensively in musical theatre. With these things in mind we crafted between us a Faustus who was a middle-aged academic, frustrated and disillusioned with the kind of status accorded by academia, a Faustus pondering the possibility of what Lois Potter, who reviewed the show kindly for *Shakespeare Bulletin*, shrewdly identified as 'life after tenure'. This was a Faustus who, having mastered his discipline(s) and outgrown the confines of his scholarly study, felt he deserved a different kind of adulation, a Faustus – in short – who wanted to be a rock star.[4]

I had read of a prominent Princeton hire, brought in at considerable expense as a kind of writer in residence, who had caused consternation by forming a band and spending all his time jamming with them and playing tiny campus clubs (Paul Muldoon, who joined with Nigel Smith to form Rackett: Muldoon has recently been made chair of a new creative arts initiative on campus). I did no research on this person at all and was not interested in consciously modelling the role on him, but the story struck me as resonant. Muldoon and Smith were, doubtless, pursuing a particular form of artistic expression, but I was intrigued by the possibility of using the analogy as a way of reconceiving Faustus's strangely public rise to power. After all, although his dealings with Valdes and Cornelius have the aura of secrecy about them, Faustus's private imaginings of what he might do with magical power are expressly public and open:

O, what a world of profit and delight,
Of power, of honour, of omnipotence
Is promised to the studious artisan!
All things that move between the quiet poles
Shall be at my command. Emperors and kings
Are but obeyed in their several provinces,
Nor can they raise the wind, or rend the clouds;
But his dominion that exceeds in this
Stretcheth as far as doth the mind of man.
A sound magician is a mighty god.
Here, Faustus, try thy brains to gain a deity.

(I.i.55–65)

Here, as elsewhere, the fantasy is not simply for power or the satisfaction of real, hedonistic desires, but for the performance of that power. As he dismisses his former professions in terms of what he might be or already is famous for (being 'eternized' for some cure, his bills hung up as 'monuments,' and so on [I.i.15,20]), so his aspirations seem grounded in show, in celebrity. Ransacking the ocean for Orient pearl, walling Germany with brass and filling the public schools with silk are less about power than they are about the performance of it, the glamour and conspicuous excess of it. If the spirits can do all that, he says, then he needs no treasure or military defences and if his gift to the schools celebrates those unappreciated people who pursue learning, it does so in a flagrantly playful and showy way. Moreover, his quasi-humanist faith that the 'the mind of man' (I.i.63) makes his power limitless is badly flawed, as the rest of the play points out. Faustus always thinks like someone from parents of base stock, imagining himself in third person terms: thus, 'What does Faustus want?' slides easily into 'What *should* Faustus want?'. What will show that he has really made it? Pursuing such questions means, of course, that Faustus spends his time performing his power for others rather than exercising it on behalf of a selfhood which is somehow asocial.

Our Faustus was thus less interested in power than in prestige, in fame rather than the actual capacity for self-determination, and this is what made him vulnerable to Mephistopheles and to the distracting spectacles built into the script. This approach to the character gave us the chance to make Faustus's predicament more sympathetic to the audience: it allowed us to seduce them theatrically, put them in Faustus's predicament so they could glimpse in those spectacles what it is that he finds so enticing and difficult to give up. What our Faustus was offered, above all, was glamour of an expressly theatrical kind. It changed his wardrobe, his sex-appeal, his social standing and it did so in ways as far from the conventionally academic as possible, particularly through the sensuous power of dance (choreographed by Delia Neil). For instance, the first dance, accompanied by exotic music, drew Faustus into the choreography itself, enacting his desires as other-worldly women in red tantalized him with cases of money and jewellery, replacing his scholarly tweed with sleek Armani and wrapping him in drapery, so that he finished centre stage above them all, the statue of an emperor or a Christ. It was a fantasy of self-fashioning that played on his weaknesses, appetites and aspirations perfectly, and even his very appetites were shaped by what he thought he should want as a celebrity.

This logic pursues him throughout the play. His decision to have sex with Helen, for instance, is made after a kind of opinion poll. It is not enough for Faustus to have sexual intercourse with someone beautiful: he has to couple with the person others have determined to be the most beautiful. This takes 'trophy wife' to a new and terrifying level, a place where hedonistic desire can be little more than a performance of what one – always thinking of oneself in the third person – thinks one *should* have.[5]

While the production used dance and large-scale puppetry for set-piece shows designed to impress Faustus during the first half of the play (up to the pageant of the Seven Deadly Sins), the second half made him the orchestrator of those shows, although always dependent on Mephistopheles. Indeed, Faustus's only real power was over summoning the devil. Mephistopheles performed all the actual illusions and Faustus, still the clear-eyed sceptical academic, was acutely aware of this. Indeed, his sense of triumph waned comparatively quickly, paralleling the larger onstage culture's awareness of (and thus creation of) his steady decline: in a society where celebrity is not clearly grounded in the celebrity's field-specific productivity, where people are famous merely for being famous, the star quickly loses his lustre when the audience turns to something else.

A motif for the show became the puncturing of glamour and spectacle. It is clear from the text that the various shows within the show, the dances, pageants, masques and Madame Tussauds-esque wheeling out of famous dead people are all supposed to be both impressive and suspect.[6] There is a sense of the snake-oil salesman in Faustus's sideshow entertainments for the emperor, but the play is clear that the same impressive ruses are used on Faustus himself, cropping up in those moments where it seems most likely he may actually turn to God again. That the play should so foreground the theatrical as deceptive and confusing suggests the way its author uses the medium to play ironically with the audience, giving them – perhaps – the morality play they expect, while subverting the logics of its orthodoxy. For our purposes, the undermining of *show* in general reinforced our concern with fame, celebrity and the performance of an externalized selfhood. We sought to underscore this idea by creating a series of moments in which dramatic expectation was frustrated or complicated by the use of spectacle. The idea was that such devices would grant a theatrical excitement to the show, while also offering a subverting caution about the seductive powers of such spectacle.

In Faustus's initial summoning of the devil, for instance, the text suggests the way that Faustus himself punctures the devil's spectacular entrance: 'Thou art too ugly to attend on me | Go and return an old Franciscan Friar'(I.iii.25–26). We opted to extend the irony and indicate Faustus's vulnerability to the grandeur of spectacle and his desire to master it. So his Latin incantation, delivered as a piece of an old Catholic service under the shadows of the three monolithic structures which were rearranged to shape each scene, was underscored by wind and mounting thunder. It ended with the conjurer dramatically shouting the devil's name from the centre of his pentagram, in a column of incense-touched light, arms spread. Nothing happened. For a few seconds, Faustus waited, then, as the audience released their breath and started to snicker, moved downstage to check over the incantation from his book, make sure the thurible was working properly and try to figure out why it had not worked. While he was doing this, the blacks upstage flew out, revealing a deep red cyclorama, the upstage trap opened and a medieval devil, all red and gold with a horned gargoyle mask, clambered out onto the stage and extended his wings.[7]

Faustus became aware of the thing behind him, steeled himself and delivered the dismissal as a show of manly fortitude. The devil returned into the trap, chastened, and Faustus delighted in his mastery, but when the devil 'returned' it unsettled him (and the audience). Mephistopheles, lightly cowled in black, rose from the front row and spoke ('Now, Faustus, what would you have me do?' [I.iii.36]) before mounting the stage. Faustus, caught off guard, backtracked, then carefully put back her hood, revealing the woman

Faustus (James Vesce) summons the devil.
Photograph by Rolland Elliot.

he had not expected in her business suit. He was momentarily unsettled, then decided that he liked the change. When Mephistopheles came to exit at the end of the scene, however, he made her affirm her hellish origins and reconnect to the kind of spectacle he was more comfortable with, by insisting that she depart through the trap – complete with the sound effects and billowing smoke which had heralded 'her' first appearance – thereby claiming mastery over her and the situation.

This was the way we tried to use spectacle throughout, attempting to find the unsettling postscript to the expected. Even the devils, glamorous in their sparkling scarlet wings, were only impressive and fun when they wanted to be so. By the end, the demons hemming Faustus in were shambling, faceless corpses: black body suits and white masks, blank but contorted into expressions of pain and misery. In the light of such changes, the revelation that 'Helen' was really Mephistopheles ironically supplied the answer to the play's most famous question: 'Was this the face that launched a thousand ships?'. No, it was not. It may look like it, but no, although by then it should be clear that appearances are never what they seem, and they certainly are not worth sacrificing self and soul for.

In our production, the character and story arcs beat out in terms not unlike a modern three act screenplay. After Act I, in which Faustus decides to practise black magic and summons the devil,[8]

Faustus began the second act by exploring all the things that his power can give him, and commenced the back-and-forth movement to and from repentance. His wrestling with Mephistopheles over cosmology was comically counterpointed by Robin's absurd parallel activities, with Faustus watching in some instances, prompting the intervention of Lucifer, and the distracting pageant of the Sins. Faustus's delighted embrace of all things demonic facilitated his rise to glory. On Lucifer's 'In meantime take this book. Peruse it thoroughly, and thou shalt turn thyself into what shape thou wilt' (II.iii.171–73), Faustus – centre stage and surrounded by both the colossal puppet forms of the Sins and the dancers who had accompanied them – turned his face upwards into a shaft of light from whence an electric guitar descended. He began a virtuosic solo which – with his (extratextual!) cry of 'Good evening, Charlotte!' transformed the theatre into a wildly enthusiastic concert venue. The fade-to-black provided his mid-point climax and led into our intermission. The second half of the production (still Act II in movie terms) continued from this most glamorous and publicly successful moment. His travels around the world (accompanied with projected holiday-style snaps of Faustus and Mephistopheles mugging in front of world-famous sites) heralded his being surrounded by photographers and news crews, most conspicuously after his disruption of the papal feast. The apotheosis of his career became his performance for the emperor – a spectacular affair with music, dance and Vegas-style showgirls performed with the press in attendance – but it also marked the beginning of his decline, as he failed to negotiate court politics successfully (his punishment of the disruptive knight was clearly a PR faux pas as far as the emperor was concerned).

The summery climate which had underscored the scenes of his success moved into the snows of winter, and these scenes (as in the first half) were undercut by the comic antics of Robin, Ralph and the Vintner. The second act concluded with a sense of failure and inadequacy after the Vanholt scene, and Act III was thus comprised of the summoning of Helen, Faustus's farewell to the scholars and his final soliloquy (as the stage cluttered slowly with numerous lurching and cadaverous devils). Mapped out like this, the production played Faustus's rise and fall in psychological terms, the tragedy hinging on the hero's inability to stop straining for validation from outside himself, and also on the full horror of what he has done along the way.

Faustus, for his part, quickly recognized that he had made a bad choice. It was clear in the emperor's court that his star was (like all celebrities too much in the public eye) on the wane, and by the time

Faustus (James Vesce) debates with Mephistopheles (Maralie Schofield).
Photograph by Rolland Elliot.

of his summoning grapes at what in our show was the Duke of Vanholt's cocktail party, he was clearly a has-been, abandoned by the paparazzi who had hounded him earlier. The pregnant duchess was bored with him, irritated by being made a party to his sideshow, and – by the time she left, handing the uneaten grapes off to a servant – exasperated that her husband would have lowered the tone of the evening by bringing him along. His date, a news anchor who had been seen interviewing him prior to the episode at the emperor's palace – was invited to stay longer, but he was pointedly paid off by the butler and shown the trademan's exit.

The emblem of Faustus's realization was a clown nose. This first appeared when Wagner opted to take Robin into her service.[9] Robin, who had first appeared in the house as a student, complaining on his cellphone about having to watch 'Dr Franken-stein', was drawn up onto the stage and into the play. His agreement to serve Wagner came with the acceptance of his (already apparent) role as clown, and the red foam nose she put on him. The same nose later passed back and forth between Robin and Rafe, moving finally to the Vintner who doubled as the Horse-Courser. In each case, the moment that the characters put on the nose signalled the impossible stupidity of their situation, their knowing recognition of that impossibility and their resultant willingness to play along. At the end of the play, with Faustus surrounded by devils poised to drag him down through the stage floor, Mephistopheles offered Faustus the nose. His horror turned to soft self-deprecating laughter as he took it, considered it and put it on. This was the cue for the hitherto slow, zombie-like devils to rush him into the trap. The moment wove together the tragic elements of the main plot and their accumulated aura of gravitas with the parallel scenes of the comic sub-plot, retrospectively weaving them together and revealing the aspirations of both protagonist and clowns as fruitless and absurd.

What happened next was – in some ways – my favourite moment of the production, and hinged on a crucial piece of casting. Our Mephistopheles was played by a female student working against all demonic type, directed to play the devil as a character with the same kinds of depths, complexities and motivations as any other. It might be objected that this is to project onto the text, but I do not believe this to be true and do not much care if it is: our job was to perform a play in the present (and therefore in the performative idiom of the present, however much the words used were sixteenth century). Speaking both theatrically and pedagogically (since campus productions are always at least as much about teaching the students involved as they are about entertaining the audience) a rounded, psychologically complex character, although more difficult to achieve if that character is a devil, is far richer and more satisfying than any hissing villain. Our Mephistopheles was thus deliberately undemonic, neither conniving nor seductive, although she was

Faustus (James Vesce) presents Alexander and his paramour to the court of the emperor (Miller McGowan) in front of the press. Photograph by Rolland Elliot.

knowing and clever in the ways someone who has seen a great deal might be clever. But her knowledge – so much deeper than Faustus's swaggering showmanship – also made her compassionate. Indeed, from a certain perspective, our production wound up being more about her than it was about the title character. Maralie Schofield's Mephistopheles was coolly poised, sometimes playful – though never deliberately sexy – and (as when she reproached Robin and his idiot friends) lethally powerful, but the core of her character was one of paradox, even division. She made no bones about the dangers Faustus was embracing, and often seemed to be counselling him to reflect more seriously on what he was doing, sometimes overtly ('O Faustus, leave these frivolous demands' [I.iii.83]) and sometimes with the pointed resonance ('And are forever damned with Lucifer' [I.iii.74]), to which Faustus had to work to turn his tin ear.

In our telling of the story we took Mephistopheles's lines on the nature of hell ('this is hell, nor am I out of it' [I.iii.78]) to suggest the devil's endless torment, a part of which was having to watch the destruction of people like Faustus. Misery, as she said, loves company, but that only intensified the misery because it increased the sense of responsibility, of guilt. A devil who feels nothing – or feels only glee – at the destruction of others cannot be said to be in hell. I wanted a devil whose torment was always just beneath the surface, a devil torn apart by the desire to save Faustus, overridden by her obligation to damn him by any means necessary. Her hell was

Faustus (James Vesce), now wearing the sign of his foolishness, is taken down through the trap at the end of the play. Photograph by Rolland Elliot.

in being forced to conspire against someone with whom she had built a relationship over time, until he was eventually damned. She thus spent her time moving between the desire to do her job and the desire to save Faustus, whose childish ambitions and bluster she saw through utterly. Sometimes she indulged him, played along (tormenting the nuns at the papal feast for his delight); sometimes she admonished him; and sometimes she looked after him (covering his legs with a blanket as the snow began to fall so that he could sleep off his sense of anticlimax after the emperor's palace).[10] Her interest was not clearly romantic, however much Faustus tried to taunt her in his dance with the devil whore early on, although she was revealed to be Helen after Faustus had taken her to bed.[11] At the end, with Faustus dragged down through the trap, she broke down and – in a long, slow and painful moment underscored by plainchant ornamented with evocative alto saxophone – wept for him and for herself. This was her hell, nor was she out of it.[12]

We should know by now that productions of Renaissance plays on the modern stage can only be partially determined by the text of the play itself and that much of the logic behind certain theatrical choices or – less consciously – theatrical moments are derived from notions of authority quite removed from the textual or historical. This is the nature of the performative beast which is of the cultural moment in which it appears, however much its roots go back for centuries. The way our play took shape on stage grew out of the sensibilities of those involved and their mission was not to tell the story of the play (as if such a thing could be done in some definitive fashion) but to tell a new story for a new audience with or through the play. It is thus a particularly painful irony that the tragedy most associated with the production which many of our audience will best remember was not Faustus's or even Mephistopheles's but Ralph's. Theatre lives on in the memory and memory reshapes all things. In this case the production is being reshaped by the as yet unsolved murder of one of the cast – Ira Yarmolenko, who played Ralph as Robin's sister – a year after the production. The killing had no direct connection to the show, of course, but many of those close to her when she died met her through rehearsals for this production and for other theatre work in which she later became involved. I mention this not because I want to somehow read the production retrospectively through this event, but to honour her memory and to underscore this most basic truth of production: that when the show first goes into rehearsal, when it first opens for the public, and when it lives on in recollection, the production is evolving, its semiotic apparatus branching and multiplying, blurring and fading as it builds meanings that are necessarily provisional and shifting, meanings which cannot and should not be held hostage to the text, its author or the original generative moment.

Notes

1   The intellectual and emotional through-line is central to modern naturalistic acting. It assumes an inherent coherence of character, a constant selfhood which – far from being jeopardized by apparent shifts from moment to moment or scene to scene – demands that the actor find reasons to explain in psychological terms what may otherwise seem discontinuous.

2   Christopher Marlowe, *'Doctor Faustus': A- and B-texts (1604, 1616)*, ed. David Bevington and Eric Rasmussen (Manchester: Manchester University Press, 1993). This quotation and all subsequent quotations from the play are taken from the A-text of this edition.

3   One of the many practical concerns that dominate any conceptual or theoretical approach to directing is casting, and the problems thereof. In this case, I cast a student actor in the title role only to lose him a week into rehearsals. I was fortunate to have James Vesce agree to step into the role, but his doing so necessarily changed the production.

4   The rock star motif underwrote the choice of music for the show, the original plan for which was to anchor it with David Bowie tunes, since they nicely evoked a sense of the importance of the rock star persona. With Vesce in the title role, however, we moved to music which was less glam, more angst-ridden and the music – the specifics of which were determined by the sound designer, Mark Howieson, who won a local theatre award for the design – emphasized nineties bands on the darker edge of pop: Soundgarden, The Cure, Marcy Playground and Everclear, to name a few.

5   The scholars who requested to see the woman considered the most beautiful in the world approached Faustus with copies of *Variety* and *People* magazine.

6   Something of this was figured in the set, a flexible arrangement of three slightly curved monolithic staircases which could be fitted together to form a semicircle or otherwise arranged to create different senses of space. Each was large, containing the stagecrew that moved them around, and they could be arranged to drastically curtain the space or open it up to create the freedom needed for the dance pieces. Spread out formally they could feel like the repeating columns of a papal palace, or tightened into a classroom auditorium, but they always created levels and – through their stairs – suggested aspiration. Since the stairs did not actually lead anywhere, however, and since they were constantly being adjusted and reconfigured, the nature and goal of that aspiration seemed far from stable. The set was designed by Anita Tripathi Easterling.

7   The devil masks and costumes for this scene were derived from medieval woodcuts and images from church architecture. The show's costume designer was Bob Croghan.

8   In three-act movie structure terms, Act I ended for us at 'Now that I have obtained what I desire, | I'll live in speculation of this art | 'Till Mephistopheles return again' (I.iii.114–16).

9   Wagner – who was also the chorus, and thus both inside and outside the play – was, like several roles, cross-cast.

10   The covering of his legs was also the way we set up the false leg, which the Vintner (Horse-Courser) would then pull off.

11   The actor playing Helen met Faustus centre stage (as she had when he first summoned her for the scholars), but after a brief embrace they parted and moved up to a central, mirrored wall. Once on the other side of the wall, the light on the mirror changed and they were revealed in bed together behind it. The scene faded to black for the speech of the Bag Lady (Old Man) and the

appearance of two devils, then came up again as they parted to return downstage. At this moment, the actor playing Helen was switched with Mephistopheles in Helen's clothes, so that Faustus had already embraced her again before realizing who she was. Indeed, although the moment produced audible gasps from the audience each night, the actors were of similar build and colouration and not everyone realized that the switch (one which took immense work to pull off!) had happened at all.

12   This was the most difficult scene for the actor concerned – one who tends to work off the simulation of emotion rather than the experience of it, an actor famous for asking what the director wants rather than generating ideas out of herself – and we had to rehearse it sparingly to keep it fresh. The poignant music aided the mood and nicely combined the ancient and ritualistic with the modern and personally expressive.

CHAPTER SEVEN

The Other Black Arts: *Doctor Faustus* and the Inky Worlds of Printing and Writing

Georgia E. Brown

Books feature prominently in *Doctor Faustus*. From the opening scene, which takes place in a scholar's study, to the magic book which Robin steals from Faustus, books are an essential part of the setting and action of the play. The phenomenon of the book invites us to think about writing and printing (among other things) and so it has always surprised me that critics pay little attention to what *Doctor Faustus* has to say about these issues. In fact, many of the stories associated with the Faust legend involve the invention of printing. Moreover, as I thought about the play's attitudes toward writing and printing it became clear that while we may sometimes forget that a piece of writing or a printed text is a material object with physical characteristics, the Renaissance does not forget this fact. *Doctor Faustus* is interested in the ways that the material aspects of writing and printing interact with the more intellectual and abstract aspects of texts. It also analyses the ways that texts might interact with another aspect of material reality – the human body. The linking of textuality with corporeality may appear to be a fanciful bit of modern theorizing until we remember that *Doctor Faustus* was produced at a time when drama was adopting new forms of cultural authority. The appearance of large numbers of plays in print threw the relationship between scripts, printed texts and actors to the fore. In *Doctor Faustus* Marlowe responds to the opportunities and dangers occasioned by his particular historical moment and he probes the relationship between textuality and corporeality at a time when writers, actors and printers were all trying to capitalize on plays. Of course scripts, in the sense of playtexts, clearly affect actors' bodies but, in this play, writing also exerts its own strange power on human bodies.

The seed for this chapter derived from my attempts to make sense of the opening lines of *Doctor Faustus*. The chorus sums up what we are about to see, or read, in terms that are repetitious, confusing and even awkward:

> Not marching now in fields of Trasimene
> Where Mars did mate the Carthaginians,
> Nor sporting in the dalliance of love
> In courts of kings where state is overturned,
> Nor in the pomp of proud audacious deeds,
> Intends our muse to daunt his heavenly verse.
> Only this, gentlemen: we must perform
> The form of Faustus' fortunes, good or bad.
>
> (Prologue 1–8)[1]

What does the phrase 'perform | The form of Faustus's fortunes, good or bad' actually mean? Does 'the form' refer to the shape of Faustus's life or does it refer to the playtext? If it refers to the playtext and the chorus announces that the players must now perform the text about Doctor Faustus, does this text create characters and generate their sphere of action or does the playtext describe a real life, a pre-existent reality? Does it perhaps adapt pre-existent texts and give life to a form derived from other books, like *The History of the Damnable Life and Deserved Death of Doctor John Faustus* (1592)? In any case, how easy is it to separate life from words, reality from textuality, in the case of John Faustus, who actually was suspected of practising black magic in early sixteenth-century Germany, but whose biography became mixed up with other stories? There are other possibilities. Does the playtext describe a prior performance? Is the form that is actualized in performance a form of words, perhaps a prose biography of John Faustus, or the playwright's own handwritten manuscript of the play, or is it a prior performance of the play which supplies some kind of template for subsequent performances? Are words constitutive or representative, in other words do they create things or describe things? Does the physical verify the textual or vice versa? Are forms substantiated and given credit through performance?

The phrase 'perform | The form' resonates in all sorts of unexpected ways with diverse aspects of the play. The verb 'to perform' can mean to fulfil a promise. In other words, the verb 'to perform' refers to an action that brings something to an end and

terminates words and promises. In this sense, it alludes to the end of
the play and the appointed time when Faustus must pay his debt. A
'form' is also a class in school, or it is the specialized term for the
subjects that are prescribed for a particular course at university,
appropriately enough for this play about the pitfalls and opportunities of bookishness, which opens in a scholar's study. Appropriately too, given Faustus's pact with the devil and his denial of the
redemptive pact between Christ and humanity defined by the New
Testament, a 'form' is also a formal agreement between two parties.
The word 'form' is also a specialized term used in printing, the name
given to a body of type, and one of the purposes of this chapter is to
show that this meaning of form is also highly appropriate to *Doctor
Faustus*. While the editors of the play confine themselves to the
simple observation that verbal repetition is characteristic of
Marlowe, in their annotations to the phrase 'perform | The form'
they suggest that Marlowe seems to be doing rather a lot through
this supposedly unremarkable piece of verbal repetition which
immediately sets the relationship between playtext and performance
into spirals of complication.[2] Moreover, the word 'form' also refers
to the shape, configuration or visible aspect of an object and, as
such, it would seem to refer to the superficial and debased aspects of
the object. However, early modern neoplatonism understands form
as the visible expression of the most profound principles of order
and truth in the universe, whereby the external aspect of a thing is a
surface that simultaneously expresses the deepest spiritual meanings.
It seems to me that *Doctor Faustus* opens by destabilizing the
priority of internal over external, depth over surface, text over
performance, but also of external over internal, surface over depth,
performance over text.

Marlowe's play is obsessed with the relationship between writing,
print and performance, and the ways that textuality and corporeality
might overlap. For all the excitement generated by its angels, devils,
magic and hell fire, *Doctor Faustus* actually starts with the most
unpromising dramatic material – a university scholar alone in his
study – and it deals in the opportunities and dangers of writing.
According to the surviving records, the play was first performed by
the Lord Admiral's Men on 30 September 1594, and this coincides
with the period when drama became a print form. *Doctor Faustus*
remarks on, and is marked by, the movement between script,
performance and print. Nine quartos of Marlowe's play were
published between 1604 and 1631, and unlike most early modern
plays *Doctor Faustus* actually stimulated positive interest from the
book-buying public. Thus the play was in the thick of drama's entry

into print to a greater degree than most other plays produced in the 1590s. It coincides with the tentative beginnings of a writerly drama and it interrogates those beginnings by probing the nature of script and of print, and by questioning the relationship of writing to performance and to bodies. Of course, the Faust myth provides the ideal subject matter with which to probe the processes whereby people, places or activities acquire cultural presence. By the late sixteenth century, the myth had become a trans-national cultural phenomenon in northern Europe, and Marlowe's play capitalizes on Faust's notoriety and relishes the power of the name. The word 'Faustus' appears frequently and even Faustus refers to himself in the third person, as Faustus. This is part of an increasingly intimate connection of person and page which Douglas Bruster identifies as characteristic of the late 1580s and 1590s and which forms the backdrop to the emergence of the author and the writerly dramatist.[3] For Bruster, print is key in enabling a new kind of literary authorship, and authorship and print are mutually supportive. Leaving aside the possibility that manuscript circulation also creates names and makes the public recognition of authorship possible, my analysis of *Doctor Faustus* suggests that the relation-ship between print and authorship is much tenser than Bruster implies because authors are anxious about the power and nature of print. Moreover, by highlighting some of the ways that texts and bodies overlap in early modern culture, this study of *Doctor Faustus* not only suggests that embodied writing is more fundamental to early modern culture than Bruster acknowledges, but also concludes that writing has powers that are strange, disturbing and impossible to control because it has a physical form. In a sense, writing also has a body.

Much critical energy has already been expended on the role of writing in Marlowe's plays, but it tends to deal with the ways that the plays promote Marlowe's personal ambitions. For example, Emily Bartels argues that the story of Faustus's fall ends by affirming the power of the writer, although the existence of two competing versions of the play renders this affirmation ironic.[4] My discussion of writing has a different focus; I focus on writing as writing, as the simple setting down of letters and words. The other sense of writing, what could be called writing with a capital W, the sense of writing as a specifically literary activity, is important but different definitions of literature are based on different understandings of the nature of writing, including the nature of writing at its most basic level.

As *Doctor Faustus* constructs the image of Christopher Marlowe for his contemporaries, it articulates reservations about writing as an agent of control and as a vehicle for personal advancement. The play analyses the relationship between words and actions. It also explores the relationship between language and materiality, not only in the body of the actor but also in the body of the text. The early modern period conceived of the text in spatial, volumetric and acoustic terms, as a physical entity with somatic effects. This chapter draws on the study of material culture, the new critical movement that studies physical objects, in an attempt to recover early modern understanding(s) of writing. In trying to work out the relationship between text and performance, and between textuality and corporeality in the early modern period, I suggest that both text-based criticism and performance studies have been impaired by their failure to incorporate the findings of cultural materialism which demonstrate that writing is itself a physical entity with somatic consequences.

In an article published in 1987, Harry Berger identifies a 'general rift between the order of the body and the order of texts' as a fundamental characteristic of early modern culture.[5] In other words, print culture and theatre culture, book and body, occupy separate spheres of existence. In *Theatre of the Book 1480–1880,* Julie Stone Peters analyses the ways that printing acted with the theatre, rather than against it, to define drama's particularity. Pointing to the demand for the *Doctor Faustus* playbook, she suggests that publication can function to stimulate theatrical enthusiasms and by exploring the conventions which govern the typography and layout of playbooks she demonstrates how printing helped to give theatre an image of itself, how it dignified the characteristics of dramatic form and contributed to the institutionalization of the theatre as a form of high literature.[6] While this essay is heavily indebted to Peters's groundbreaking work, it argues that we need to keep in mind the limitations hedging the following kind of statement: 'To print is (even in the early sixteenth century) to transcend the requirements of theatrical presence, to draw nearer to incorporeal being, to explore the limits of material space and time and enter the realm of the spirit'.[7] Peters's premise that printing is immortal while performance is ephemeral is true only in so far as a stream of Renaissance writers laboured to make it appear true. The status of print and the nature of text were much more uncertain in the early modern period than such statements might suggest. As Adrian Johns has shown, the early modern scientific revolution depended on belief in the truth of the printed text, but fixity was not normally associated with print, and the authority of the text and its claims to reliability and stability were based on mobilizing a range of strategies that aimed to prove the creditability of those involved in producing the text.[8] Print, as well as performance, presented problems to the early modern mind.

Doctor Faustus registers contesting views of text and of writing. Books may be idealized in the play, but they are also exposed to misuse, to the perversions of different readers and to the kinds of corruption, or instability, epitomized by the puns and malapropisms of the comic scenes. In one sense Faustus's conjuring books may last forever, just as copies of the Gutenberg Bible still exist, but in what sense do books of high magic last when they change and become different things for different readers? The play exposes the way that the same book can mean different things in different contexts when the working men and clowns appropriate highbrow volumes. At one point, Robin steals one of Faustus's books:

> O, this is admirable! Here I ha'stol'n one of Doctor Faustus' conjuring books, and, i'faith, I mean to search some circles for my own use. Now will I make all the maidens in our parish dance at my pleasure stark naked before me, and so by that means I shall see more than e'er I felt or saw yet.
>
> (II.ii.1–6)

The fact that Robin cannot read, as Rafe points out (II.ii.15–16), is beside the point as the book still serves Robin's purposes. The word circle has bawdy associations in early modern English, and Robin expects that the book will bring him sex.[9] Even if the spells do not work, the book still brings him sexual satisfaction as the vehicle for his happy erotic fantasies. What is more, even though the words Robin later reads aloud appear to be gibberish and a misreading of the book, they still succeed in raising Mephistopheles:

> I'll tell you what I mean. *He reads.*
> *Sanctobulorum Periphrasticon*! Nay, I'll tickle you, Vintner.
> Look to the goblet, Rafe. *Polypragmos Belseborams framanto pacostiphos tostu Mephistopheles! etc.*
> *Enter to them* MEPHISTOPHELES.
>
> (III.ii.25–28)

In fact, the canonical status of a book seems to rest on its flexibility, rather than its stability, on its ability, as John Guillory asserts, to fulfil a variety of needs and to satisfy the demands of a range of readers.[10] It is this kind of flexibility that gives a text cultural presence and gives it the illusion of permanence, although it is a permanence derived from impermanence and fluidity.

The material nature of writing comes to the fore when Faustus casts his spells. In this scene, writing is represented on stage, both the act of writing and the product of that action, in other words writing as both an activity and an object:

Within this circle is Jehovah's name,
Forward and backward anagrammatised,
The breviated names of holy saints,
Figures of every adjunct to the heavens,
And characters of signs and erring stars,
By which the spirits are enforced to rise,
Then fear not, Faustus, but be resolute,
And try the uttermost magic can perform.

Sint mihi dei Acherontis propitii! Valeat numen triplex Jehovae! Ignei, aerii, aquatici, terreni, spiritus, salvete! Orientis princeps Lucifer, Beelzebub, inferni ardentis monarcha, et Demogorgon, propitiamus vos, ut appareat et surgat Mephistopheles!

(I.iii.8–20)

This scene highlights the sensual enjoyment of the acoustic and visual aspects of both performance and writing. First, for those unfamiliar with Latin, the incantatory quality of the Latin defamiliarizes language as it promotes its ritualistic and sonic elements at the expense of its representational elements. Second, given that notation is being represented in this scene, the thing represented and the vehicle of its representation are indistinguishable. A diagram of an apple, for example, produces a representation of an apple, something that is clearly not an apple, but a diagram or tracing out of a circle and symbols on the stage is just what the real Faustus would have done when casting a spell and reproduces what Faustus reproduces. This scene really does accomplish magic in that it collapses the differences between reality and representation, meaning and sign, text and performance. It questions what is real by suggesting that the thing representing is none other than the thing represented. Writing is of course a special case because writing performs what it means; its form has meaning and the execution of the form has meaning. In this case the text is generated by performance at the same time as performance is generated by text. Textual and performative modes of communication are superimposed, and this scene of writing is further glossed by the imagery of the 1619 title page which depicts Faustus, in his study, standing in a circle filled with symbols. The text, the performance and the visual image are parodies of each other, different ways of framing the story which bring out different relations and emphases.

Writing occupies different kinds of space in *Doctor Faustus*. It can be found in Faustus's study, or on his arm, but it also occupies another sort of physical space, one that is determined by the shape and size of the letters. This is literal space, in the now obsolete sense of literal which means pertaining to letters, or expressed by letters, and this literal space, the space of letters, is not only available to readers of the printed text of the play, but is also represented to the audience of *Doctor Faustus* in Faustus's conjuring:

> Within this circle is Jehovah's name,
> Forward and backward anagrammatised,
> The breviated names of holy saints,
> Figures of every adjunct to the heavens,
> And characters of signs and erring stars,
> By which the spirits are enforced to rise.
>
> (I.iii.8–13)

Faustus may well be tracing out the various letters and shapes as he speaks these lines, or he may hold up a paper or a page of a book to the audience which bears these mystical names and symbols. Even if the actor does neither of these things, the lines themselves remind the audience that words are composed of letters, of sequences of signs that can be reversed and reordered, 'Forward and backward anagrammatized'. The lines remind the audience that letters are shapes that resemble other kinds of figure, character and sign; that they make patterns and may be arranged to form a circle, as well as the usual horizontal lines of writing. The phrase 'Within this circle is Jehovah's name' may suggest that the word 'Jehovah' is written out so that its letters form a circle. The lines also remind the audience that ideas can be indicated by 'breviated names', or abbreviations, which make words, if abbreviated words still are words, less familiar, more oblique and more like the other kinds of symbol that Faustus deals with. These lines bring letters back into view and turn our attention to the means of representation as well as the thing being represented, so that writing is presented as a visual object that occupies space in particular ways. Rather than presenting writing as something transparent, these lines conceive of writing as an opaque medium, as something that has its own material form and unexpected potential.

It is perhaps surprising that critics who deal with the issues of text and performance in Marlowe ignore *Doctor Faustus*, a play in which the interaction between texts and bodies lies at the very heart of the story. Texts are brought on stage and characters try to act out the parts already scripted for them in a book, as they try to follow the spells set down in the conjuring book, and the recitation of pre-scripted words brings the bodies of Mephistopheles, Alexander and Helen onto the stage. Like Marlowe, Faustus creates roles for actors. The problem with *Doctor Faustus* and the reason for its neglect may be that it questions both the nature of text and the nature of performance and so it does not conform to a critical model that traces the establishment of a hierarchy of text over performance, but neither does it support the reverse hierarchy of performance over text. Books certainly carry weight in *Doctor Faustus*, but authority also takes non-verbal forms: it lies in vision as well as in the book. Seeing is believing, and there are multiple centres of authority in the play, including those who see and confirm. As the emperor tells Faustus:

> Master Doctor Faustus, I have heard strange report of thy knowledge in the black art – how that none in my empire, nor in the whole world, can compare with thee for the rare effects of magic. They say thou hast a familiar spirit by whom thou canst accomplish what thou list. This, therefore, is my request: that thou let me see some proof of thy skill, that mine eyes may be witnesses to confirm what mine ears have heard reported.
> (IV.i.1–8)

Doctor Faustus also registers the ways that non-verbal rituals and gestures can organize space and incorporate memory. Magic, like religion, has its own rituals and incantations that preserve and transmit values, as gesture and orality acquire their own forms of authority. Knowledge, which may or may not be derived from books, passes into experiential knowledge and is communicated in customs and in the performance of rites, rather than through texts.

Nevertheless, the play remains sceptical about any kind of idealization and uses parody as its basic structural principle as events and themes shift between tragic and comic contexts, to be reviewed through the perspective of another form. The comic antics of Robin and the clowns clearly puncture intellectualism; conversely, Faustus's aspirations and grandeur of emotion, especially in his final speech, point up the triviality of the clowns and the limitations of bodily existence as opposed to the flight of the mind. The play is also obsessed with the ways that words, whether in the form of spells or playtexts, can conjure up materiality and it plays with the paradox of the actor as both a real and a virtual presence. When, for example, Faustus conjures up Alexander and his paramour, he reminds the emperor that the characters he sees both are, and are not, there before him:

> But if it like your Grace, it is not in my ability to present before your eyes the true substantial bodies of those two deceased princes, which long since are consumed to dust [] But such spirits as can lively resemble Alexander and his paramour shall appear before your Grace in that manner that they best lived in, in their most flourishing estate – which I doubt not shall sufficiently content your Imperial Majesty.
>
> (IV.i.47–50, 53–57)

Writing occupies ideological as well as physical spaces; in fact, writing occupies an unstable position in the literary canon. On the one hand, we are only now emerging from a system that privileged text over performance. On the other hand, the processes of canonization depend on the expurgation of the material aspects of writing, including the look and sound of the words and letters, since it is the material and corporeal nature of texts (and performance) that drags writing into the debased realm of temporal existence and the canon prefers its texts to come without bodies because only then can it talk about the timeless essence of meaning. The place of writing in Marlowe's play is also a point in a social hierarchy where bookishness can help a scholar advance up the social ladder. Books and the knowledge of writing are deployed to mediate social relationships, as they are in the scene when Faustus, as a courtly client, demonstrates his skills to the emperor (IV.1). As Robin knows, books can turn him into a made man: 'Come, Rafe, did not I tell thee we were for ever made by this Doctor Faustus' book?' (III.ii.1–2), and familiarity with books can help him to climb the social ladder.[11] Robin and Rafe are 'ever made by this Doctor Faustus' book' in other senses as well. First, they exist through the story and only come to life as characters in this particular play. Moreover, in a play which, as Patrick Cheney has shown, is pieced together from quotation and self-quotation, all the characters constructed by the play, including the author Christopher Marlowe, are already inscribed in language and are pieced together from words.[12] In a humanist universe where people read for action and incorporate the writings of authorities into their own conduct, words are incorporated into bodies and become the substance of action and feeling. In the Renaissance, words are embodied and bodies are textualized in all kinds of ways.

In trying to recuperate the physical and emotive force of acting, which can lend authority to a play, Robert Weimann attacks performance studies that are based on literary preconceptions. He condemns their tendency to reduce everything, even material reality, to a text waiting to be deciphered and, moreover, to one that can only be deciphered by invoking other texts.[13] Instead, he promotes performance studies based on the acknowledgement that performance practice has a cultural poetics of its own and that it cannot be reduced to the textual. An important part of the meaning of a performance for Weimann lies in what he calls 'the game, the craft, and the craftiness of playing' and not in representation.[14] Performance is an act in its own right and deals in the immediacy of a rapport with a particular social occasion that a text cannot foresee. For Weimann, Renaissance theatre is made up of the interplay of presentation and representation. In the case of presentation, actors seek applause as the performer of a role in a game or entertainment, whereas in the case of representation actors attempt to give the illusion of character, but the two modes are permeable. Weimann's identification of two modes of performance makes sense of the so-called 'bad' bits of *Doctor Faustus*, including its moments of melodramatic exaggeration, of emotional grandstanding and of comedy. As Weimann notes, a bad text does not necessarily make a bad performance. Thus, we may well need to reconsider our dismissal of the comic scenes of *Doctor Faustus* which exploit the actors' slapstick skills and their affinity with jugglers, singers, mountebanks and other kinds of showmen because these comic scenes may succeed as impressive shows, even if they do not fulfil our literary expectations. In its repeated staging of performance, of spectatorship and of the charismatic presence of the hero, *Doctor Faustus* invites the audience to judge the play as playing and to consider the actor's charisma and its impact on the audience at a time when actors like Edward Alleyn, who took the role of Faustus, were making a name and acquiring prominent social and economic profiles.

Weimann's analysis is a significant contribution to the study of early modern drama and its analysis of the interplay of presentational and representational codes of performance is a brilliantly suggestive piece of criticism but, in other ways, Weimann's argument is impaired by a failure to incorporate the findings of the study of material culture. This is especially true of his characterization of writing, which is typical of performance studies in general. While playwrights were certainly exploring new ways of justifying their own claims to cultural significance, the rift between playing and writing, and between materiality and writing, is more characteristic of our post-Cartesian culture than of the Renaissance, when the philosophy of René Descartes had not yet privileged mind and separated it from what he saw as the debasement of nature and body. The study of material culture will eventually change performance studies as it highlights the fact that the Renaissance conceived of the relationship between materiality and meaning in ways that are unfamiliar to us, and recognized different problems and different opportunities in the relationships between texts and bodies.

At several points in his argument Weimann exaggerates the discrepancy between what is written and what is done, and this correlates uneasily with his argument that a play does not privilege either text or performance. For example, Weimann criticizes Derrida because 'the physical, corporeal, and, finally, existential components of [] histrionic transaction' cannot be subsumed under 'the absent imaginary world of the text', words which betray a tendency in Weimann, however much he states the necessity of doing the opposite, to reduce writing to an immaterial presence.[15] His desire to defend performance which has historically been devalued ends by creating the kind of imbalance that he criticizes. *Doctor Faustus,* and Renaissance attitudes to writing more generally, seem to confuse, if not to obliterate, the distinctions between the imaginary and the real, the abstract and the concrete, text and materiality. The business of distinguishing playwrights from acting practices and text from performance is more complicated than modern critics who wish to promote the text, like Harry Berger, would have us believe but, equally, more complex than critics who wish to promote performance, like Robert Weimann, would have us believe. Weimann still conceives of a text as being something without a body, as something that is alien to ritual and performance and has no somatic consequences. In the Renaissance, the text is not simply the conveyor of voice and we need to look again at the ways that writing was understood to relate to the world. In the Renaissance, writing is not something fixed and immutable with inherently more authority than orality, not just because of the vagaries of printing and manuscript production, but also because of the different ways that Renaissance readers and audiences understood writing.

The claim that there is a 'general rift between the order of the body and the order of texts' in the early modern period is not substantiated in *Doctor Faustus* where, to coin Weimann's own phrase, there is a 'mutual engagement of text and bodies'.[16] Faustus writes the deed whereby he covenants his soul to the devil in his own blood. When he cuts his arm and the blood congeals, Faustus queries, 'What might the staying of my blood portend? | Is it unwilling I should write this bill?' (II.i.64–65). His blood is eventually liquidized by the application of heat and Faustus completes the deed, a word which itself confuses text, in the form of a written deed, or deed of gift, with action, in the form of a deed as a gesture. However, once he has completed the deed, Faustus suddenly sees the following inscription on his arm: '*Homo, fuge!*'(II.i.81). Writing in blood resurfaces at the end of the play when Faustus repeats the bloody deed to confirm his vow to Lucifer (V.i.70–75). This scene is closer to the reality of Renaissance practice than might at first appear, because the Renaissance used body parts to create artefacts. For example, human hair was sometimes used for embroidery instead of silk thread and bracelets were also woven out of hair. Blood serves as ink in Faustus's deed of covenant, and the separation of world and word in this phrase, written in blood on a human arm, is impossible as the body becomes a text and the text becomes a body. Content and surface merge as meaning is inscribed on the surface of the skin and the boundaries between the physical object and the high matter of meaning collapse. The word becomes the world in the Renaissance in other ways as well, in the incorporation of biblical phrases into the articulation and practice of the self, for example. Books are physical objects with weight and volume and they make an appeal to the senses. Indeed, Renaissance books sometimes had lavender stuffed under their covers and could even appeal to the sense of smell.

Anagrams and ciphers play with language as a visual system, while puns play with language as an acoustic system. Puns run riot in the comic scenes of *Doctor Faustus*. For example, Robin's speech at I.iv.35–37, 'Mass, but for the name of French crowns a man were as good have as many English counters. And what should I do with these?' puns on crowns and counters. A 'crown' is the name of a French coin; the symbol of sovereignty; an alternative to the word 'summit'; a head, perhaps suggesting a head that has lost its hair because of venereal disease; and something with a circular form, which once again recalls the bawdy associations of the circle or ring. A 'counter', a word which also exists in the potentially obscene form of 'cunter', is one who counts; anything used in counting; anything used to keep a record in a game of chance; a piece in a game; an imitation coin of inferior metal; a counterfeit; something with no intrinsic value; the prison attached to the court of a mayor; the specific name of a prison in Southwark and in other towns and boroughs of England; and the contrary or opposite. The verb 'to counter' means to contradict; to dispute; to encounter, and so Robin hopes for a good many English enc(o)unters. The puns are both acoustic and visual and are related to slips of the tongue, eye and ear, to the kind of productive misunderstanding that sees and hears the word 'fustian' in the word 'Faustus' (I.iv.75). Slips of the tongue and eye are a place where the pressure of the body is registered on the text, just as Wagner mispronounces the name for the devil, Belial, and calls on 'Balioll and Belcher', with puns on belly-all and belching (I.iv.45–53). In both anagrams and puns, meanings fan out from the forms of words and meaning is an effect of language, and not something that exists behind, or prior to, its transposition into words. A playtext is not just transcribed speech, not only because, as Weimann claims, the actor exceeds the script, but also because there are occasions when writing exceeds speech. In anagrams and puns, the form of writing itself generates and embodies meaning.[17] When audiences and readers look at the characters in *Doctor Faustus* they see things that we do not see, and acknowledge dangers and opportunities that we do not readily acknowledge. While the performance of the actors certainly exceeds the script, the text also exceeds the actors and is more than the record of their speeches. *Doctor Faustus* stages effects that derive from the visual and acoustic shape of language, from words not only understood as transparent vehicles of reference but as pattern and form, and these effects can escape the control of actors as well as authors.

Doctor Faustus is a play that highlights the magical powers of language. Not only does the play remind us that Virgil was a magician (III.i.13–15), it is also constructed out of the pun on the word 'spell'. A 'spell' is a magical formula; a narration; or a sermon; while the verb 'to spell' means to talk; to contemplate; to preach; to dismantle words into their component elements; and to construct words by putting their components in order. The punning word 'spell' suggests that words precede reality, and that spelling, or the dis-assembly and re-assembly of words, can conjure up materiality. Marlowe's choice of a story of magic multiplies the possibilities for fruitful variation on the relation between performance, text and reality. For example, if we read *Doctor Faustus* out loud, or perform the play, do we then also raise the devil by reciting the same spells as Faustus does? According to some reports, during one early performance of *Doctor Faustus* there was an excess of embodiment as an extra devil suddenly appeared on stage. Writing after the event, William Prynne recalls:

the visible apparition of the devil on the stage at the Belsavage playhouse, in Queen Elizabeth's days, to the great amazement both of the actors and spectators, whiles they were there playing the History of Faustus, the truth of which I have heard from many now alive, who well remember it, there being some distracted with that fearful sight.[18]

The terrible event recorded by Prynne is a case of the action exceeding the script, but perhaps also a case of the script exceeding the action, an implicit acknowledgement that words do not always produce the intended results because they have the power to produce more than the audience, or the actors, or indeed the authors, bargained for. In other words, text can exceed performance, and the text itself is not fixed, flattening or delimited.

In *The Light in Troy*, Thomas Greene analyses the necromantic imagery that obsessed Renaissance culture.[19] The resurrection of Helen of Troy and Alexander the Great are expressions of this desire to talk with the dead, but the fact that the dead are relayed in manuscripts and print confers magical powers of resurrection and conjuration not only on writing, but on another kind of black art, the art of printing. Printing is inscribed in the text of *Doctor Faustus* in unexpected ways. Explosions were not only caused by fireworks and alchemical experiments in the Renaissance but also by the process used to make printer's ink. In the opening chorus there is a typographical error in the 1604 quarto which prints negromancy for necromancy (Prologue 25). I would prefer to think of such errors as motivated errors, as something akin to the pun, which displaces the opposition between accident and meaningful relation. Necromancy is a black art, a form of negromancy, as is printing. In *The Academy of Armory*, an encyclopedia of knowledge published in 1688, Randle Holme notes that the word 'devil' was printer's slang for the boys who remove printed sheets from the press:

the Press-Man sometimes have a Week Boy to take Sheets as they are Printed off the the [*sic*] Tympan; or run of Arrants: These Boys do in a Printing-House commonly black and dawb themselves; whence the Workmen do jocosely call them Devils, and sometimes Spirits, and sometimes Flies.[20]

Holme's book draws on the fashion for 'books of secrets' which transmitted trade secrets to a wider public. The genre was created by the printers who compiled the information and produced a new kind of technical literature. In the Renaissance, craft and manual industry had demeaning associations with the lower orders and ambitious authors, like Marlowe, are supposed to have avoided any associations with craft. However, books of secrets link artisanal knowledge with high science and offer readers empirical knowledge and another way of knowing nature. Similarly, in its explorations of the black arts, *Doctor Faustus* is not wholly divorced from the world of industry and acknowledges how bodies may become blackened or dirty through activity, and how bodies may bear the traces of the craft of writing which involves the exertion of pressure on the arm or on the page and leaves marks on the body.

The play may or may not be aware of 'devil' as printer's slang, but it nonetheless explores the devilish potential of printing, which was an activity that Protestantism, in particular, sought to recuperate for God. According to John Foxe, printing is essential to the Protestant reform movement, but *Doctor Faustus* is sceptical about print's ability to reform and civilize, and is responsive to its magical and dangerous properties, and to its ability to generate meanings that are distanced from mimetic referents. In the *Book of Martyrs*, Foxe argues that printing, writing, and reading produce enlightenment:

> Briefly, if there were no demonstration to lead, yet by this one argument of printing, the bishop of Rome might understand the counsel and purpose of the Lord to work against him, having provided such a way in earth, that almost how many printing presses there be in the world, so many block-houses there be against the high castle of St. Angelo; so that either the pope must abolish knowledge and printing, or printing at length will root him out.[21]

Earlier in this section, which is entitled 'The Invention and Benefit of Printing', Foxe states that the person responsible 'for the divine and miraculous invention of printing' (p. 718) was one John Faustus, although this is a different Faustus from the scholar who is the hero of the various stories of the damnation of Faust:

> The first inventor thereof (as most agree) is thought to be a German, dwelling first in Strasburg, afterwards citizen of Mentz [i.e., Mainz], named John Faustus, a goldsmith. The occasion of this invention first was by engraving the letters of the alphabet in metal; who then, laying black ink upon the metal, gave the form of letters in paper. The man being industrious and active, perceiving that, thought to proceed

further, and to prove whether it would frame as well in words, and in whole sentences, as it did in letters.

(p. 718)

William Camden has a different version of Faustus's contribution to the invention of printing, one in which Faustus is a thief. Camden's account is based on Adrien de Jonghe's *Batavia* (1588), a celebration of Dutch Protestantism and a polemical defence of the city of Harlem. Camden notes that printing was picked up by travellers to China but identifies the first European to cut letters as Lawrence Hans of Harlem, who,

> first cutt the formes of the lettres in tables, and so printed a small dutch booke called The looking glasse of saluation. Afterward he began to cast them in tynne and lead, and when he had brought them to some perfection he was robbed on a Christmas daye att night, of all his instrumentes by John Faustus who fled to Mentz in Germany.[22]

The wicked apprentice, John Faustus, stole his master's trade secret and ran away to profit from his misdeed. The publication of de Jonghe's story of the birth of printing in Harlem and the nefarious dealings of Faustus coincided with the appearance of the Faust legend with the result that myths of magic and printing gradually became interlinked. The printing press, like the emperor's court and Faustus's study, is a site where knowledge is created and transmitted, but contrary to Foxe's claims that print will advance the godly revolution, print is parodied as black magic in *Doctor Faustus*, both a way of dealing with the devil and a way of reproducing matter without order. *Doctor Faustus* does not present a normative history of the press but associates print with the multiplication of error and degeneration into heresy.

In *Doctor Faustus* meaning is not deducible from the text alone, but neither is it deducible from performance and spectacle alone. I remain sceptical about the rift between writing and performing in the Renaissance, a rift that suits the ideological investments of a post-Cartesian world where the senses and materiality are subordinated to intellect and meaning. Form can alter meaning, as different productions of the play make clear, because form itself is meaning, but this also applies to the form of writing. Writing is the transcription of speech, but it also has acoustic, symbolic and pictographic potential that separates it from mimesis. In all sorts of ways that are unfamiliar to us, *Doctor Faustus* reconfigures the relationship between playtext and performance, the metaphysical and the physical, meaning and the world, writing and the body.

Notes

1   All quotations are from David Bevington and Eric Rasmussen 'Doctor Faustus': A- and B-texts (1604, 1610) (Manchester: Manchester University Press, 1993). Although I quote from the A-text in this chapter, my argument applies to both A- and B-texts, and I find both texts to be equally valid. In the B-text, these lines are 'Only this, gentles: we must now perform | The form of Faustus' fortunes, good or bad' (Prologue 7–8).

2   Douglas Bruster and Robert Weimann, Prologues to Shakespeare's Theatre (London: Routledge, 2004), pp. 24–25, note that the actor who spoke a prologue traditionally wore black, was crowned with bay leaves and may have held a book, scroll, paper or staff. The appearance of the actor adds to the prologue's ambiguity. These props suggest competing sources of authority, for instance, in the playwright's words, or even a magician's staff, even as the actor appeals to the goodwill of the audience. Bruster and Weimann devote a chapter to Marlowe's prologues but do not discuss Doctor Faustus in detail except to note that the Prologue to Faustus plays with thresholds, notably the threshold between playing and writing (p. 89), and that the chorus is unreliable (p. 174).

3   Douglas Bruster, Shakespeare and the Question of Culture (New York: Palgrave Macmillan, 2003), pp. 65–93.

4   Emily C. Bartels, Spectacles of Strangeness: Imperialism, Alienation, and Marlowe (Philadelphia, PA: University of Pennsylvania Press, 1993), pp. 111–42.

5   Harry Berger, Jr, 'Bodies and Texts', Representations 17 (1987), pp. 144–66.

6   Julie Stone Peters, Theatre of the Book 1480–1880: Print, Text and Performance in Europe (Oxford: Oxford University Press, 2000).

7   Peters, Theatre of the Book, p. 109.

8   Adrian Johns, The Nature of the Book: Print and Knowledge in the Making (Chicago: University of Chicago Press, 1998).

9   Eric Partridge's Shakespeare's Bawdy: A Literary & Psychological Essay and a Comprehensive Glossary (1947) (London, Routledge, 1968), p. 79, notes that the word 'circle' means 'pudend'.

10   John Guillory, Cultural Capital: The Problem of Literary Canon Formation (Chicago: University of Chicago Press, 1993), pp. 3–82.

11   Both the clowning in the play and Faustus's attempts to materialize bodies through language parody sixteenth-century debates about the Eucharist. For a discussion of the Eucharist in relation to embodiment in Doctor Faustus, see Marjorie Garber, ' "Here's Nothing Writ": Scribe, Script, and Circumscription in Marlowe's Plays', Theatre Journal 36 (1984), pp. 308–20.

12   Patrick Cheney's Marlowe's Counterfeit Profession: Ovid, Spenser, Counter-Nationhood (Toronto: University of Toronto Press, 1997), pp. 190–220 offers a brilliant analysis of the play's engagement with Spenser and Ovid. On citation in Doctor Faustus, see also Clare Harraway, Re-citing Marlowe: Approaches to the Drama (Aldershot: Ashgate, 2000), pp. 31–33.

13   Robert Weimann, Author's Pen and Actor's Voice: Playing and Writing in Shakespeare's Theatre. See also Robert Weimann, 'Playing with a Difference: Revisiting "Pen" and "Voice" in Shakespeare's Theater', Shakespeare Quarterly 50 (New York, Cambridge University Press, 2000), pp. 415–32.

14   Weimann, 'Playing with a Difference', p. 426.

15   Weimann, 'Playing with a Difference', p. 427.

16   Weimann, 'Playing with a Difference', p. 420.

17   See Jonathan Culler, ed., Introduction, in On Puns: The Foundation of Letters, ed. Jonathan Culler (Oxford: Blackwell, 1988), p. 14 for a discussion of this

almost magical potential in words.

18   Quoted from David Bevington and Eric Rasmussen, Introduction, in *Doctor Faustus,* ed. David Bevington and Eric Rasmussen (Manchester: Manchester University Press, 1993), p. 2. The quotation is from Prynne's *Histrio-Mastix* (1633), Part 1, 556.

19   Thomas M. Greene, *The Light in Troy: Imitation and Discovery in Renaissance Poetry* (New Haven, CT: Yale University Press, 1982), pp. 28–53.

20   Randle Holme, *The Academy of Armory, or, A Storehouse of Armory and Blazon,* bk. 3, ch. 3 (Chester, 1688), p. 120. I have normalzsed the use of *s.*

21   *The Acts and Monuments of John Foxe,* ed. Rev. George Townsend, 8 vols (New York: AMS Press, 1965), III, pp. 720–21. For an extremely interesting discussion of the relationship between the Faust legend and printing, see also Harraway, *Re-citing Marlowe,* pp. 36–38 and especially Johns, *The Nature of the Book,* pp. 324–79.

22   Camden's notes on the history of printing are found in a miscellany, which includes drafts and notes for *The Remaines.* The section on printing consists of 30 lines and was written before 28 November 1598. It was first published in the 1614 edition of *The Remaines.* All details about Camden's notes on printing are taken from R. D. Dunn, 'Fragment of an Unpublished Essay on Printing by William Camden', *The British Library Journal* 12 (1986), pp. 145–49. The quotation is from p. 147.

CHAPTER EIGHT

A Survey of Resources

Sarah K. Scott

Doctor Faustus continues to be Marlowe's most popular and critically discussed play, owing to its captivating portrayal of the dangerously attractive Faustian bargain that promises to fulfil our least rational and most forbidden desires but instead results in our utter annihilation. Its fascinating depth and rich questioning are further complicated by the marked differences between its two notoriously different versions, known as the A-text (the 1604 quarto) and the B-text (the 1616 quarto). For these reasons and others, *Faustus* is a perennial favourite, appearing more frequently than any other work by Marlowe on university and college syllabi. In what follows, I offer a selection of resources that includes editions, critical studies, pedagogical essays and media-based resources to suggest pedagogical strategies, critical approaches and interpretative perspectives for those who teach the play.

Compared to Marlowe's other works, *Doctor Faustus* poses the greatest set of textual problems which, when considered in detail, can make the relatively easy task of selecting a text a challenging one. Of the two major versions, the 1616 quarto contains approximately 600 more lines than the 1604 quarto, mostly consisting of additional comic episodes inserted by revisers. The two playtexts are also dissimilar in numerous instances of phrasing, punctuation and spelling. They diverge in ideology and theology as well, which results in substantive differences in interpretation. In the past, the prevalence of conflated editions promoted the misinterpretation that a single, authoritative play could exist, which therefore pre-empted discussion of such textual issues. Presently, the dominant scholarly view holds that the A-text is the more authoritative, yet advocates that both versions are products of collaboration and are unique theatrical experiences, distinct yet related and equally worthy of study.

New and revised editions of *Doctor Faustus* are scheduled for release, in addition to the great number of those produced in the last quarter-century. Roma Gill, Michael Keefer, Ros King, David Ormerod and Christopher Wortham, Frank Romany and Robert Lindsey, and David Wooton produce versions that present the A-text in a single volume. Some include an appendix of the most significant additions and variants of the B-text. Sylvan Barnet and James H. Lake offer a version of the B-text. Other volumes print A and B in succession, which promotes the idea that each one can be studied either independently or in concert. Such editions include those by David Bevington and Eric Rasmussen, Mark Thornton Burnett, W. W. Greg and David Scott Kastan. A trend that may emerge is the parallel text format that displays the A- and B-texts on facing pages. Bevington and Rasmussen intend to publish in 2010 a Revels edition that responds to an increase in scholarly and pedagogical interest in textual studies.

In reaction to these developments, several recent essays offer useful strategies for teaching *Faustus*. Andrew Duxfield's 'Teaching & Learning Guide for Modern Problems of Editing: The Two Texts of Marlowe's *Doctor Faustus*' presents a 12-week syllabus exploring the current state of textual scholarship in early modern studies. The course asks that students analyse editing decisions that lead to the creation of texts that depart substantively from source texts. As students engage in their study, they become familiar with editing and printing practices, develop an understanding of the problems involved in producing texts and acquire fluency with important early modern works. Complementing this syllabus is Duxfield's essay 'Modern Problems of Editing: The Two Texts of Marlowe's *Doctor Faustus*', which examines many theoretical challenges faced by scholars and editors. Leah Marcus shares her approach to teaching the textual complexities of *Doctor Faustus* in her essay 'Texts That Won't Stand Still'. Students who investigate differences in the treatment of predestination and free will in the A- and B-texts engage in the important work of comparative close reading, which in turn enables them to be 'better able to understand the complexity of moral choice in the play and feel more confident in drawing their own conclusions'.[1] Marcus finds that this practice can then lead to a study of the ways that modern editors influence our readings. They reflect, for example, gender biases in the editorial treatment of Helen of Troy's second appearance to Faustus. Although she argues that such an approach works best for graduate and upper-division honours courses, Marcus finds that engaging in more concentrated editing exercises with a broader student population is equally rewarding because students engage in lines of questioning that lead to the development of their own interpretative lenses. Stevie Simkin and Lisa Hopkins also advocate this approach in small increments in introductory or survey courses. Both observe that much can be gained by asking students to analyse the implications of the difference of a single word. A world of theological questioning may emerge from a discussion of the Good Angel's use of 'can' at II.iii.79 in the A-text ('Never too late, if Faustus can repent') versus the use of 'will' at II.iii.80 in the B-text ('Never too late, if Faustus will repent').[2] Such conversations lead, for instance, to discussions of Renaissance theology and to questions of free will.

Thomas Akstens proposes a useful cultural studies approach that responds to student inquiry into the nature and role of devils in 'Contextualizng the Demonic: Marlowe's *Dr. Faustus* in the Classroom'. To explore early modern conceptions of the demonic that students find at once familiar and strange, Akstens encourages examination of the play's treatment of devils in III.24–27, IV.44–53, and V.144–47 (Roma Gill's B-text), along with a study of medieval and early modern visual art (including the 1616 quarto woodcut) as a means to discover early modern conceptions of the demonic. He asks students to consider early modern theatregoers' complex understandings of these issues in the context of the cycle plays, which frequently combine comic treatments of devils with deadly serious ones, and to compare these understandings to present-day representations of the demonic in popular film, including *Damn Yankees*, *Bedazzled* and *The Exorcist*.

Lisa Hopkins offers three approaches to teaching *Faustus* in the chapter 'Marlowe' in *Teaching Shakespeare and Early Modern Dramatists*. She first suggests that the drama be read together with John Ford's *'Tis Pity She's a Whore* to present a contrast between two forms of illicit knowledge (i.e. necromancy and incest, respectively). Second, she writes that students may make profitable comparisons between attitudes toward the New World by examining *Faustus* in conjunction with Thomas Hariot's *A briefe and true report of the new found land of Virginia*. Hopkins also advocates pairing the play with *Hamlet* to illuminate both the significance of Wittenberg during the Reformation and the ways that the two plays subtly pose political questions through their use of the *translatio imperii*, the widely circulating fictional story serving to legitimize English rule by claiming that English monarchs derive their power from Aeneas's grandson, Brutus of Troy. Other plays frequently studied in conjunction with *Doctor Faustus* include *Everyman*, *Mankind*, Nathaniel Woodes's *The Conflict of Conscience* and William Shakespeare's *Macbeth* and *The Tempest*.

A Preface to Marlowe by Stevie Simkin features user-friendly discussions of the playwright and his work that act as another resource to understanding the drama's central themes and questions. Part One, 'The Writer and His Setting', addresses the facts and myths surrounding Marlowe's life and the religious, political and social climate of early modern England as it relates to the role of the theatre and the business of playgoing. Part Two, 'Critical Survey', provides critically informed discussions of the sources, cultural contexts and major themes of the works. The chapter 'Of Gods and Men: *Doctor Faustus*' surveys the Faust legend, the *English Faust Book* and the morality play tradition from which the play emerges. It includes an investigation into the A- and B-texts, the idea of Faustus as tragic hero, the treatment of the questions of free will and predestination and the play's structure with an eye to performance history.

Patrick Cheney's *The Cambridge Companion to Christopher Marlowe* is another valuable guidebook. Several essays address aspects of *Doctor Faustus*: 'Marlovian Texts and Authorship' by Laurie E. Maguire discusses the complicated history of modern edited editions; 'Marlowe and the Politics of Religion' by Paul Whitfield White analyses the play's sceptical attitudes toward religion and politics; Richard Wilson's 'Tragedy, Patronage, and Power' investigates Faustus's desire for power and Marlowe's relationship to authority; Garrett A. Sullivan Jr's 'Geography and Identity in Marlowe' explores the interrelatedness of the physical and mental landscapes of *Doctor Faustus* to reveal a fascination with the new global geography analogous to Faustus's aspiring, worldly mind; and Lois Potter's 'Marlowe in Theatre and Film' discusses the play's performance history. Thomas Healy's '*Doctor Faustus*', the one essay in the volume dedicated solely to the play, examines the relationships of the A and B versions to the world of the early modern commercial theatre and its audiences. Healy interprets both playtexts as metaphysical tragedies that seek to teach and delight as a response to the moral, religious and political issues of the period. He argues further that the versions deliberately leave open the challenging and potentially dangerous questions that they pose.

Several online resources related to Marlowe studies could be incorporated into such pedagogical approaches to the play, although one must take care to avoid the numerous websites presenting non-professional scholarship, such as those attempting to advance unsubstantiated claims that Marlowe wrote under the name 'Shakespeare' after faking his death in a tavern brawl.

Of those sites most reputable and instrumental to *Doctor Faustus*, the best is *The Complete Works of Christopher Marlowe*, developed by Perseus Project at Tufts University under the guidance of Hilary Binda.³ Since its construction, the site remains the most noteworthy and useful for investigations into the play's textual complexities. Both the A- and B-texts are represented in fully searchable linked versions in modern and original spelling thus allowing for easily accessible comparisons. Additionally, these versions are linked to the *English Faust Book*, allowing analysis of the play's primary source material. Another useful internet resource is 'The Magician, the Heretic, and the Playwright' located on the area of the W. W. Norton site dedicated to sixteenth-century studies.⁴ These pages contain biographical and cultural background specific to the study of Marlowe and *Doctor Faustus*. Excerpts of material from the period on the topics of necromancy and divine punishment provide opportunities to inquire more fully and directly into the worlds of Marlowe, Faustus and early modern England. The pages dedicated to Marlowe on Luminarium also present helpful starting points for initial investigations into Marlowe's life and work.⁵ Perhaps the most useful aspect of the site is the set of links directing viewers to present-day critical essays on the drama, affording exploration into an array of topics.

Another resource for students and scholars is the Marlowe Society of America (MSA) website, www.mightyline.org. A non-profit organization composed primarily of academics, scholars and upper-level graduate students, the MSA offers its members information regarding recent and current events related to Marlowe as well as access to present and back issues of the *Marlowe Society of America Newsletter*, a publication that includes book and performance reviews and an annual listing of recent scholarship in all areas of Marlowe studies.

The internet presents more websites and pages related to Marlowe than most other early modern English writers. A section on Marlowe's works, for instance, is under consideration for inclusion in the Metadata Offer New Knowledge (MONK) Project (http://monkproject.org), a scholarly web engine. An ambitious project supported by numerous cooperating academic organizations, MONK will allow for 'both micro analyses of the verbal texture of an individual text and macro analyses that [...] locate texts in the context of a large document space consisting of hundreds or thousands of other texts'.[6] The addition of Marlowe's works to WordHoard would supply yet another outlet for textual investigations. Developed by Northwestern University under the sponsorship of Martin Mueller, WordHoard allows for the annotation of texts 'by morphological, lexical, prosodic, and narratological criteria'.[7] The presence of the Marlowe canon in these engines would create sites that complement the work of the Perseus Project while providing users the ability to engage in further levels of questioning and thus the ability to conduct more complex queries.

Despite the play's continued popularity on the professional and amateur stage, only one film of *Doctor Faustus* exists, the 1968 Richard Burton and Nevill Coghill production. Educational recordings of selected scenes are also available: *Marlowe's Faust: Parts I and II*, directed by Carl Heap with the Bridge Lane Theatre in London (1997) and *Marlowe's Doctor Faustus: Parables of Power: Part III*, directed by John D. Mitchell with the Institute for Advanced Studies in the Theatre Arts (1988). Although these films afford opportunities to analyse the play through juxtaposition of dramatic performance and textual study, many students will find them rather dusty and outmoded, thus possibly limiting rather than enhancing their engagement. Another approach to incorporating film media in the classroom (though copyright issues may complicate availability) would be to contact the directors of recent productions to request copies of performances for educational purposes. Videos can also prove helpful when used in concert with performance-based methods for study. Encouraging students to perform various scenes may illuminate central themes and demonstrate the importance of textual variations while making Marlowe's drama come alive. Despite the scarcity of media resources specifically related to *Doctor Faustus*, the popularity of its foundational myth continues in its numerous and wide-ranging adaptations in opera, popular music, film and television, all of which may provide opportunities for the development of courses exploring the trajectory and import of the Faust story.

In addition to these pedagogically orientated essays and media resources, many other important contributions to the study of the play by leading scholars can be fruitfully integrated into classroom discussions to address the pleasures, powers and intricacies of *Doctor Faustus*. The annotated bibliography below suggests further book chapters and critical essays that interrogate a range of topics through an even wider variety of interpretive lenses.

Annotated Bibliography

Collected works

Bevington, David and Rasmussen, Eric, eds, *Christopher Marlowe: Doctor Faustus and Other Plays* (Oxford: Oxford University Press, 1998). A modern spelling version of the A- and B-texts with a general introduction to Marlowe's life and plays (excluding *Dido, Queen of Carthage* and *The Massacre at Paris*). Includes a discussion of the textual problems of *Faustus* and a glossary.

Bowers, Fredson, ed., *The Complete Works of Christopher Marlowe*, 2 vols (Cambridge: Cambridge University Press, 1973). Volume 2 presents an old spelling edition of the B-text and an important essay detailing the rationale for understanding the B-text as produced from authorial manuscript, with exceptions including additions by William Birde and Samuel Rowley. The 1981 edition includes textual emendations.

Burnett, Mark Thornton, ed., *Christopher Marlowe: The Complete Plays* (London: J. M. Dent, 1999). A modern spelling Everyman edition of both A and B versions featuring an introduction, glossary, play summaries and listing of geographical, historical and mythological names.

Gill, Roma, ed., *The Complete Works of Christopher Marlowe*, 5 vols (Oxford: Clarendon University Press, 1987–98). Volume 2 (1990) features the A-text in original spelling with some normalization. Contains an introduction and commentary as well as appendices of the *English Faust Book* and B-text additions.

Romany, Frank and Lindsey, Robert, eds, *Christopher Marlowe: The Complete Plays* (New York: Penguin, 2003). Presents a modern spelling version of the A-text with an introduction, glossary and list of mythological, historical and geographical names.

Single text editions

Barnet, Sylvan, ed., *Christopher Marlowe: Dr. Faustus* (New York: Signet, 2001). Offers a modern spelling edition following the B-text and includes an introduction, selections from the *English Faust Book* and critical essays on the play's form and structure as well as two discussions on performance.

Bevington, David and Rasmussen, Eric, eds, *'Doctor Faustus': A- and B-texts (1604, 1616)* (Manchester: Manchester University Press, 1993). The present gold standard. A modern spelling version of the A- and B-texts. Substantial introduction includes a thorough discussion of sources, history, form, structure, style, performance history and central themes. A new Revels student edition featuring the A- and B-texts on facing pages is scheduled for 2009/10.

Greg, W. W., ed., *Marlowe's Doctor Faustus. 1604–1616: Parallel Texts* (1950) (Oxford: The Clarendon Press, 1968). This groundbreaking modern spelling, parallel text edition of the A- and B-texts includes an extensive introduction that argues for the superiority of the B-text.

Kastan, David Scott, ed., *Christopher Marlowe: Doctor Faustus* (New York: W. W. Norton, 2005). A modern spelling version of the A- and B-texts featuring a well selected collection of texts from the period, including the Baines note, excerpts of the *English Faust Book* and Reginald Scot's *The Discoverie of Witchcraft,* as well as critical essays by early and modern critics on topics including magic, religion and performance.

Keefer, Michael, ed., *Doctor Faustus: A 1604-Version* (Peterborough, Ontario: Broadview Press, 2007). An edition of the A-text including substantial introduction, scenes from the B-text, excerpts from the *English Faust Book* and selections from the writings of Cornelius Agrippa and John Calvin.

King, Ros, ed. *Doctor Faustus*, New Mermaids Series (London: Methuen, 2009). A modern spelling edition of the A-text with introduction, notes, and scenes from the B-text.

Lake, James H. and Ribner, Irving, eds., *Christopher Marlowe's Doctor Faustus: With Introduction, Essays, and Notes* (Newburyport, MA: Focus Publishing, 2004). A revised edition of Irving Ribner's modern spelling edition of the B-text (*Christopher Marlowe's Doctor Faustus: Texts and Major Criticism* [New York: Macmillan, 1985]). Features an introduction, questions for critical study of text and performance and interviews with Ralph Alan Cohen, director of the American Shakespeare Center's 2000 production and Andreas Teuber, actor performing Mephistopheles in Nevill Coghill's 1966 Oxford Playhouse production and the 1967 film.

Ormerod, David and Wortham, Christopher, eds, *Christopher Marlowe: Dr. Faustus: The A-Text* (Nedlands: University of Western Australia Press, 1985). The first of recent modern spelling editions of the A-text. Includes an extensive introduction focusing on early modern magic and the occult.

Wootton, David, ed., *Christopher Marlowe: Doctor Faustus with the English Faust Book* (Indianapolis, IN: Hackett, 2005). A modern spelling edition of the A-text and the *English Faust Book* with an introduction that includes a discussion of early modern magic and religion.

Texts on Early English books Online

The English Faust Book
THE / HISTORIE / of the damnable / life, and the deserued death of / *Doctor Iohn Faustus*, / Newly imprinted, and in conueni- / *ent places imperfect matter amended*. / according to the true Copie printed / at Franckfort, *and translated into* / *English by* P.F. *Gent*. / Seene and allowed. / [Device] / *Imprinted at London by Thomas Orwin, and are to be* / solde by Edward White, dwelling at the little North / doore of Paules, at the signe of the Gun. 1592. STC 10711.

The 1604 A-text
THE / TRAGICALL / History of D. Faustus. / *As it hath bene Acted by the Right* / *Honourable the Earle of Nottingham his seruants*. / Written by Ch. Marl. / [Device] / LONDON / Printed by V. S. for Thomas Bushell. 1604. STC 17429.

The 1616 B-text
The Tragicall History / of the Life and Death / of *Doctor Faustus*. / Written by Ch. Marklin. / [Woodcut of Faustus conjuring a devil] / *LONDON*, / Printed for *Iohn Wright*, and are to be sold at his shop / without Newgate, at the si[gne] of the Bibl[e] 1616. STC 17432.

Concordances
Fehrenbach, Robert J., *et al*., eds., *A Concordance to the Plays, Poems, and Translations of Christopher Marlowe* (Ithaca, NY: Cornell University Press, 1983). An index based upon Bowers's *Complete Works, supra*.

Ule, Louis, ed., *A Concordance to the Works of Christopher Marlowe*, The Elizabethan Concordance Series (Hildesheim: Georg Olms Verlag, 1979). Includes an A- and B-text index drawn from C. F. Tucker Brooke's A-text (in *The Works of Christopher Marlowe* [Oxford: The Clarendon Press, 1910]) and the British Library 1616 quarto. Available at Google Books Online.

Selected textual scholarship and criticism (essays and book chapters)

Akstens, Thomas, 'Contextualizing the Demonic: Marlowe's *Doctor Faustus* in the Classroom', in *Approaches to Teaching English Renaissance Drama*, ed. Karen Bamford and Alexander Leggatt (New York: Modern Language Association, 2002), pp. 186–90. Illustrates the merits of a cultural studies approach to teaching *Doctor Faustus* with a multiple-staged assignment addressing comparisons between present-day and early modern conceptions of the demonic.

Bartels, Emily, 'Demonizing Magic: Patterns of Power in *Doctor Faustus*', in *Spectacles of Strangeness: Imperialism, Alienation, and Marlowe* (Philadelphia, PA: University of Pennsylvania Press, 1993), pp. 112–42. Demonstrates that Marlowe's depiction of Faustus as a practitioner of black magic shows the European subject as Other to himself and asserts that it is Mephistopheles and not God (or Protestant beliefs about God) who exerts power over Faustus to create an internal conflict that ultimately controls and contains him.

Belsey, Catherine, 'Doctor Faustus and Knowledge in Conflict', in *Marlowe*, ed. Avraham Oz (New York: Palgrave, 2003), pp. 163–71. Examines discursive, empirical and contemplative forms of knowledge in medieval plays including *Mankind*, *Apius and Virginia*, *The Castle of Perseverance* and *The Marriage of Wit and Wisdom*, leading to a discussion of the problematization of these forms in *Doctor Faustus*. Appeared originally in Catherine Belsey, *The Subject of Tragedy: Identity and Difference in Renaissance Drama* (London: Methuen, 1985), pp. 55–75.

Bevington, David, '*The Conflict of Conscience* and *Doctor Faustus*', in *From 'Mankind' to Marlowe: Growth of Structure in the Popular Drama* (Cambridge, MA: Harvard University Press, 1962), pp. 245–62. Discusses *Doctor Faustus* as part of a long morality play and *psychomachia* tradition. Examines the drama's structural logic and homiletic characteristics and compares the play to Nathaniel Woodes's *The Conflict of Conscience*.

Bevington, David, 'Staging the A- and B-texts of *Doctor Faustus*', in *Marlowe's Empery: Expanding His Critical Contexts*, ed. Sara Munson Deats and Robert A. Logan (Newark, DE: University of Delaware Press, 2002), pp. 43–60. Compares the staging requirements of the A- and B-texts, exploring early modern audience expectations and examining resulting variations in ideological and doctrinal messages. Finds that enhancements to the B-text, including the increased presence of devils, comic additions and the graphic rendering of hell, create a more deterministic, theatrically charged play.

Bevington, David, 'One Hell of an Ending: Staging Last Judgment in the Towneley Plays and in *Doctor Faustus* A and B', in *'Bring furth the pagants': Essays in Early English Drama Presented to Alexandra F. Johnston*, ed. David N. Klausner and Karen Sawyer Marsalek (Toronto: University of Toronto Press, 2007), pp. 292–310. Examines the parallels between the B-text's depiction of hell and those of the Wakefield Master's *Harrowing of Hell* and *Last Judgment*, finding that the B-text, like the medieval plays discussed, emphasizes the importance of good works for salvation. Argues that the play's revisions were made to promote commercial success.

Deats, Sara Munson, 'The Rejection of the Feminine in *Doctor Faustus*', in *Sex, Gender, and Desire in the Plays of Christopher Marlowe* (Newark, DE: University of Delaware Press, 1997), pp. 202–24. An important feminist psychoanalytical argument that the A-text depicts the horrors of a world devoid of feminine characteristics, including those associated with benevolent Christianity and a range of transgressive phenomena. Deats also reads the play as an integration of two competing theatrical modes, the 'emblematic' (medieval, allegorical) and the 'illusionist' (psychological realism).

Deats, Sara Munson, '"Mark this show"': Magic and Theater in Marlowe's *Doctor* Faustus', in *Placing the Plays of Christopher Marlowe: Fresh Cultural Contexts*, ed. Sara Munson Deats and Robert A. Logan (Aldershot: Ashgate, 2008), pp. 14–24. Asserts that the play interrogates conflicting early modern attitudes toward the magician and the poet, and magic and the theatre, concluding that Faustus's complex relationship toward magic comments upon Marlowe's ambivalence toward the theatre.

Dollimore, Jonathan, '*Dr Faustus* (c. 1589–92): Subversion Through Transgression', in *Radical Tragedy: Religion, Ideology and Power in the Drama of Shakespeare and his Contemporaries* (Chicago: University of Chicago Press, 1984), pp. 109–19. Argues that *Doctor Faustus* interrogates early modern Protestant ideologies through its depiction of Faustus's transgression against constructed notions of a Protestant God, creating a deep, inescapable internal conflict leading to damnation. Appears in the following Marlowe essay collections: Avraham, Oz, ed., *Marlowe* (New York: Palgrave, 2003) and Richard Wilson, ed., *Christopher Marlowe* (Harlow: Longman, 1999).

Duxfield, Andrew, 'Modern Problems of Editing: The Two Texts of Marlowe's *Doctor Faustus*', *Literature Compass* 2 (2005), pp. 1–14. A lively, informative analysis of the editorial challenges and poststructuralist textual debates surrounding the play.

Duxfield, Andrew, 'Teaching & Learning Guide for: Modern Problems of Editing: The Two Texts of Marlowe's *Doctor Faustus*', *Literature Compass* 5 (2008), pp. 681–84. Provides a 12-week syllabus for an upper-division textual studies course on 'Marlowe, Shakespeare and the Modern Edition'.

Gatti, Hilary, 'Bruno and Marlowe: *Doctor Faustus*', in *Christopher Marlowe*, ed. Richard Wilson (London: Longman, 1999), pp. 246–65. A new historicist approach that traces parallels between Faustus and Giordano Bruno and compares Mephistopheles to the Grand Inquisitor. Reprinted from Hilary Gatti, *The Renaissance Drama of Knowledge: Giordano Bruno in England* (London: Routledge, 1989), pp. 89–113.

Greenblatt, Stephen, 'Marlowe and the Will to Absolute Play', in *Renaissance Self-Fashioning: From More to Shakespeare* (Chicago: University of Chicago Press, 1980), pp. 193–221. A new historicist examination of ways in which Marlowe stages rebellious characters and subversive acts that are solidly contained within the dominant culture.

Halpern, Richard, 'Marlowe's Theatre of Night: *Doctor Faustus* and Capital', *English Literary History* 71 (2004), pp. 455–95. A Marxist-influenced investigation into the material and economic conditions of the playwright, the stage and the theatre. Argues that the metatheatrical aspects of *Doctor Faustus* reflect both the playwright's relationship to forms of capital exchange and the drama's representations of commodification. Discusses theological and philosophical forms of privation (lack of the good) as expressed by St Augustine, Cornelius Agrippa and Francis Bacon.

Hamlin, William H., 'Casting Doubt in Marlowe's *Doctor Faustus*', *Studies in English Literature* 41(2001), pp. 257–75. Investigates the question of early modern scepticism as it relates to *Doctor Faustus* through the study of early modern Pyrrhonian and academic texts. Explores the relationships between desire and doubt, in part through an analysis of the effects of Faustus's employment of first- and third-person pronouns.

Hammill, Graham L., ' "The Forme of Faustus Fortunes": Knowledge, Spectatorship, and the Body in Marlowe's *Doctor Faustus*', in *Sexuality and Form: Caravaggio, Marlowe, and Bacon* (Chicago: University of Chicago Press, 2000), pp. 97–127. Asserts that Faustus's relationship to the subjectivity of literary language and forms of capital creates his downfall. Understands the play to participate in the early modern hermeneutics of sodomy.

Harraway, Clare, 'Rewriting *Doctor Faustus*', in *Re-citing Marlowe: Approaches to the Drama* (Aldershot: Ashgate, 2000), pp.

25–50. A deconstructionist and psychoanalytical approach to reading *Doctor Faustus* that responds to a heightened awareness of the relationships between textual and interpretative issues. Finds that Faustus's failure to recognize the limits of memory, which are related to written texts, the processes of writing and the instability of language, is the cause of his tragic fall.

Hopkins, Lisa, 'Marlowe', in *Teaching Shakespeare and Early Modern Dramatists*, ed. Andrew Hiscock and Lisa Hopkins (Basingstoke: Palgrave, 2007), pp. 42–53. Offers teachers of Marlowe a brief chronology, a summary of criticism since the 1960s and a number of approaches to teaching the plays. Includes lists of complementary readings as well as helpful questions for discussion.

Keefer, Michael H., 'The A and B Texts of Marlowe's *Doctor Faustus* Revisited', *Papers of the Bibliographical Society of America* 100 (2006), pp. 227–57. Reasons that the A-text was likely printed from 'heterogeneous manuscript' and that speeches in II.i, II.iii and III.i in the B-text afford fuller, more authentic readings than those appearing in the A-text.

Kuriyama, Constance, 'Dr. Greg and *Doctor Faustus*: The Supposed Originality of the 1616 Text', *English Literary Renaissance* 5 (1975), pp. 171–97. An early argument for the superiority of the A-text on aesthetic and textual grounds.

Kuriyama, Constance, 'Omnipotence', in *Hammer or Anvil: Psychological Patterns in Christopher Marlowe's Plays* (New Brunswick, NJ: Rutgers University Press, 1980), pp. 95–135. Presents a psychoanalytical lens through which to read Marlowe and *Doctor Faustus*. Discusses Faustus's problematic father-son relationships, fears of effeminization and submission, and attraction to dark magic.

Levin, Harry, 'Science Without Conscience', in *The Overreacher: A Study of Christopher Marlowe* (Cambridge, MA: Harvard University Press, 1952), pp. 108–35. An important study of Faustus as overreacher and magician. Compares Faustus to the figures of Icarus, Simon Magus and Cornelius Agrippa and to the Faust of Goethe and the *English Faust Book*. Discusses the drama in relation to the medieval morality play tradition as well as to plays of the period, including Robert Greene's *Friar Bacon and Friar Bungay*, John Lyly's *Galatea*, William Shakespeare's *The Tempest* and *Hamlet* and Pedro Calderón's *El Mágico Prodigioso*. Considers also *Doctor Faustus*'s structural design and textual issues.

Logan, Robert A., ' "Glutted with Conceit": Imprints of *Doctor Faustus* on *Macbeth* and *The Tempest*', in *Shakespeare's*

Marlowe: The Influence of Christopher Marlowe on Shake-speare's Artistry (Aldershot: Ashgate, 2008), pp. 197–229. A thorough examination of the linguistic, dramaturgical and doctrinal influences of *Doctor Faustus* on William Shakespeare's *Macbeth* and *The Tempest*. Includes a valuable discussion of the psychological semblances of Faustus to Macbeth and Prospero. Appears also in *Placing the Plays of Christopher Marlowe*, ed. Sara Munson Deats and Robert A. Logan.

Lopez, David, 'The Philosophy of Death in Christopher Marlowe's *Doctor Faustus*', in *Spanish Studies in Shakespeare and His Contemporaries*, ed. José Manuel González (Newark, DE: University of Delaware Press, 2006), pp. 219–33. Argues Faustus refuses to recognize death as a form of being, thus resulting in damnation best characterized as nothingness.

Lucking, David, 'Our Devils Now are Ended: A Comparative Analysis of *The Tempest* and *Doctor Faustus*', *Dalhousie Review* 80 (2000), pp. 15–67. An exploration of the parallels between the two dramas, with particular emphasis on the uses of magic, time, metadrama and sub-plot.

Marcus, Leah S., 'Textual Instability and Ideological Difference: the Case of *Doctor Faustus*', in *Unediting the Renaissance: Shake-speare, Marlowe, Milton* (London: Routledge, 1996), pp. 38–67. An important investigation into the ways in which the 1604, 1616 and 1668 editions can be understood to reflect the ideologies that produced them as well as the biases of present-day editors, many of whom attempt to recover the play's alleged textual integrity as though a definitive version exists as a lost original. Questions the notion of single authorship. An earlier version of this chapter appears in Leah Marcus, 'Textual Indeterminacy and Ideological Difference: the Case of *Doctor Faustus*', *Renaissance Drama* (1989), pp. 1–29.

Marcus, Leah S., 'Texts That Won't Stand Still', in *Approaches to Teaching English Renaissance Drama*, ed. Karen Bamford and Alexander Leggatt (New York: Modern Language Association, 2002), pp. 29–34. Provides useful undergraduate- and graduate-level approaches for practising textual studies in the classroom that utilize both A- and B-texts. Also suggests an approach to examining relationships between editorial choices and the representation of gender.

Melnikoff, Kirk, ' "[I]ygging vaines" and "riming mother wits": Marlowe, Clowns and the Early Frameworks of Dramatic Authorship', *Early Modern Literary Studies*, Special Issue, 16 (2007): 1–37. Investigates ways in which the English clowning tradition informs the worlds of the A-text *Doctor Faustus* and *The Jew of Malta*.

Mitchell, Michael, 'Standing and *Falling*: Marlowe's *Doctor Faustus*', in *Hidden Mutualities: Faustian Themes from Gnostic Origins to the Postcolonial* (Amsterdam: Rodopi, 2006), pp. 51–77. Analyses *Doctor Faustus* within the gnostic-hermetic tradition. Utilizes Jungian psychology of archetypes to interpret Faustus's desires and drives.

Pettitt, Thomas, 'Formulaic Dramaturgy in *Doctor Faustus*', in *Marlowe: A Poet and a Filthy Play-maker*, ed. Kenneth Friedenreich, Roma Gill and Constance Brown Kuriyama (New York: AMS Press, 1988), pp. 167–91. Finds that Elizabethan drama employs formulas similar to those used in oral narratives. Examines the function of dramaturgical elements in the A- and B-texts, including formalized action, dumb shows and clowning scenes.

Poole, Kristen, 'Dr. *Faustus* and Reformation Theology', in *Early Modern English Drama: A Critical Companion*, ed. Garrett A. Sullivan Jr, Patrick Cheney and Andrew Hadfield (Oxford: Oxford University Press, 2006), pp. 96–107. Discusses Faustus as a Renaissance man caught in the tangle of doctrinal contradictions produced by competing medieval and Reformation theologies. Asserts that the play's representation of these conflicts produces a deliberately unclear moral lesson in the B-text.

Poole, Kristen, 'The Devil's in the Archive: *Doctor Faustus* and Ovidian Physics', *Renaissance Drama* 35 (2006), pp. 191–219. Argues that the drama's depictions of the demonic reflect early modern Ovidian conceptions of metamorphosis through the play's emphasis on literal, physical and psychological forms of transformation.

Proser, Matthew, 'Dr. *Faustus* and The Limits of Learning', in *The Gift of Fire: Aggression and the Plays of Christopher Marlowe* (New York: Peter Lang, 1995), pp. 139–65. A psychoanalytical approach demonstrating that Faustus's fall results from his recognition of disillusionment.

Ricks, Christopher, '*Doctor Faustus* and Hell on Earth', *Essays in Criticism* 35 (1985), pp. 101–20. Examines the significance of the composition and performance of *Doctor Faustus* during a period riddled by the plague. Addresses the ironies of the Faustian bargain in this context.

Roberts, Gareth, 'Necromantic Books: Christopher Marlowe, *Doctor Faustus* and Agrippa of Nettesheim', in *Christopher Marlowe and English Renaissance Culture*, ed. J. A. Downie and

J. T. Parnell (Burlington, VT: Ashgate, 1996), pp. 148–71. Finds that Agrippa's *De Occulta* and *De Vanitate* are reflected in Faustus's attitudes toward magic. Suggests that Marlowe knew these works well.

Roberts, Gareth, 'Marlowe and the Metaphysics of Magicians', in *Constructing Christopher Marlowe*, ed. J. A. Downie and J. T. Parnell (Burlington, VT: Ashgate, 2000), pp. 55–73. Shows that *Doctor Faustus* exhibits a pluralistic understanding of early modern magic in both the 1604 and 1616 versions.

Shepherd, Simon, 'Making Persons', in *Marlowe and the Politics of Elizabethan Theatre* (New York: St Martin's Press, 1986), pp. 72–109. An investigation into early modern constructions of social, political, moral and emotional identities and an examination of public and private forms of governance that create and disrupt order. Analyses *Doctor Faustus* as an example of the powers of theatrical presentation and the dynamics of audience reception.

Sinfield, Alan, 'Reading Faustus's God', in *Critical Essays on Christopher Marlowe*, ed. Emily Bartels (New York: G. K. Hall, 1997), pp. 192–99. An important essay interpreting both the A- and B-texts as solidly Protestant plays deeply concerned with registering the problems of predestination and repentance as expressed by Lutheran and Calvinist doctrine. Asserts that since the plays are products of Protestant theology, Faustus's efforts to repent are futile because he is already damned. Recognizes, however, that both texts are indeterminate enough to allow for modernist questions of free will. Reprinted from Alan Sinfield, *Faultlines: Cultural Materialism and the Politics of Dissident Reading* (Berkeley, CA: University of California Press, 1992), pp. 230–37.

Snow, Edward A, ' "Doctor Faustus" and the Ends of Desire', in *Christopher Marlowe*, ed. Harold Bloom (New York: Chelsea House, 1986), pp. 171–81. A phenomenological investigation into Marlowe's deliberately ambiguous use of the word 'end' in the play, finding it to be related to a wide range of phenomena associated with forms of desire. Provides a detailed reading of Faustus's opening soliloquy.

Stockholder, Kay, ' "Within the massy entrails of the earth": Faustus's Relation to Women', in *A Poet and a Filthy Play-maker: New Essays on Christopher Marlowe*, ed. Kenneth Friedenreich, Roma Gill and Constance Kuriyama (New York: AMS Press, 1988), pp. 203–19. A psychoanalytically informed discussion examining the relationship between Faustus's practice of forbidden magic and his heterosexual desires. Concludes that

Faustus chooses a state of unconsummated, heterosexual hell rather than submit to a paternalistic, domineering God.

Sullivan, Garrett A., ' "If he can remember": Spiritual Self-forgetting and *Dr. Faustus*', in *Memory and Forgetting in English Renaissance Drama: Shakespeare, Marlowe, Webster* (Cambridge: Cambridge University Press, 2005), pp. 65–87. Argues that Faustus's fall results from acts of forgetting that distance him from his spiritual self.

Tromly, Fred B., 'Damnation as Tantalization: *Doctor Faustus*', in *Playing with Desire: Christopher Marlowe and the Art of Tantalization* (Toronto: University of Toronto Press, 1998), pp. 133–52. Discusses the ways in which the Tantalus myth can be understood to inform elements of desire and deprivation in the play, which are used to exert forms of power. Focuses primarily on the B-text, finding it to use the myth to greatest effect.

Wall-Randell, Sarah, '*Doctor Faustus* and the Printer's Devil', *Studies in English Literature* 48 (2008), pp. 259–81. Shows the play's use of books and magic to participate in early modern beliefs surrounding the dangers and powers of printing.

Warren, Michael J., '*Doctor Faustus*: The Old Man and the Text', *English Literary Renaissance* 11 (1981), pp. 111–47. A persuasive argument against conflation of the A- and B-texts. Demonstrates that differences between the two versions are significant enough to warrant that each be analysed and interpreted independently.

Weil, Judith, ' "Full Possession": Service and Slavery in *Doctor Faustus*', in *Marlowe, History, and Sexuality: New Critical Essays on Christopher Marlowe*, ed. Paul Whitfield White (New York: AMS Press, 1998), pp. 143–54. An examination of the relationships of possession, slavery and service in the drama that is based upon the substitution of 'oeconomy' in the B-text for 'on kai me on' in the A-text in Faustus's opening speech in I.i.

Willis, Deborah, '*Doctor Faustus* and the Early Modern Language of Addiction', in *Placing the Plays of Christopher Marlowe: Fresh Cultural Contexts*, ed. Sara Munson Deats and Robert A. Logan (Aldershot: Ashgate, 2008), pp. 136–48. Investigates the ways the play participates in early modern discourses of addiction, especially as they relate to demonology. Finds the B-text to be especially revealing.

Additional resources

Cheney, Patrick, ed., *The Cambridge Companion to Christopher Marlowe* (Cambridge: Cambridge University Press, 2004). Part of the Cambridge Companion series, an accessible collection of essays on Marlowe's life and writings. 'Doctor Faustus' by Thomas Healy considers the central textual and thematic issues posed by the A- and B-texts by examining them within the worlds of early modern England and the commercial theatre.

Jones, John Henry, ed., *The English Faust Book: A Critical Edition, Based on the Text of 1592* (Cambridge: Cambridge University Press, 1994). A modern spelling edition of P. F.'s *English Faust Book* that details additions to and departures from its source, the *German Faust Book*. The introduction offers arguments for the dating of Marlowe's play, a discussion of the identity of P. F. and a bibliographical study and printing history of the *English Faust Book*.

Rasmussen, Eric, *A Textual Companion to Doctor Faustus* (Manchester: Manchester University Press, 1993). A careful textual analysis including type and spelling evidence and function-word testing that demonstrates the authenticity of the A-text by showing it to be set from authorial manuscript. Finds the B-text to contain multiple non-authorial revisions.

Simkin, Stevie, *A Preface to Marlowe* (Harlow: Longman, 2000). Part of the Analysing Texts series, the volume offers students a pragmatic approach to the critical study of Marlowe's life and works. 'Of Gods and Men: *Doctor Faustus*' provides an overview of the textual issues surrounding the A and B versions as well as a discussion of the play's most important themes.

Thomas, Vivien and William Tydeman, eds., *Christopher Marlowe: The Plays and Their Sources* (New York: Routledge, 1994). A modern spelling collection of sources most directly informing the plays that includes discussions of the ways in which the materials influence the playtexts. Prints P. F.'s *English Faust Book* in its entirety and excerpts of John Foxe's *Acts and Monuments* and Nathaniel Woodes's *The Conflict of Conscience*.

Internet resources

Christopher Marlowe (1564–93), www.luminarium.org/renlit/marlowe.htm. Features links to essays and articles, biographical background and images.

Christopher Marlowe, www.theatrehistory.com/british/marlowe001.html. Supplies biographical background and some helpful links to Marlowe studies.

Christopher Marlowe and the creation of *Doctor Faustus*, www.teachersfirst.com/lessons/marl-1.htm. Provides a well-conceived, goal-based unit for teaching *Doctor Faustus* to high-school students.

Marlowe Society of America (MSA), www.mightyline.org. A non-profit organization devoted to the life, works and time of Christopher Marlowe. Publishes the *Marlowe Society of America Newsletter*, which contains book reviews and scholarly news related to Marlowe studies, other playwrights of the period and staging history.

The Complete Works of Christopher Marlowe: An Electronic Edition, www.perseus.tufts.edu/Texts/Marlowe.html. A searchable edition of original and modern spellings of the A- and B-texts as well as Marlowe's other works. Developed by Tufts University Perseus Project and edited by Hilary Binda. Presently the most valuable internet resource of its kind.

The Life of Christopher Marlowe, The Literature Network: Christopher Marlowe, www.online-literature.com/marlowe/. Offers a biography of Marlowe and his works. Includes versions of the 1604 and 1616 quartos with footnotes.

The Norton Anthology of English Literature, 'The Sixteenth Century: Topics': 'The Magician, the Heretic, and the Playwright', www.wwnorton.com/college/english/nael/16century/topic_1/welcome.htm. Presents an introduction to Marlowe's life and artistry, excerpted texts and illustrations providing cultural context to *Doctor Faustus*, questions for reading and links to web resources.

Video recordings

Doctor Faustus, dir. Nevill Coghill and Richard Burton, Sony Pictures Home Entertainment, 1968. The only full-length film adaptation.

Marlowe's Doctor Faustus: Parables of Power: Part III, dir. John D. Mitchell, The Institute for Advanced Studies in the Theatre Arts, 1988. A brief introduction to Marlowe's life, *Doctor Faustus* and the early modern theatre. Includes performed excerpts of Faustus's opening speeches at I.i and I.iii; Mephistopheles's speech at I.iii ('That was the cause'); exchanges between Faustus and Mephistopheles in I.iii and II.i; and Faustus's eleventh-hour speech at V.ii. Follows the B-text, with the exception of Faustus's final speech, which adheres to the A-text. Faustus is performed by Paul Jackel and Mephistopheles by George Gitto. Available through Fordham University Press.

Marlowe's Faust: Parts I and II, dir. Carl Heap with the Medieval Players at Bridge Lane Theatre, London, 1997. Features scenes from *Dr. Faustus*. Part I presents a staged performance of the Prologue, Faustus's speeches at I.i and I.iii; the catechistic exchange between Faustus and Mephistopheles at I.iii; and the clowning of Wagner and Robin at I.iv. Part II features Act V in its entirety. Follows the A-text. Players: Lucy Allen; Anna Hemey; Mark Knox; Neil Savage; Kevin Walton; and Roy Weskin.

Notes

1   See *Approaches to Teaching English Renaissance Drama*, ed. Karen Bamford and Alexander Leggatt (New York: Modern Language Association, 2002), pp. 31, 29–34.

2   *Doctor Faustus A- and B-texts (1604, 1616)* ed. David Bevington and Eric Rasmussen (Manchester: Manchester University Press, 1993), pp. 155, 227; Lisa Hopkins, 'Marlowe', in *Teaching Shakespeare and Early Modern Dramatists*, ed. Andrew Hiscock and Lisa Hopkins (Basingstoke: Palgrave, 2007), pp. 50–51; Stevie Simkin, *A Preface to Marlowe* (Harlow: Longman, 2000), pp. 117–18.

3   www.perseus.tufts.edu/Texts/Marlowe.html.

4   www.wwnorton.com/college/english/nael/16century/topic_1/welcome.htm.

5   www.luminarium.org/renlit/marlowe.htm.

6   MONK, monkproject.org.

7   wordhoard.northwestern.edu/userman/index.html.

Bibliography

Adler, D., 'The acts of *Doctor Faustus* as monuments of the moment', *Selected Papers from the West Virginia Shakespeare and Renaissance Association* 10 (1985), pp. 1–24.

Alexander, N., 'The performance of Christopher Marlowe's *Dr. Faustus*', *Proceedings of the British Academy* 62 (1971), pp. 331–49.

Altman, J., *The Tudor Play of Mind: Rhetorical Inquiry and the Development of Elizabethan Drama* (Berkeley, CA: University of California Press, 1978).

Appleby, J. C., 'War, Politics, and Colonization, 1558–1625', in *The Oxford History of the British Empire: Volume I: The Origins of Empire: British Overseas Enterprise to the Close of the Seventeenth Century*, ed. N. Canny (Oxford: Oxford University Press, 1998).

Aubrey, J., *The Natural History and Antiquities of the County of Surrey* (London: for E. Curll, 1718–19).

Baines, B. J., 'Sexual Polarity in the Plays of Christopher Marlowe', *Ball State University Forum*, 23.3 (1982), pp. 3–17.

Bakeless, J., *The Tragicall History of Christopher Marlowe*, 2 vols (Cambridge, MA: Harvard University Press 1942).

Banerjee, P., 'I Mephastophilis: Self, Other, and Demonic Parody in Marlowe's *Doctor Faustus*', *Christianity and Literature* 42 (1993), pp. 221–41.

Barber, C. L., 'The Form of Faustus' Fortunes Good or Bad', *Tulane Drama Review* 8.4 (1964), pp. 92–119.

Barber, C. L. and Wheeler, R. P., eds., *Creating Elizabethan Tragedy: The Theater of Marlowe and Kyd* (Chicago: University of Chicago Press, 1988).

Bartels, E. C., *Spectacles of Strangeness: Imperialism, Alienation, and Marlowe* (Philadelphia, PA: University of Pennsylvania Press, 1993).

Beall, C., 'Definition of Theme by Unconsecutive event: Structure as Induction in Marlowe's *Doctor Faustus*', *Renaissance Papers* (1962), pp. 53–61.

Beckerman, B., 'Scene patterns in *Doctor Faustus* and *Richard III*', in *Shakespeare and His Contemporaries: Essays in Comparison*, Revels Plays Companion Library, ed. E. A. J. Honigmann (Manchester: Manchester University Press,1986).

Belsey, C., *The Subject of Tragedy: Identity and Difference in Renaissance Drama* (London: Methuen 1985).

Bentley, G. E., *The Jacobean and Caroline Stages*, 5 vols (Oxford: Clarendon, 1941–56).

Berger, Jr., H., 'Bodies and Texts', *Representations* 17 (1987), pp. 144–66.

Bevington, D., *From 'Mankind' to Marlowe: Growth of Structure in the Popular Drama of Tudor England* (Cambridge, MA: Harvard University Press, 1962).

Bevington, D. and Rasmussen, E. (1993), 'Introduction', in *'Doctor Faustus': A- and B-texts (1604, 1616)*, ed. D. Bevington and E. Rasmussen (Manchester: Manchester University Press, 1995), pp. 1–102.

Bevington, D. and Rasmussen, E., eds, *'Doctor Faustus': A- and B-texts (1604, 1616)*, (Manchester: Manchester University Press, 1993).

Birringer, J. H., 'Between Body and Language: "Writing" the Damnation of Faustus', *Theatre Journal* 36 (1984), pp. 335–55.

Black, C. V., *Pirates of the West Indies* (Cambridge: Cambridge University Press, 1989).

Black, J., *The British Seaborne Empire* (New Haven, CT: Yale University Press, 2004).

Bluestone, M., 'Libido speculandi: Doctrine and Dramaturgy in Contemporary Interpretations of Marlowe's *Doctor Faustus*', in *Reinterpretations of Elizabethan Drama: Selected Papers from the English Institute*, ed. N. Rabkin (New York: Columbia University Press, 1969), pp. 33–88.

Boas, F. S., ed., *The Tragical History of Doctor Faustus* (New York: Lincoln MacVeagh; Dial Press, 1932).

Bodley, J. H., *The Power of Scale: A Global History Approach* (Armonk, NY: M.E. Sharpe, 2003).

Bowers, F., 'Marlowe's *Doctor Faustus*: The 1602 Additions', *Studies in Bibliography: Papers of the Bibliographical Society of the University of Virginia* 26 (1973), pp. 1–18.

Bowers, F. ed., *The Complete Works of Christopher Marlowe*, vol. 2 (Cambridge: Cambridge University Press, 1973).

Bowers, R. H., 'Marlowe's *Dr. Faustus*, Tirso's *El Condenado por Desconfiado*, and the Secret Cause', *Costerus: Essays in English and American Language and Literature* 4 (1972), pp. 9–27.

Brandt, B. E., 'Marlowe's Helen and the Soul-in-the-kiss conceit', *Philological Quarterly* 64 (1985) pp. 118–21.

Brooke, C. F. T., 'The Marlowe Canon', *PMLA* 37 (1922), pp. 367–417.

Brooke, N., 'The Moral Tragedy of *Doctor Faustus*', *Cambridge Journal* (1952), pp. 662–87.

Brookes, C., 'The Unity of Marlowe's *Dr. Faustus*', in *To Nevill Coghill from Friends*, ed. J. Lawler and W. H. Auden (London: Faber & Faber, 1966), pp. 109–24.

Bruster, D., *Shakespeare and the Question of Culture* (New York: Palgrave Macmillan, 2003).

Bruster, D. and Weimann, R., *Prologues to Shakespeare's Theatre* (London: Routledge, 2004).

Butler, E. M., *The Fortunes of Faust* (Cambridge: Cambridge University Press, 1952).

Campbell, L. B., '*Doctor Faustus*: A Case of Conscience', *PMLA* 67 (1952), pp. 219–39.

Canny, N., ed., *The Oxford History of the British Empire: Volume I: The Origins of Empire: British Overseas Enterprise to the Close of the Seventeenth Century* (Oxford: Oxford University Press,1998).

Cartelli, T., *Marlowe, Shakespeare, and the Economy of Theatrical Experience* (Philadelphia, PA: University of Pennsylvania Press, 1991).

Chambers, E. K., *The Elizabethan Stage*, 4 vols (Oxford: Clarendon,1923).

Cheney, P., 'Love and Magic in *Doctor Faustus*: Marlowe's Indictment of Spenserian idealism', *Mosaic* 17.4 (1984), pp. 93–109.

Cheney, P., 'Un-script(ur)ing Christian Tragedy: Ovidian Love, Magic, and Glory in *Doctor Faustus*', in *Marlowe's Counterfeit Profession: Ovid, Spenser Counter-Nationhood* (Toronto: University of Toronto Press, 1997), pp. 190–220.

Cheney, P., *Marlowe's Counterfeit Profession: Ovid, Spenser, Counter-Nationhood* (Toronto: Toronto University Press, 1997).

Cheung, K., 'The Dialectic of Despair in *Doctor Faustus*', in *'A Poet and a filthy Play–Maker': New Essays on Christopher Marlowe*, ed. K. Friedenreich, R. Gill and C. B. Kuriyama (New York: AMS, 1988), pp. 193–201.

Cole, D., *Suffering and Evil in the Plays of Christopher Marlowe* (Princeton, NJ: Princeton University Press, 1962).

Cooper, B., 'An ur–Faustus?', *Notes & Queries* 104 (1959),pp. 6, 66–68.

Covella, F. D., 'The Choral Nexus in *Doctor Faustus*', *Studies in English Literature* 26 (1986), pp. 201–15.

Cox, G. H., III, 'Marlowe's *Doctor Faustus* and "sin against the Holy Ghost"', *Huntington Library Quarterly* 36 (1973), pp. 119–37.

Cox, J. D., 'Devil and Power in Marlowe and Shakespeare', *Yearbook of English Studies* 23 (1993), pp. 46–64.

Crabtree, J. H., Jr., 'The Comedy in Marlowe's *Dr. Faustus*', *Furman Studies* 9 (1961), pp. 1–9.

Craik, T. W., 'Faustus' Damnation Reconsidered', *Renaissance Drama* 2 (1969), pp. 189–96.

Culler, J., ed., *On Puns: The Foundation of Letters* (Oxford: Blackwell, 1988).

Cunningham, J. S., ed., *'Tamburlaine the Great', by Christopher Marlowe*, The Revels Plays (Manchester: Manchester University Press, 1981).

Dabbs, T., *Reforming Marlowe: The Nineteenth-Century Canonization of a Renaissance Dramatist* (Lewisburg, PA: Bucknell University Press, 1991).

Danson, L., 'Christopher Marlowe: The Questioner', *English Literary Renaissance* 12 (1982), pp. 3–29.

Davidson, C., 'Renaissance Dramatic Forms, Cosmic Perspective, and Alienation', *Cahiers Elisabéthains* 27 (1985), pp. 1–16.

De Bruyn, L., *Woman and the Devil in Sixteenth–Century Literature* (Tisbury: Compton, 1979).

Deats, S. M., '*Doctor Faustus*: From Chapbook to Tragedy', *Essays in Literature* 3 (1976), pp. 3–16.

Deats, S. M., *Sex, Gender, and Desire in the Plays of Christopher Marlowe* (Newark, DE: University of Delaware Press, 1997).

Deats, S. M., 'Marlowe's Interrogative Drama: *Dido, Tamburlaine, Doctor Faustus*, and *Edward II*', in *Marlowe's Empery: Expanding His Critical Contexts*, ed. S. M. Deats and R. A. Logan (Newark, DE: University of Delaware Press, 2002), pp. 107–30.

Deats, S. M., ' "Mark this show": Magic and Theater in Marlowe's *Doctor Faustus*', in *Placing the Plays of Christopher Marlowe: Fresh Cultural Contexts*, ed. S. M. Deats and R. A. Logan (Aldershot: Ashgate, 2008), pp. 13–24.

Diehl, H., *Staging Reform, Reforming the Stage: Protestantism and Popular Theatre in Early Modern England* (Ithaca, NY: Cornel University Press,1997).

Dollimore, J., *Radical Tragedy: Religion, Ideology and Power in the Drama of Shakespeare and His Contemporaries* (Chicago: University of Chicago Press, 1984).

Dollimore, J., '*Doctor Faustus*: Subversion Through Transgression', in *Christopher Marlowe*, ed. R. Wilson (London: Longman, 1999), pp. 235–45.

Donaldson, P. S., 'Conflict and Coherence: Narcissism and Tragic Structure in Marlowe', in *Narcissism and the Text: Studies in Literature and the Psychology of Self. Psychoanalytic Crosscurrents*, ed. L. Layton and B. A. Schapiro (New York: New York University Press, 1986), pp. 36–63.

Duane, C. L., 'Marlowe's Mixed Messages: A Model for Shakespeare?', *Medieval and Renaissance Drama in England* 3 (1986), pp. 51–67.

Dunn, R. D., 'Fragment of an Unpublished Essay on Printing by William Camden', *The British Library Journal* 12 (1986), pp. 145–49.

Duthie, G. I., 'Some Observations on Marlowe's *Doctor Faustus*', *Archiv für das Studium der Neueren Sprachen und Literaturen* 203 (1966) pp. 81–96.

Duxfield, A., ' "Resolve me of all ambiguities": *Doctor Faustus* and the Failure to Unify', *Early Modern Literary Studies*, Special Issue 16.7 (2007), pp. 1–21.

Ellis-Fermor, U., *Christopher Marlowe* (London: Methuen, 1927).

Ellis-Fermor, U., *The Frontiers of Drama* (New York: Oxford University Press, 1946).

Empson, W., *Faustus and the Censor: The English Faust-book and Marlowe's 'Doctor Faustus'* (Oxford: Basil Blackwell, 1987).

Eriksen, R. T., 'Giordano Bruno and Marlowe's *Doctor Faustus* (B)', *Notes & Queries* 32 (1985), pp. 463–65.

Eriksen, R. T., *The Forme of Faustus Fortunes: A Study of 'The Tragedie of Doctor Faustus' (1616)* (Oslo: Solum Forlag A.S.; Atlantic Highlands, NJ: Humanities Press International, 1987).

Euclid, *The Elements of Geometrie*, 2nd edn (London: STC, 1570).

Fehrenbach, R. J., 'A pre-1592 English Faust Book and the Date of *Doctor Faustus*', *Library: The Transactions of the Bibliographical Society* 2.4 (2001), pp. 327–35.

Findlay, A., *A Feminist Perspective on Renaissance Drama* (Oxford: Blackwell Publishers, 1999) pp. 11–25.

Fitz, L. T., 'Humanism Questioned: A Study of Four Renaissance characters', *English Studies in Canada* 5 (1979), pp. 388–405.

Fleissner, R. H., 'Robert Frost and the Dramatic', *New England Quarterly* 10 (1937), pp. 202–9.

Fleissner, R. H., *The Prince and the Professor: The Wittenberg Connection in Marlowe, Shakespeare, Goethe, and Frost* (Heidelberg: Carl Winter, 1986).

Forsyth, N., 'Heavenly Helen', *Etudes de Lettres* 4 (1987), pp. 11–21.

Foxe, J., *The Acts of Monuments of John Foxe*, 8 vols, ed. Rev. G. Townsend (New York: AMS Press, 1965).

French, P., *John Dee: The Life of an Elizabethan Magus* (London: Routledge & Kegan Paul, 1972).

Friedenrich, K., *Christopher Marlowe: An Annotated Bibliography of Criticism Since 1950* (Metuchen, NJ: Scarecrow, 1979).

Frye, R. M., 'Marlowe's *Dr. Faustus*: The Repudiation of Humanity,' *South Atlantic Quarterly* 55 (1956), pp. 322–28.

Garber, M., ' "Here's nothing writ": Scribe, Script, and Circumscription in Marlowe's Plays', *Theatre Journal*, 36 (1984), pp. 308–20.

Gardner, H., 'Milton's Satan and the Theme of Damnation in Elizabethan tragedy', *English Studies* (1948), pp. 46–66.

Gatti, H., 'Bruno and Marlowe: *Doctor Faustus*', in *Christopher Marlowe*, ed. R. Wilson (London: Longman, 1999), pp. 246–65.

Geckle, G. L., 'The 1604 and 1616 Versions of *Dr. Faustus*: Text and Performance', in *Subjects on the World's Stage: Essays on British Literature of the Middle Ages and the Renaissance*, ed. D. G. Allen and R. A. White (Newark, DE: University of Delaware Press, 1995), pp. 146–61.

Gill, R., ed., *Dr Faustus*, New Mermaids (London: Ernest Benn, 1965).

Gill, R., ed., *Dr Faustus*, 2nd edn, New Mermaids (London: A & C Black, 1989).

Gilman, E. B., *The Curious Perspective: Literary and Pictorial Wit in the Seventeenth Century*, (New Haven, CT: Yale University Press, 1978).

Golden, K. L., 'Myth, Psychology, and Marlowe's *Doctor Faustus*', *College Literature* 12 (1985), pp. 202–10.

Grantley, D., ' "What means this shew?": Theatricalism, Camp, and Subversion *in Doctor Faustus* and *The Jew of Malta*', in *Christopher Marlowe and English Renaissance Culture*, ed. D. Grantley and P. Roberts (Aldershot: Scholar, 1996), pp. 224–38.

Greenblatt, S., *Renaissance Self-Fashioning: From More to Shakespeare* (Chicago: University of Chicago Press, 1980).

Greene, T. M., *The Light in Troy: Imitation and Discovery in Renaissance Poetry* (New Haven, CT: Yale University Press, 1982).

Greg, W. W., 'The Damnation of Faustus,' *Modern Language Review* 41 (1946), pp. 97–107.

Greg, W. W., ed., *Marlowe's 'Doctor Faustus,' 1604, 1616: Parallel Texts*. Oxford: Clarendon, 1950).

Grotowski, J. '*Doctor Faustus* in Poland', trans. R. Schechter, *Tulane Drama Review* 8.4 (1964), pp. 120–33.

Guillory, J., *Cultural Capital: The Problem of Literary Canon Formation* (Chicago: University of Chicago Press, 1993).

Harraway, C., *Re-citing Marlowe: Approaches to the Drama* (Aldershot: Ashgate, 2000).

Hattaway, M., 'The Theology of Marlowe's *Doctor Faustus*', *Renaissance Drama* 3 (1970), pp. 51–78.

Hirst, D. L., *Tragicomedy*, The Critical Idiom 43 (London: Methuen, 1984).

Hjort, A. M., 'The Interests of Critical Editorial Practice', *Poetics* 15 (1986), pp. 259–77.

Holme, R., *The Academy of Armory, or, A Storehouse of Armory and Blazon* (Chester, 1688).

Honderich, P., 'John Calvin and Doctor Faustus', *Modern Language Review* 68 (1972), pp. 495–519.

Houk, R. A., 'Doctor Faustus and A Shrew', *PMLA* 62 (1947), pp. 950–57.

Huebert, R., 'Tobacco and Boys and Marlowe', *Sewanee Review* 150 (1984), pp. 206–24.

Hunter, G. K., 'Five Act Structure in *Doctor Faustus*', *Tulane Drama Review* 8.4 (1964), pp. 77–91.

Hunter, R. G., *Shakespeare and the Mystery of God's Judgments* (Athens, GA: University of Georgia Press, 1976).

Ingram, R. W., ' "Pride in learning goeth before a fall": Dr. Faustus' Opening Soliloquy', *Mosaic* 13.1 (1979), pp. 73–80.

Jackson, M. P., 'Three Old Ballads and the Date of *Doctor Faustus*', *Journal of the Australasian Universities Language and Literature Association: A Journal of Literary Criticism, Philology & Linguistics* 36 (1971), pp. 187–200.

Jackson, R., '*Doctor Faustus* in Manchester', *Critical Quarterly* 23.4 (1981), pp. 3–9.

Jantz, H., 'An Elizabethan Statement on the Origin of the *German Faust Book*', *Journal of English and Germanic Philology* (1952), pp. 137–53.

Jarrett, H. S., 'Verbal Ambiguities in Marlowe's *Dr. Faustus*', *College English* 5 (1944), pp. 339–40.

Johns, A., *The Nature of the Book: Print and Knowledge in the Making* (Chicago: University of Chicago Press, 1998).

Jump, J. D., ed., *The Tragical History of the Life and Death of Doctor Faustus*, The Revels Plays (London: Methuen 1962, reprinted 1968).

Keefer, M. H., 'Verbal Magic and the Problem of the A- and B-texts of *Doctor Faustus*', *Journal of English and Germanic Philology* 82 (1983), pp. 324–46.

Keefer, M. H., 'History and the Canon: The Case of *Doctor Faustus*', *University of Toronto Quarterly: A Canadian Journal of the Humanities* 56 (1987), pp. 498–522.

Keefer, M. H., ed., *Christopher Marlowe's 'Doctor Faustus': A 1604-version Edition* (Peterborough, Ontario: Broadview, 1991).

Kernan, A. B., *The Playwright as Magician: Shakespeare's Image of the Poet in the English Public Theater* (New Haven, CT: Yale University Press, 1979).

Kiessling, N., '*Doctor Faustus* and the Sin of Demoniality,' *Studies in English Literature* 15 (1975), pp. 205–11.

Kirschbaum, L. (1943), 'Marlowe's *Faustus*: A Reconsideration', *Review of English Studies*, 19, 225–41.

Kirschbaum, L. (1946), 'The good and bad quartos of *Doctor Faustus*', *The Library*, 4th ser., 26, 272–94.

Kocher, P. H., 'The *English Faust Book* and the date of Marlowe's *Faustus*', *Modern Language Notes* 55 (1940), pp. 95–101.

Kocher, P. H., 'The Witchcraft Basis in Marlowe's *Doctor Faustus*', *Modern Philology* 38 (1940), pp. 9–36.

Kocher, P. H., 'Nashe's Authorship of the Prose Scenes in *Faustus*', *Modern Language Quarterly* 3 (1942), 17–40.

Kocher, P. H., 'The Early Date for Marlowe's *Faustus*', *Modern Language Notes* 58 (1943), pp. 539–42.

Kocher, P. H., *Christopher Marlowe: A Study of his Thought, Learning, and Character* (New York, Russell & Russell, 1946, reprinted 1962).

Kuriyama, C. B., 'Dr. Greg and *Doctor Faustus*: The Supposed Originality of the 1616 Text', *English Literary Renaissance* 5 (1975), pp. 171–97.

Kuriyama, C. B, *Hammer or Anvil: Psychological Patterns in Christopher Marlowe's Plays* (New Brunswick, NJ: Rutgers University Press, 1980).

Lake, D. J., 'Three Seventeenth-century Revisions: *Thomas of Woodstock, The Jew of Malta,* and *Faustus* B', *Notes & Queries* 30 (1983), pp. 133–43.

Langston, B., 'Marlowe's *Faustus* and the *Ars Moriendi* Tradition', in *Tribute to George Coffin Taylor,* ed. A. Williams (Chapel Hill, CA: University of North Carolina Press, 1952), pp. 148–67.

Levin, H., *The Overreacher: A Study of Christopher Marlowe* (Cambridge, MA: Harvard University Press, 1952, reprinted 1964).

MacLure, M., *Marlowe: The Critical Heritage 1588–1896* (London: Routledge & Kegan Paul, 1979).

Mahood, M. M., *Poetry and Humanism* (Port Washington, NY: Kennikat, 1950, reprinted 1967).

Marcus, L., 'Textual Indeterminacy and Ideological Difference: The Case of *Doctor Faustus*', *Renaissance Drama,* 20 (1989), pp. 1–29.

Marcus, L., *Unediting the Renaissance: Shakespeare, Marlowe, Milton* (London: Routledge, 1996).

Margaret, A. O., 'Christian Belief in *Doctor Faustus*', *ELH* 37 (1970), pp. 1–11.

Marlowe, C., *'Doctor Faustus': A- and B-texts (1604, 1616),* ed. D. Bevington and E. Rasmussen (Manchester: Manchester University Press, 1993).

Marlowe, C., *'Doctor Faustus,'* in *English Renaissance Drama,* ed. D. Bevington, L. Engle, K. E. Maus and E. Rasmussen (New York: Norton, 2002), pp. 245–86.

Marlowe, C., *Doctor Faustus,* ed. D. S. Kastan (New York: Norton, 2005).

Matalene, H. W., III, 'Marlowe's *Faustus* and the Comforts of Academicism', *ELH* 39 (1972), pp. 495–519.

Maxwell, J. C., 'The Sin of Faustus', *The Wind and the Rain* 4 (1947), pp. 49–52.

McAdam, I., *The Irony of Identity: Self and Imagination in the Drama of Christopher Marlowe* (Newark, DE: University of Delaware Press, 1999).

McAlindon, T., 'The Ironic Vision: Diction and Theme in Marlowe's *Doctor Faustus*', *Review of English Studies* 32 (1981), pp. 129–41.

McAlindon, T., *English Renaissance Tragedy* (Vancouver: University of British Columbia Press, 1986).

McAlindon, T., '*Doctor Faustus*: The Predestination Theory', *English Studies* 3 (1993), pp. 215–20.

McCloskey, J. C., 'The Theme of Despair in Marlowe's *Faustus*', *College English* 4 (1942), pp. 110–13.

McCullen, J. T., '*Dr. Faustus* and Renaissance Learning', *Modern Language Review* 51 (1956), pp. 6–16.

McNeely, J. T., 'The Integrated Design of *Dr. Faustus*: An Essay in Iconoclasm', *Cahiers Élisabéthains* 41 (1992), pp. 1–16.

Mebane, J., *Renaissance Magic and the Return of the Golden Age: The Occult Tradition in Marlowe, Jonson, and Shakespeare* (Lincoln: University of Nebraska Press, 1989).

Muir, K., 'Three Marlowe Texts', *Notes & Queries* 43 (1996), pp. 142–44.

Nosworthy, J. M., 'Some Textual Anomalies in the 1604 *Doctor Faustus*', *Modern Language Review* 41 (1946), pp. 1–8.

O'Brien, M. A., 'Christian Belief in *Doctor Faustus*', *ELH* 37 (1970), pp. 1–11.

Oliver, L. M., 'Rowley, Foxe, and the *Faustus* Additions', *Modern Language Notes* 60 (1945), pp. 391–94.

Ormerod, D. and Wortham, C., eds. (1985), *Christopher Marlowe: 'Dr Faustus': The A–Text.* Nedlands: University of Western Australia Press.

Ornstein, R., 'The Comic Synthesis in *Doctor Faustus*', *ELH* 22 (1955), pp. 165–72.

Ornstein, R., 'Marlowe and God: The Tragic Theology of *Dr. Faustus*', *PMLA* 83 (1968), pp. 1378–85.

Owens, M. E., 'Desperate Juggling Knacks: The Rehearsal of the Grotesque in *Doctor Faustus*', *Medieval and Renaissance Drama in England,* 8 (1996), pp. 63–93.

Pagden, A., 'The Struggle for Legitimacy and the Image of Empire in the Atlantic to c.

1700', in *The Oxford History of the British Empire: Volume I: The Origins of Empire: British Overseas Enterprise to the Close of the Seventeenth Century*, ed. N. Canny (Oxford: Oxford University Press, 1998), pp. 34–54.

Palmer, P. M. and More, R. P., *The Sources of the Faust Tradition* (New York: Octagon Books, 1936, reprinted 1966).

Partridge, E., *Shakespeare's Bawdy: A Literary & Psychological Essay and a Comprehensive Glossary* (London: Routledge, 1947, reprinted 1968).

Peters, J. S., *Theatre of the Book 1480–1880. Print, Text and Performance in Europe* (Oxford: Oxford University Press, 2000).

Pettitt, T., 'Formulaic Dramaturgy in *Doctor Faustus*', in '*A Poet and a filthy Play-maker': New Essays on Christopher Marlowe*, ed. K. Friededreih, R. Gill and C. B. Kuriyama (New York: AMS, 1988), pp. 167–91.

Phillips, E., *Theatrum Poeteareum, or, A Complete Collection of the Poets*, 2 vols (London: for Charles Smith, 1675).

Poole, K., '*Dr. Faustus* and Reformation Theology', in *Early Modern English Drama: A Critical Companion*, ed. G. A. Sullivan, P. Cheney and A. Hadfield (Oxford: Oxford University Press, 2005), pp. 96–107.

Proser, M. N., *The Gift of Fire: Aggression and the Plays of Christopher Marlowe* (New York: Peter Lang, 1995).

Puhvel, M., 'Marlowe's *Doctor Faustus*, V.i', *Explicator* 46.4 (1988), pp. 3–5.

Rasmussen, E., 'The Black Book and the Date of *Doctor Faustus*', *Notes & Queries* 235, n.s., 37 (1990), pp. 168–70.

Rasmussen, E., 'Rehabilitating the A-text of Marlowe's *Doctor Faustus*', *Studies in Bibliography: Papers of the Bibliographical Society of the University of Virginia* 46 (1993), pp. 221–38.

Rasmussen, E., *A Textual Companion to 'Doctor Faustus'*, The Revels Plays Companion Library (Manchester: Manchester University Press, 1993).

Rayburn, S. E., 'Marlowe's *Doctor Faustus* and Medieval Judgment Day Drama', *Publications of the Mississippi Philological Association* (1985), pp. 33–39.

Reynolds, J. A., *Repentance and Retribution in Early English Drama*, Jacobean Drama Studies 96 (Salzburg: Universität Salzburg, Institut für Anglistik und Amerikanistik, 1982).

Ribner, I., 'Marlowe's "tragic glasse"', in *Essays on Shakespeare and Elizabethan Drama in Honor of Hardin Craig*, ed. R. Hosley (Columbia, MO: University of Missouri Press, 1962), pp. 91–114.

Ribner, I., 'Marlowe and the Critics', *Tulane Drama Review* 8.4 (1964), pp. 211–24.

Ribner, I., ed., *The Complete Plays of Christopher Marlowe* (New York: Odyssey, 1963).

Riehle, W., 'Marlowe's *Doctor Faustus* and Renaissance Italy: Some Observations and Suggestions', *Medieval Studies Conference*, Aachen 1983: Language and Literature. Bamberger Beitrage zur Englischen Sprachwissenschaft 15 (Frankfurt: Peter Lang, 1984) pp. 185–95.

Roberts, G., 'Necromantic Books: Christopher Marlowe, *Doctor Faustus* and Agrippa of Nettesheim', in *Christopher Marlowe and English Renaissance Culture*, ed. D. Grantley and P. Roberts (Aldershot: Scolar Press, 1996), pp. 148–69.

Roberts, G., 'Marlowe and the Metaphysics of Magicians', in *Constructing Christopher Marlowe*, ed. J. A. Downie and J. T. Parnell (Cambridge: Cambridge University Press, 2000), pp. 55–73.

Rosador, K. T., 'Supernatural Soliciting: Temptation and Imagination in *Doctor Faustus* and *Macbeth*', in *Shakespeare and His Contemporaries: Essays in Comparison*, ed. E. A. J. Honigmann, The Revels Plays Companion Library (Manchester: Manchester University Press, 1986), pp. 42–59.

Rose, W., 'Introduction', in *The Historie of the Damnable Life and Deserved Death of Doctor John Faustus, by P. F. Gent*, ed. W. Rose (Notre Dame: University of Notre Dame Press, 1963).

Roy, E., 'Faustus' Dream of Punishment', *American Imago* 34 (1977), pp. 158–69.

Rozett, M. T., *The Doctrine of Election and the Emergence of Elizabethan Tragedy* (Princeton, NJ: Princeton University Press, 1984).

Sachs, A. (1964), 'The Religious Despair of *Doctor Faustus*', *Journal of English and Germanic Philology*, 63, 625–47.

Sams, E., 'The Timing of the Shrews', *Notes & Queries* 32 (1985), pp. 33–45.

Santayana, G., *Three Philosophical Poets: Lucretius, Dante, and Goethe* (Cambridge, MA: Harvard University Press, 1910).

Scott, M., *Renaissance Drama and a Modern Audience* (London: Macmillan,1982).

Sellin, P. R., 'The Hidden God: Reformation Awe in Renaissance English Literature', in *The Darker Vision of the Renaissance*, ed. R. S. Kinsman, (Berkeley, CA: University of California Press, 1974), pp. 147–94.

Shepherd, S., *Marlowe and the Politics of Elizabethan Theatre* (New York: St Martin's Press, 1986).

Sheppeard, S., 'Faustus and the Fall of Troy', *CCTE Studies* 54 (1994), pp. 68–74.

Simpson, P., 'Marlowe's *Tragical History of Doctor Faustus*', *Essays and Studies* 14 (1929), pp. 20–34.

Sinfield, A., *Literature in Protestant England, 1560–1660* (London: Croom Helm, 1983).

Smith, R. A. H., 'A Note on *Doctor Faustus* and *The Taming of a Shrew*', *Notes & Queries* 26 (1979), pp. 116.

Smith, R. A. H., ' "Faustus end" and The Wounds of Civil War', *Notes & Queries* 32 (1985), pp. 16–17.

Smith, R. A. H., '*Doctor Faustus* and *The Merry Wives of Windsor*', *Review of English Studies* 43 (1992), pp. 395–97.

Smith, W. D., 'The Nature of Evil in *Doctor Faustus*', *Modern Language Review* 60 (1965), pp. 171–75.

Snow, E. A., 'Marlowe's *Doctor Faustus* and the Ends of Desire', in *Two Renaissance Mythmakers: Christopher Marlowe and Ben Jonson*, ed. A. Kernan, Selected Papers from the English Institute, 1975–76. n.s. 1 (Baltimore, MD: Johns Hopkins University Press, 1977), pp. 41–69.

Snyder, S., 'Marlowe's *Doctor Faustus* as an Inverted Saint's Life', *Studies in Philology* 63 (1966), pp. 565–77.

Speaight, R., *William Poel and the Elizabethan Revival* (London: Heinemann, 1954).

Spinrad, P. S., 'The Dilettante's Lie in *Doctor Faustus*', *Texas Studies in Literature and Language* 24 (1982), pp. 243–54.

Spinrad, P. S., *The Summons of Death on the Medieval and Renaissance English Stage* (Columbus, OH: Ohio State University Press, 1987).

Spivack, B., *Shakespeare and the Allegory of Evil* (New York: Columbia University Press, 1958).

Stock, L. K., 'Medieval Gula in Marlowe's *Doctor Faustus*', *Bulletin of Research in the Humanities* 85 (1982), pp. 372–85.

Stockholder, K., ' "Within the massy entrailes of the earth": Faustus's Relation to Women', in *'A Poet and a Filthy Play-maker': New Essays on Christopher Marlowe*, ed. K. Friedenreich, R. Gill and C. B. Kuriyama (New York: AMS, 1988), pp. 203–19.

Streete, A., 'Calvinist Conceptions of Hell in Marlowe's *Doctor Faustus*', *Notes and Queries* 47 (2000), pp. 430–32.

Stull, W. L., 'Marlowe's Adlerian Tragedies', *Soundings* 73 (1990), pp. 443–64.

Summers, C. J. and Pebworth, T. L., 'The Conversion of St. Augustine and the B-text of *Doctor Faustus*', *Renaissance and Renascences in Western Literature* 1.2 (1979), pp. 1–8.

Tanner, J. T. F., '*Doctor Faustus* as Orthodox Christian Sermon', *Dickinson Review* 2 (1969), pp. 23–31.

Tate, W., 'Solomon, Gender, and Empire in Marlowe's *Doctor Faustus*', *Studies in English Literature* 37 (1997), pp. 257–76.

Traci, P. J., 'Marlowe's Faustus as Artist: A Suggestion About a Theme in the Play', *Renaissance Papers* (1966), pp. 3–9.

Traister, B. H., *Heavenly Necromancers: The Magician in English Renaissance Drama* (Columbia, MO: University of Missouri, 1984).

Trismegistus, H., *Hermis Mercuries Trismegistus his Divine Pymander in Seventeen Books* (London: Wing, 1657).

Tromley, F. B., *Playing with Desire: Christopher Marlowe and the Art of Tantalization* (Toronto: University of Toronto Press, 1998).

Tupper, F., Jr., 'Legacies of Lucian', *Modern Language Notes* 21.3 (1906), pp. 76–77.

Tydeman, W., *'Doctor Faustus': Text and Performance* (Basingstoke: Macmillan, 1984).

Ule, L., 'Recent Progress in Computer Methods of Authorship Determination', *Association for Literary and Linguistic Computing Bulletin* 10.3 (1983), pp. 73–89.

Versfeld, M., 'Some Remarks on Marlowe's *Faustus*', *English Studies in Africa* 1 (1958), pp. 134–43.

Warren, M., '*Doctor Faustus*: The Old Man and the Text', *English Literary Renaissance* 11 (1981), pp. 111–47.

Webb, D. C., 'Damnation in *Doctor Faustus*: Theological Strip Tease and the Histrionic Hero', *Critical Survey* 11.1 (1999), pp. 31–47.

Weil, J., *Christopher Marlowe: Merlin's Prophet* (Cambridge: Cambridge University Press, 1977).

Weimann, R., *Shakespeare and the Popular Tradition in the Theater: Studies in the Social Dimension of Dramatic Form and Function*, ed. Robert Schwartz (Baltimore, MD: Johns Hopkins University Press, 1978).

Weimann, R., 'Playing with a Difference: Revisiting "pen" and "voice" in Shakespeare's Theater', *Shakespeare Quarterly* 50 (1999), pp. 415–32.

Weimann, R., *Author's Pen and Actor's Voice: Playing and Writing in Shakespeare's Theatre* (Cambridge: Cambridge University Press, 2000).

Wilks, J. S., *The Idea of Conscience in Renaissance Tragedy* (London: Routledge, 1990).

Winstanley, W., *The Lives of the Most Famous English Poets* (London: H. Clark for S. Manship, 1687).

Wion, P. K., 'Marlowe's *Doctor Faustus*, the Oedipus Complex, and the Denial of Death', *Colby Library Quarterly* 16 (1980), pp. 190–204.

Woods, G., *A History of Gay Literature: The Male Tradition* (New Haven, CT: Yale University Press, 1998).

Woolley, B., *The Queen's Conjuror: The Life and Magic of Dr Dee* (London: Flamingo, 2002).

Wortham, C., ' "Read, read the scriptures": *Doctor Faustus* and the Retreat from Humanism', *The Aligarh Critical Miscellany* 6.2 (1993), pp. 157–74.

Yates, F. A., *The Occult Philosophy in the Elizabethan Age* (London: Routledge & Kegan Paul, 1979).

Zimansky, C. A., 'Marlowe's *Faustus*: The Date Again', *Philological Quarterly* 41 (1962), pp. 181–78.

Notes on Contributors

David Bevington is the Phyllis Fay Horton Distinguished Service Professor of Humanities at the University of Chicago. He is the author of many books, including *From 'Mankind' to Marlowe*, *Tudor Drama and Politics* and *Action is Eloquence: Shakespeare's Language and Gesture*. He has edited *The Complete Works of Shakespeare* for Bantam and is editor of *Medieval Drama* and *The Macro Plays*. He is also senior editor of the *Norton Anthology of English Renaissance Drama* and the Student Revels editions, co-editor of *Shakespeare: Script, Stage, Screen* and one of the senior editors of the *Complete Works of Ben Jonson* (forthcoming 2009). He has also published numerous journal articles and book chapters on Marlowe and Shakespeare and has twice served as president of the Shakespeare Association of America.

Bruce E. Brandt is a professor of English at South Dakota State University. He received his BA and MA from the University of Denver and his PhD from Harvard University. His publications include two books on Marlowe: *Christopher Marlowe in the Eighties: An Annotated Bibliography of Marlowe Criticism from 1978 through 1989* and *Christopher Marlowe and the Metaphysical Problem Play*. Professor Brandt has also presented papers on Marlowe at a number of professional forums. Complementing his Marlowe scholarship, he has long been active in the Marlowe Society of America, having served as membership chair, editor, vice-president and president.

Georgia E. Brown has been a lecturer at Lincoln College, Oxford, and fellow and director of studies in English at Queens' College

Cambridge. She has also lectured at universities in Greece, Switzerland, Poland and the United States. She is the author of a study of English literary culture in the 1590s, entitled *Redefining Elizabethan Literature*. She has a particular interest in the ways that the Renaissance adapted classical models and her book includes an analysis of Ovid's influence on the Elizabethan avant-garde. She has also published essays on classical literature, teaching the epyllion, Queen Elizabeth I's activities as a translator, Christopher Marlowe, John Marston and Shakespeare. She has been active in the Marlowe Society of America for many years and is currently serving as vice-president of that organization.

Sara Munson Deats is the Distinguished University Professor at the University of South Florida, former chair of the Department of English and associate dean of the College of Arts and Sciences and of the Graduate School. She is also a former president of the Marlowe Society of America and has published numerous articles and book chapters on Marlowe and Shakespeare in referred journals and anthologies. She has published nine books: a feminist study entitled *Sex, Gender, and Desire in the Plays of Christopher Marlowe*, for which she received the Roma Gill Award for Outstanding Contribution to Marlowe Scholarship; five co-edited collections relating literature to social issues; a collection of essays on *Antony and Cleopatra* for Routledge Press; and two collections of essays co-edited with Robert A. Logan entitled *Marlowe's Empery: Expanding His Critical Contexts* and *Placing the Plays of Christopher Marlowe: Fresh Cultural Contexts*.

Andrew Duxfield is an associate lecturer at Sheffield Hallam University. His publications include the essays ' "Resolve me of all ambiguities": *Doctor Faustus* and the Failure to Unify' in *Early Modern Literary Studies* and 'Modern Problems of Editing: The Two Texts of Marlowe's *Doctor Faustus*' in *Literary Compass*. He is the contributor on Christopher Marlowe to *The Year's Work in English Studies* and has delivered papers on textual issues in *Doctor Faustus* and on the play's treatment of early modern hermeticism. In 2008 he submitted his PhD thesis, which focuses on reduction and ambiguity in the plays of Christopher Marlowe, and he is currently working on a chapter on Shakespeare's contemporary writers in a forthcoming multi-volume *Companion to Shakespeare*.

Toni Francis received her PhD from the University of South Florida in 2007 and is currently an assistant professor of English Studies at

The College of the Bahamas, where she teaches early modern drama, modern drama, literary theory and advanced writing. Professor Francis's research areas include transatlantic studies, postcolonial theory, early modern drama and composition pedagogy. She has presented papers at a number of professional forums, including the Shakespeare Institute in Stratford-upon-Avon, the Modern Language Association, the American Dialect Society, the New College Medieval/Renaissance Conference and the Convention of the Conference on College Composition and Communication.

Andrew James Hartley is the Distinguished Professor of Shakespeare Studies and the director of the Shakespeare in Action Centre at the University of North Carolina at Charlotte. His PhD is in English from Boston University, but Professor Hartley now teaches primarily in the Theatre Department, where he also works as a director and dramaturg. He is the author of *The Shakespearean Dramaturg* and the editor of the performance journal *Shakespeare Bulletin* published by Johns Hopkins University Press. In addition to writing scholarly articles on early modern drama in performance, he also publishes mystery/thrillers with Penguin Berkley.

Robert Logan teaches at the University of Hartford where he has served as chair of the English Department and director of the university's Humanities Centre. From 1999 to 2003, he was president of The Marlowe Society of America. Professor Logan has written several articles and book chapters on Marlowe and Shakespeare, served as guest editor, published numerous reviews and co-edited with Sara Munson Deats two collections of essays: *Marlowe's Empery: Expanding His Critical Contexts* and *Placing the Plays of Christopher Marlowe: Fresh Cultural Contexts*. In 2007, he published a critical work entitled *Shakespeare's Marlowe: The Influence of Marlowe on Shakespeare's Artistry*. At present, he is working on a book tentatively entitled *Measuring Up: Shakespeare's Antony and Cleopatra and the Phenomenon of Celebrityhood*. He is also general editor for a series of six books on the University Wits and is himself editing the volume on Marlowe.

Sarah K. Scott is assistant professor of English at Mount St Mary's University where she teaches courses in Shakespeare, early modern poetry and drama, and cultural, gender and sexuality studies. Her current projects include the forthcoming edited collection with M. L. Stapleton, *Christopher Marlowe the Craftsman: Lives, Stage, and Page*, a monograph examining the relationship between city comedy and the dynamics of *caritas*, and a study that explores the implications of adulterated wine in *The Dutch Courtesan*. She has published in *Early Theatre* and *Research Opportunities in Renaissance Drama* and presented papers at the Modern Language Association, the Sixteenth-Century Studies Conference, and the Group for Early Modern Cultural Studies. She currently serves as assistant editor for the New Variorum Shakespeare *Julius Caesar* and as membership chair for the Marlowe Society of America.

Index